# Divorce and Money

## Everything You Need to Know
## About Dividing Property

FIRST EDITION

BY VIOLET WOODHOUSE, CFP

AND VICTORIA FELTON-COLLINS, PhD, CFP

WITH M.C. BLAKEMAN

*Edited by Robin Leonard and Stephen Elias*

NOLO PRESS      BERKELEY, CALIFORNIA

## Your Responsibility When Using a Self-help Law Book

We've done our best to give you useful and accurate information in this book. But laws and procedures change frequently and are subject to differing interpretations. If you want legal advice backed by a guarantee, see a lawyer. If you use this book, it's your responsibility to make sure that the facts and general advice contained in it are applicable to your situation.

## Keeping Up To Date

To keep its books up to date, Nolo Press issues new printings and new editions periodically. New printings reflect minor legal changes and technical corrections. New editions contain major legal changes, major text additions or major reorganizations. To find out if a later printing or edition of any Nolo book is available, call Nolo Press at (510) 549-1976 or check the catalog in the Nolo News, our quarterly newspaper.

To stay current, follow the "Update" service in the Nolo News. You can get the paper free by sending us the registration card in the back of the book. In another effort to help you use Nolo's latest materials, we offer a 25% discount off the purchase of any new Nolo book if you turn in any earlier printing or edition. (See the "Recycle Offer" in the back of the book.)

| First Edition | JANUARY 1992 |
|---|---|
| Editors | ROBIN LEONARD & STEPHEN ELIAS |
| Illustrations | MARI STEIN |
| Book Design | JACKIE MANCUSO |
| Cover Design | TONI IHARA |
| Index | JENNY JONES |
| Printing | DELTA LITHOGRAPH |

Woodhouse, Violet, 1948-
    Divorce & money / by Violet Woodhouse, Victoria Felton-Collins, and M. C. Blakeman : edited by Robin Leonard : illustrations by Mari Stein. -- 1st national ed.
      p. cm.
    Includes index.
    ISBN 0-87337-143-7 : $19.95
    1. Marital property--Valuation--United States--Popular works.
2. Equitable distribution of marital property--United States--Popular works. 3. Divorce settlements--United States--Popular works. I. Felton-Colllins, Victoria. II. Blakeman, M. C., 1952- . III. Leonard, Robin. IV. Title. V. Title: Divorce and money.
KF524.Z9W66 1991
346.73'04--dc20
[347.3064]
          91-31761
          CIP

recycled paper

## Dedication

We dedicate this book to

Our clients—who were the compelling reason for this book

Our families and friends—who kept us sane through its writing

## Thank You

Thanks must first go to those very special people at Nolo—Steve Elias, for his vision and unflagging efforts, Jake Warner, for giving the big "Yes," Sandy Coury, for reading the entire manuscript, Mary Randolph, who helped with the estate planning sections, and of course, Robin Leonard, our editor, friend and inspiration. Robin's astute input, challenging questions and ongoing encouragement meant a lot to us personally and helped make this book the very best it could be.

Salli Rasberry freely gave us wise advice and the benefit of her experience as a much-published author. Our appreciation also goes to support staffers Debbie Robinson, Linda Lee and Sophia Hall for their timely and cheerful assistance, and to Michael Anne Conley for her outstanding desktop publishing skills.

Our professional colleagues were a source of valuable information and constructive ideas. Certified Family Law Specialists Mark Minyard, Randy Morrison, Wilma Presley, Karen Rhyne and Diana Richmond deserve special thanks, as does Ginita Wall, CFP, CPA, for her expertise, ideas and support. Other professionals who participated in interviews and contributed their time include Certified Business Appraisers Gary Allen and Bud Garvin; stockbroker Laurie Renny; and attorneys Brian Berg, Thomas Bernauer, Steven Briggs, Gary Friedman (Director of the Center for Mediation in Law), Douglas Page, Sidney Radus and Marc Tovstein.

Thanks also to Mary Rowland, a well-known writer herself, for her confidence and Mimi Modisette, an attorney, who has been wonderfully supportive of our efforts.

For on-going support, we want to thank Dean Ronald Talmo and the professors and staff at Western State University, College of Law, Irvine, California.

A very special thanks go to our clients who shared questions, concerns, stories, hopes, fears and insights during this process. Dee Foltz, Lynne Fisher and Pamela Frogge gave us valuable feedback which helped shape this book.

Finally, we must thank those who have been with us through the ups and downs of book writing and who have provided never-ending encouragement—Larry, Brooke and Tyler Woodhouse; David Collins; Kimberly and Todd Felton; Jennifer, David and Nicole Collins; and Robert Neumann.

—V.W., V.F.C., M.C.B.

P.S. We wish to extend special recognition to the tireless efforts of Mary Claire Blakeman, the writer of this book, who persevered through numerous drafts and even a theft of the edited manuscript. We thank her for her insights and ideas, as well as her clear, warm writing style.

—V.W., V.F.C.

# Table of Contents

Introduction

## Decisions To Make in the First 30 Days

## The First 30 Days: The Hardest Part—Is My Marriage Really Over?

## The First 30 Days: The Separation—Who Must Move Out, and By When?

## The First 30 Days: Closing the Books—What To Do With Joint Accounts

## CHAPTER 12

## The First Thirty Days: Going From "We" to "Me"

## CHAPTER 13

## Your Property and Expenses

## CHAPTER 14

## What Will Happen to the House?

## CHAPTER 15

## Retirement Benefits: Who Gets What?

CHAPTER 20

# Negotiating the Settlement

CHAPTER 21

# After the Divorce

APPENDIX

# Resources Beyond the Book

# Introduction

*You've just been through the worst week of your life when the person you're divorcing suddenly calls and demands copies of your tax returns for the past five years.*

You brown-bag your lunch and take the bus to work so you can make ends meet while the divorce settlement is pending. One day, you receive an unexpected bill in the mail. Your soon-to-be ex-spouse charged an expensive vacation trip on your joint credit card, and now you have to pay for it.

No... divorce is not the best time in the world to deal with money. But it may be the most crucial. In fact, making financial decisions is possibly the most important job you have when a marriage ends.

How can you make the right decisions? How can you deal with tedious financial details when you're going through such a stressful event? Unfortunately, it's hard to find answers to those questions.

Legal advice is plentiful and therapists or support groups can help you through emotional upheavals. But who can show you how to make sense of your financial life?

That's where this book comes in. It explains what you must know to avoid the financial disasters of divorce. Specifically, our goal is to help you understand:

- what you own and owe
- how divorce affects you tax-wise
- how best to divide your property, investments and other assets
- what can happen to your retirement nest egg or your business

- what to do about alimony and/or child support
- how to prepare for negotiating a final settlement
- and how to gain financial stability in your new life as a single person or single parent.

Each divorce is different, of course, so we cannot promise to make complex calculations for every possible situation you may encounter. At the very least, however, we *can* let you know what—and who—to turn to in finding answers for yourself.

As we see it, divorce is a crash course in managing personal finances—a course you must take whether you signed up for it or not. And the first lesson in that course is to understand that there is a big difference between legal reality and financial reality.

The financial truth about divorce is this—just because you "get it in writing," doesn't mean you will get it for real. In other words, even though your settlement may be perfectly legal and fair, it can still be costly in financial terms. For example:

*How will you pay for debts that mounted during the marriage if your spouse refuses to come up with his or her share—even if you were not supposed to pay those bills under your settlement agreement?*

*If you leave the division of your property up to the courts, the future tax consequences of your transactions will most likely be ignored. But the IRS will still collect those taxes.*

*What will you do if your spouse agreed to pay child support but is consistently late?*

As you divorce, you must be on the alert for the limitations of the law. Throughout this book, we will be showing you how to craft a strong financial settlement without ignoring the blind spots of the legal system.

Keep in mind that divorce does not have to be messy and expensive. Even if you have a great deal of property you need not spend a fortune. One couple we worked with had $5 million in assets yet they spent only $5,000 in legal fees. This couple evaluated their property, analyzed tax consequences and negotiated fairly.

By contrast, another couple, whose property totalled only $100,000, ended up spending $20,000 on attorneys fees alone—all because they could not be realistic about the financial realities of their lives, and they let their emotions interfere with reason.

Whether you and your spouse have a little money or a lot, it is important that you look at your divorce from the perspective of financial reality. It means protecting your financial well-being, whether your spouse cooperates or not. Without this perspective, you may one day find yourself painted into a financial corner, saddled with debts or burdened with assets you cannot afford or hope to sell.

The choice is yours. Divorce is painful enough. Don't let money problems make it worse.

## If you are feeling overwhelmed . . .

Congratulations. You're normal. Feeling overwhelmed is a *very* common experience during divorce. Even people who are extremely capable under other circumstances may suddenly find it difficult to balance a checkbook or perform a simple task.

If that happens to you, try to slow down.

Although every divorce is different, the process seems to have one universal effect: temporary paralysis. Whether you're a hard-driving executive or a stay-at-home spouse, in the midst of a traumatic separation, competent people become immobilized by the gravity of the financial questions they face. Should the house be sold? How much alimony will be awarded? What will happen at tax time? Who will support the children?

Confused, overwhelmed, angry or depressed, people respond normally to the stress of divorce. Our advice, as with any large undertaking, is to break it down into small, manageable pieces. And because the hectic pace of life today puts so many demands on our time, we present this plan in step-by-step segments. When you complete several small goals each day, you are less likely to become overwhelmed and immobilized. That feeling of accomplishment helps you stay out of the crises mode and works to your benefit both emotionally and financially.

## How To Use This Book

Before you jump ahead and try to figure out what your house is worth or what you will need to do about alimony or child support, we recommend that you read Chapters 1 and 2, which give the framework on legal and financial reality which you *must* understand as your divorce progresses.

For tips on dealing with emotional upheavals, read Chapter 3.

Chapters 4 through 12 cover "The First 30 Days" and are especially important if you are in the initial stages of divorce.

In Chapter 13, you begin to seriously analyze your assets and debts, and income and expenses. Whether you are a "do-it-yourselfer" or you consult an attorney, you must figure out what you own and owe, and what it costs you and your family to live. We've provided several worksheets in the chapter to help you.

Chapters 14 through 17 cover specific assets—family home, retirement benefits, investments and business assets. Chapter 18 offers the complement of dealing with your debts. And in Chapter 19, you will evaluate the likelihood of paying or receiving alimony and/or child support—and in what amounts.

Your analysis and calculations from Chapter 13 through 19 are brought together in Chapter 20 to help you structure your final settlement. Finally, Chapter 21 gives you guidelines for establishing a healthy financial life once the marriage has officially ended.

## Icons

Throughout the book, we use icons to alert you to certain information. These icons are:

 **Fast track**
We use this icon to let you know when you can skip information that may not be relevant to your case.

 **Warning**
Our warning icon alerts you to financial pitfalls during divorce or other information that needs emphasizing because of the potential consequences.

 **Attorney**
This icon lets you know when you probably need the advice of an attorney.

 **Steps**
This icon alerts you to the steps necessary for settling particular issues. Be sure to read these steps.

 **Additional Resources**
When you see this icon, a list of additional resources that can assist you in researching a particularly technical point follow.

 **Time**
This icon lets you know it's time to make a decision about how to divide your assets.

# 1

# Legal vs. Financial Realities of Divorce

Sooner or later during a divorce, you will discover the one insight that is central to this book *and* to the successful outcome of your settlement:

*Legal reality and financial reality are fundamentally different.*

A seemingly simple idea—but you'd be surprised at how long it takes to sink in. To help you understand why this concept is so important, take a few moments to consider the following real-life divorce stories. In each, read the Legal Reality first. Then, see the true outcome in the Financial Reality side.

| Legal Reality | Financial Reality |
|---|---|
| Jonathan and Penny were married for five years before they divorced. During that time, Penny frequently ran her credit cards to the limit buying clothing, and had trouble balancing her checkbook.<br><br>When they reached the final settlement hearing, Jonathan was greatly relieved when the court ordered Penny solely responsible for paying the $10,000 in credit card debts she had accumulated during their marriage. The settlement was included in the final divorce judgment, which made Jonathan feel safe. | After the divorce, however, Penny didn't pay off the credit cards and the creditors began hounding Jonathan for the money. Jonathan ended up footing the bills, because a divorce settlement assigning debts—even one included in a divorce judgment—cannot change a couple's original obligation to their creditors.<br><br>Had Jonathan raised the issue before their settlement was finalized, he could have demanded more property in exchange for paying Penny's debts or insisted that they sell some jointly-held property to pay off the creditors. |

*Moral of the story:*
*Getting something "in writing" from the court
doesn't always mean you'll get it for real.*

| Legal Reality | Financial Reality |
|---|---|
| In the divorce trial of Francesca and Franklin, the judge divided the couple's property and gave Franklin the family home. The judge also declared that Franklin owed Francesca $300,000 to balance out the property settlement. Franklin duly signed a promissory note to comply with the order. With the settlement finalized, Francesca and Franklin each went their respective merry ways. | The day after the trial ended, Franklin declared bankruptcy, and listed the note to Francesca as one of his debts. Ultimately, the bankruptcy court erased Franklin's obligation to make good on his debts— including the promissory note—and Francesca never received a penny of the $300,000. |

*Moral of the story: The law may be fair, but life isn't.*

| Legal Reality | Financial Reality |
|---|---|
| At the end of a 15 year marriage, Bill insisted on keeping the family home because he'd put so much care into his basement workshop and outdoor putting green. Bill and his wife Sharon had built up $150,000 in equity in the house. He offered to pay Sharon $75,000 for her share of the house and she accepted. Sharon also asked that the couple split the stocks they owned equally.<br><br>Because Sharon avidly followed the market, she wanted to keep a batch of stocks she had recently purchased and asked Bill to take stocks of equal value which they had purchased early in their marriage. After negotiating over a few other assets, Bill and Sharon reached an agreement in which each of them would receive the exact same dollar amount in cash or assets at the end of the divorce. The court accepted the terms of their settlement and the books on their marriage were quickly closed. | Sharon paid attention to a basic financial fact which Bill apparently ignored: taxes. Bill's company transferred him to another city shortly after the divorce and he had to sell the house. When he moved to the new town, he rented. He eventually paid a huge amount of taxes on the capital gains (profit) which accrued on the house during the 15 years of his marriage. He could have avoided these taxes had he purchased a new home of equal or greater value within two years of selling the first house.<br><br>While Sharon got $75,000 for her share of the house, Bill pocketed only $36,000 by the time he paid taxes, real estate commissions, closing costs and other expenses. Worse, Bill found himself in a similar boat with the stocks. Sharon wisely picked the stocks which had not yet built up a high tax liability. Bill, however, had blithely accepted the older stocks. Had he taken the time to figure his potential tax burden before agreeing to the settlement, he would not still be struggling to pay the IRS. |

*Moral of the story: A 50-50 settlement isn't always equal.*

## A. Lessons In Legal Reality

Ending a marriage with no assets or huge debts is the hard way to learn about divorce. Your lessons do not have to be so costly. You would never try to play basketball with football rules, or cook Chinese food using classic French recipes—would you? Similarly, you must learn to follow the correct "rules" for playing in the legal league versus the financial arena.

To get you started, the following five guidelines explain the basics of the legal reality of divorce.

- Most divorces are settled out of court.
- Divorce law is local.
- Don't expect the legal system (or a lawyer) to do everything for you.
- Your future is in your hands—not the court's.
- It's easier to write laws than to enforce them.

### 1. Most Divorces Are Settled Out of Court

You may imagine that you'll have a divorce trial like those on an old *Perry Mason* television show—everything settled in an hour with the "good guys" winning. Perhaps you're waiting for your day in court when you can explain to a wise and kindly judge the exact wrongs your spouse has visited upon you.

Don't count on it.

An estimated *90 percent* of divorce cases are settled without a court trial. Most of your settling will be done through meetings between you and your spouse, or between your lawyers. As the final settlement date nears, you will quite likely be rushed into conferences in the courtroom hall or coffee shop. In these frantic meetings, your spouse and/or the attorneys may confront you, demanding instant decisions on issues that will affect the rest of your life.

Realize, too, that divorce courts today are primarily concerned with money, not morals. The main job of the legal system is to oversee the division of property and to insure the welfare of any children. Spousal misconduct, of course, still affects custody;

and, economic mischief (such as hiding assets) can change the outcome of the final settlement. But, by and large, the personal side of marriage has become less important.

The impersonal atmosphere of the legal world may baffle you. But in fact, it is often to your advantage to stay out of the courtroom. As long as you and your spouse continue working toward a settlement without involving the court, you can trade property and negotiate terms. You each have control over your destiny. *If you cannot reach a settlement and must have a trial, however, you put your fate into the hands of a judge.* You'll have to live with whatever a judge decides regarding your home, retirement plan, business and children.

### 2. Divorce Law Is Local

Divorce laws not only differ from state to state, but interpretations of divorce law can vary from judge to judge. Whether or not you ultimately hire an attorney, you should ask local lawyers to assess the most likely outcome of a divorce like yours. Ask about the types of rulings local judges tend to make. Find out how the local courts and individual judges view settlement conferences and mediation. You should also ask about judges' attitudes toward women or men, and the prevailing mood regarding child custody.

You may not like what you hear. A lawyer may tell you that the things you want in your divorce are impossible to get. Another attorney may promise you everything, but ultimately deliver nothing. Interviewing several people for a cross section of opinion can give you a more accurate picture of your situation. (See the Appendix, for information on hiring an attorney.)

By knowing how the courts normally rule in your locale, your expectations will be more realistic. Even if you don't have a trial to settle matters (remember, 90% of cases are resolved before a trial), divorce lawyers tend to give advice that is consistent with local court rulings. Granted, it's hard to ignore sensational newspaper stories about big dollar divorces in other parts of the country. But those cases are irrelevant. You must concentrate on what happens in your backyard, because that is where your divorce and your financial future will be decided.

---

### Affording Attorneys

Throughout this book, we may tell you to "check with an attorney" on various questions. Partly we say this because we are financial planners, not legal advisors. Moreover, the individual circumstances of your divorce may require legal information beyond the scope of this book.

But who is going to pay for this costly legal advice?

Attending a brief consultation with a lawyer should not bankrupt you. Organize your thoughts and questions before you seek legal advice so you can save time when the attorney's meter is running. At an initial visit, spend an hour—not a day. Then go home and think about how much more you may have to spend on an attorney.

In some cases, your spouse may have to pay all or some of your lawyer's fee. The lawyer should be able to advise you about this at the initial consultation.

If you have very little money and feel you truly need advice from an attorney, consider borrowing money, holding a garage sale or taking a short-term second job to get some money to pay legal fees. As an inexpensive alternative, see if a local law school has a divorce clinic where law students can assist you.

For more information on finding—and working with lawyers, See Chapter 9, Section B.1.

---

## 3. Don't Expect the Legal System To Do Everything for You

One of the most costly illusions in divorce is the idea that the judicial system will protect all of your rights and meet all of your needs. You cannot afford to make that assumption. *You* are the one who must make the decisions in your divorce because *you* are the one who will live with them.

Attorneys and other professionals can help you understand your rights during divorce, but they should not determine what your financial needs will be once the marriage ends. Just because you are "entitled" to a property (say, a house), does not mean you can afford to keep it. Even though you may want to remain a freelancer, you may have to get a steady job so you can support your family after a divorce. Only you can make these decisions.

Instead of passively going through the motions of divorce, you might do better by adopting the active attitude of an entrepreneur. Business people starting a new company go to lawyers to have them formalize agreements and assess legal risks—not to ask whether they are making a good deal or not. The entrepreneur sits down with accountants and financial professionals to crunch the numbers and determine whether a business will turn a profit. Only then, after examining the financial aspects of a venture, do they consult with attorneys about potential legal problems.

Likewise, you must be the one to call the shots in your divorce. Don't expect the legal system to take care of you because it is not designed to do that.

### Don't Be Afraid To Ask Questions

Don't be intimidated or afraid to ask questions if something is unclear. One divorcing woman admitted that some of her troubles resulted from her own unwillingness to appear ignorant. In an interview with sociologist Terry Arendell in the book *Mothers and Divorce*, the woman recalled her divorce and commented: "Part of the problem was my own fault. I gave the appearance of being knowledgeable. I knew more about buying property and bank accounts than my lawyer did, but I didn't understand all the tax things. And so I was reluctant to ask some of the things I should have asked."

Legally, the implications of future taxes on property are not taken into account in settlement agreements in most states. Generally, only existing—or impending—taxes can be factored into a division of assets. Anything beyond these taxes are considered speculation—and speculation is not normally welcome in the courtroom. For example, if, as part of the divorce settlement, you and your spouse will sell $20,000 of stock at a profit, the taxes owed on the profit (called gain) will be factored into the settlement and could be split between you. If you agree to keep the house, however, and sell it in five years with a likely profit of $75,000, the court will not speculate about the taxes that you may have to pay.

## 4.  Your Future Is In Your Hands—Not the Court's

While attorneys can make predictions about how a judge might rule in a particular jurisdiction, or even about the best settlement you are likely to get, their crystal-ball gazing tends to stop the day your marriage ends.

Yes, you may be able to find out how much you would pay or receive in alimony, but beyond that, the legal system is not designed to plot your financial future once the divorce is final. As far as the law is concerned, your divorce is a snapshot, a frozen moment of the present.

But what happens after that moment?

You may legally and fairly split the benefits of a pension plan in a divorce settlement , but when the time comes to retire you may have less income than you need to live on. The court will not resolve that problem for you. Or, suppose you take assets (like some stocks), which generate income. In a few years, the court could decide to cut the amount of alimony you receive because of the income you are earning from the stocks. In either case, you cannot leave complex, multifaceted money questions about your future to the one-dimensional perspective of divorce law.

### Definition—Settlement Agreement

Throughout this book, we refer to marital settlement agreements, property settlement agreements, settlement agreements or simply agreements. They all mean the same thing. A settlement agreement is a written contract outlining how you will divide your property and debts, who will pay or receive—and how much—alimony and child support, who will have custody of or visitation with the children and other major issues. If you and your spouse are unable to reach an agreement on these issues, you will have to go to court to have a judge resolve them. Once issues are finalized, they are incorporated into the final divorce decree.

## 5.  It's Easier To Write Laws Than To Enforce Them

Laws concerning child support payments are among the most stringent on the books. Yet every year, millions of parents never receive the money to which they are legally entitled. Non-enforcement of court orders is one aspect of legal reality for which you must prepare yourself. As you go through each step of your negotiations, ask, "How will I handle this if my ex doesn't come through? What leverage do I have to enforce this agreement?"

And most importantly, "How much will enforcement cost me?"

In recognizing these risks ahead of time, you can take steps to minimize them.

To enforce your divorce agreement, you will probably have to go to court. The process is expensive, time-consuming and emotionally draining. If at all possible, keep animosity to a minimum after the divorce so that both parents' custodial or visitation time with the children goes smoothly and that alimony and child support payments are paid.

## B. Your Best Strategy: Think Financially—Act Legally

Make your financial concerns the centerpiece of your divorce and work within the framework of the law. That is the most powerful position you can take. If you think financially and act legally, you will be able to anticipate risks and assess your needs, before a financial disaster hits.

No one wants to negotiate for an asset in a divorce and then be unable to sell it because they'd owe too much in taxes. Why should you go through the nightmare of settlement negotiations only to end up losing everything you fought for six months after the divorce is over?

Remember: The legal process of divorce is something you will live *through*—but the financial reality is what you will have to live *with* for the rest of your life.

In a divorce, it's not what you *get* that counts— it's what you *keep*.

## C. Legal vs. Financial Stages of Divorce

Use the following table to help understand the relationship between the legal and financial stages of divorce. These stages will be explored in more detail throughout the book. Keep in mind that few divorces will follow these steps in this exact order.

| Legal Stages | Financial Stages |
|---|---|
| Consult an attorney or do some research at law library to learn about your legal rights and responsibilities. In particular, investigate your state's laws regarding separation —their impact on custody, alimony, child support, debts incurred after separation and increases and decreases in the value of marital assets after separation. | Gather together your financial papers and make copies of all documents. Investigate the financial impact of separation. Close or freeze access to joint accounts.[1] Open accounts in your own name. |
| Separate. Keep track of debts incurred, joint bills paid and improvements made to property during separation. | Separate. Keep track of moving and other expenses. Update insurance as necessary. Begin to think about taxes—will you file jointly or separately? |
| One spouse files complaint or petition requesting divorce. Formal divorce begins. Other spouse files answer or response.[2] | |
| One spouse files a motion for temporary alimony and/or child support. Motion may also include request that other spouse pay his or her attorney fees. | Document all temporary alimony payments made. These payments are tax deductible as long as there is an agreement in writing or a court order concerning the payments. |
| Conduct legal discovery, the procedures used to obtain information during a lawsuit. Determine the amount of alimony or child support you will pay or receive, if applicable. | Conduct financial fact finding. Complete the Net Worth and Cash Flow Statements in Chapter 13. Hire forensic accountant if necessary to search for hidden assets. Analyze your assets—use appraisers, accountants, tax advisors, actuaries and others to help you evaluate tax consequences and other risks of keeping or giving up property. |
| Begin settlement negotiations. Use one of these possible scenarios:<br>• Spouses negotiate through their attorneys.<br>• Spouses use mediation to negotiate the settlement.<br>• Spouses negotiate between themselves.<br>• Spouses unable to settle all issues. Unresolved issues brought to judge for trial. | Begin settlement negotiations. Be sure to carefully analyze the tax ramifications and other financial pitfalls of each offer and counteroffer. Settling without lawyers will save the most money. Having a trial will be very expensive. You'll have to pay lawyers fees as well as the fees of the experts (accountants, actuaries and the like) whom you bring in to testify. |
| Marital settlement agreement is drafted to incorporate terms of settlement or court order. Agreement is incorporated into final judgment of divorce. | |
| Divorce is over. Double check all legal papers, including deeds, registration forms and other ownership documents. | Divorce is over. Double check all financial papers, such as insurance, wills and the like. Update financial goals. |

---

[1]If you are concerned that your spouse might empty out a joint account or otherwise take assets to which you are entitled, you may need to obtain a temporary restraining order prohibiting the removal, sale, transfer or other use of the property. Not only can restraining orders be placed against your spouse, but they can also be served on third parties, such as bank managers and others with control over your assets. Restraining orders are also used to bar a violent or abusive spouse or parent from having contact with the other spouse or children. Domestic violence organizations can help you obtain that kind of restraining order. See the Appendix for more help.

[2]A common way to get an uncontested divorce is for one spouse to file the complaint or petition while the other spouse does not file any response. This procedure lets the first spouse "take the other spouse's default," and get the divorce under the terms of a marital settlement agreement drafted by the parties before the complaint was filed at the court. If you're contemplating this route, be sure you fully understand the terms of your settlement agreement.

# 2

# Financial Realities
# No One Talks About

*The end of a marriage is no longer a family se-*
*cret mentioned in hushed tones when the chil-*
*dren leave the room.*

Yet the true cost of divorce is rarely discussed openly.

You probably know more about negotiating to buy a car than you do about negotiating a divorce settlement. At least when buying a car, you have an idea of what to expect. Entering a showroom, you see a sticker price on a shiny automobile. But that price is not the final one. There's the "dealer markup" which can often be reduced. At the same time, you fully expect to pay taxes or other fees before you actually drive the car off the lot. And once you get the car home, you will have to spend money on insurance, licenses, repairs and maintenance.

In divorce, however, many transactions are conducted as though the "sticker" price was the total cost.

When it comes to property settlements, the courts do not consider the taxes, maintenance fees, insurance, commissions and other expenses that are a normal part of any money exchange today.

Look at the family home, for instance. If you were going to sell your house under any conditions other than divorce, you would plan to fix up the place and pay a commission to a real estate agent (unless you sold it yourself). You might have to repair the roof or get a termite inspection. If you'd ever sold a house before, you'd know that taxes on capital gains would have to be paid—unless you were going to buy another house of equal or greater value within two years.

In divorce, however, no one seems to talk about these very real costs which they would routinely discuss under any other circumstances. Spouses commonly pay their ex-partners for a full share of the equity—totally ignoring the other normal costs of a house sale, especially taxes. Only after selling the house do they recognize the burden of carrying these costs alone. In our experience, most people *do* sell

the family home, often within five years of the divorce.

*At divorce, you and your spouse are essentially selling everything you own—either to each other or to an outsider.*

If you were making a deal at any other time in your life, you would no doubt consider the hidden or additional costs that might crop up. That is the financial reality of divorce—looking at your situation from a realistic perspective that takes many factors into account.

Financial reality begins where legal reality ends. To help you close the gap between the two, we will provide you with worksheets and instructions on specific issues. We also suggest that you keep in mind five general observations on financial reality. We call them the basic "truths" about money and divorce, and you should refer to them any time you have to make tough decisions:

- In divorce, everything takes longer and costs more.
- When you're connected to another person financially, you're at risk.
- The IRS is watching your divorce—even when you're not.
- Cash is king.
- You're playing for keeps; don't sell off tomorrow for today.

## A. In Divorce, Everything Takes Longer and Costs More

One of the universal misconceptions about divorce is the idea that it will be over quickly. Then everyone can get on with their lives as though nothing happened.

In fact, your divorce can cost more money and take a longer time to settle than you ever imagined. For most of our clients, the whole process usually takes one to two years—even for simple divorces in which both parties thought it would be over in three or four months. The cost can range from $2,000 to $20,000. (One couple we knew took three years, spent $1 million and still hadn't settled when last seen....)

To understand the costly nature of divorce, you must recognize the high price of splitting one economic unit in half. On the surface, an equitable property division would mean each person walks away with half of what was shared by two, and is therefore left with enough to support one.

But in the mathematics of divorce, the equation does not work out that way. Spouses have unequal salaries and earning potential. And, many people today live beyond their means. When it comes time to divide one household into two, there is simply not enough money to go around. That holds true as much for young married couples with little property as it does for wealthy couples with assets accumulated over many years. When a catastrophic event such as divorce hits, the fragile economic base for these couples is torn apart much as an earthquake loosens a house from its foundation, leaving everything in disarray.

Recognizing that "everything takes longer and costs more" can help you through those moments when you are suddenly faced with an unexpected debt or an unwanted delay in your divorce.

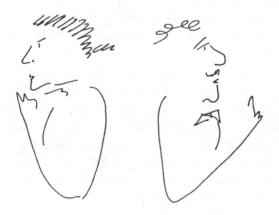

### Accept the Fact that Money Is Tight

Maybe you can accept the idea that your divorce will cost you dearly. What do you do with that knowledge?

Be willing to accept a change in your lifestyle. Face it, you may have to borrow money, move, get a second job or a used car. True, women may suffer a more dramatic drop in status than men, but both sexes must be prepared for an economic pinch—at least for a while.

You will have to resist the very understandable temptation to splurge when your marriage is ending. You must conserve your financial resources. The fact that you have to prepare for lean times also means that you must pay special attention to each financial decision you will make in divorce. In the end, your spouse may cover some of your divorce expenses, but you still must be careful with money.

## B. When You're Connected to Another Person Financially, You're At Risk

This truth seems obvious, yet it's often ignored. Divorcing partners tend to resist or "forget" the fact that they must cut or minimize the financial ties that bind them. And they pay for those ties long after the marriage ends.

You are at risk any time you hold joint interest in, have responsibility with or are financially dependent upon your spouse or ex-spouse. You have no control over what may happen in the future should your former husband or wife default on payments, commit fraud, go bankrupt, die or become disabled and thereby jeopardize your financial position.

There are many reasons for overlooking these risks: Simple resistance to change is one of them. If you've been accustomed to a joint checking account for 20 years, it may feel strange to suddenly close it.

Sometimes, financial procedures create such a feeling of finality that you're forced to recognize the marriage is really over.

If you're denying the divorce, you'll also avoid the things you need to do—like closing the joint account or having your spouse's name taken off charge cards.

---

### Women and Men—Divorce and Money

Throughout this book, we aim to provide an objective, professional view of money issues in divorce without regard to gender. We cannot honestly address personal financial realities, however, without giving recognition to the current economic conditions of the larger society.

If you are a woman with children, your standard of living is likely to drop, sometimes by as much as 73 percent, according to a thought-provoking study by Lenore Weitzman—*The Divorce Revolution* (Free Press). While Weitzman's data may be debated, the overall picture of female poverty induced by divorce cannot be denied. And in the U.S., women still earn less than men, dollar for dollar.

A divorcing woman, then, must mentally prepare for a possible drop in income if she is to have enough money to survive on once the final settlement is reached. This economic reality also underscores the necessity of accurately calculating potential income, child care needs, housing costs and other financial commitments during the divorce process.

Certainly, some women have used their divorce settlements as a launching pad to begin a business or pursue an education and thus increase their earning potential. But such an outcome takes careful planning and tough negotiating. Only by pursuing a divorce strategy that focuses on long-term financial interests can most women hope to avoid economic disaster.

---

In other cases, a spouse feels overly responsible for the other partner's welfare—and so continues paying for something like a car long after it's appropriate. Resentments over an affair or some other perceived wrongdoing, such as lying, losing money, gambling or abusing alcohol, can also cause one partner to remain financially entangled with the other.

Very commonly, however, people leave themselves at risk with their former partners because they simply do not think about it. Usually, no one talks about risks either. As you work through this book and your divorce, we will point out the most common financial risks divorcing couples face and give you tools for protecting yourself. Because your divorce is unique, however, you must stay alert to the risks in your particular case. Identify the areas where you and your spouse could remain connected financially, then work to break those connections whenever possible.

## C. The IRS Is Watching Your Divorce

Throughout the process of a divorce, you must consider the tax implications of each major financial move you make. To you, selling your property may seem like a simple business transaction—but to the Internal Revenue Service, those actions create something called a "taxable event." Be sure you're managing those "events" to your best advantage. Factor in tax costs anytime you make a financial decision in your divorce, because some day, the IRS will want to be paid.

As a general rule, a transfer of property between spouses incident to divorce is a non-taxable event. There will be major tax consequences to face in the future, however, when that asset is sold. With anything you keep as part of your settlement, you become totally and solely responsible for the taxes due on all gain (profit) on that asset from the time the two of you originally purchased it.

It is in your interest to consult with tax accountants or other financial professionals who can help you calculate the impact of divorce on your tax position.

You will also need to decide how you will file taxes once a divorce is underway. If you expect refunds on joint returns, decide how you will split the money. Be sure you know how the tax bill will be paid if money is due. And get all agreements in writing.

Investigate the implications of alimony or support payments. The point is not to become paralyzed with worry about the IRS, but to recognize that your changing marital status definitely affects your tax status. Throughout the rest of the book, we will be giving you guidance and formulas regarding tax matters.

## D. Cash Is King

Quick—which would you rather have:

* a retirement plan that promises to pay $125,000 in ten years or $100,000 today?

* a Mercedes currently valued at $35,000 or a mutual fund with a current market value of $35,000? (While the $35,000 mutual fund is not exactly in cash, a mutual fund is a liquid asset—it can be converted to cash much more quickly than a car which is depreciating in value. "Cash is king" holds true whether you are speaking of actual cash or liquid assets.)

* a secured note from your spouse promising to pay you $500 a month for the next five years or a lump sum payment of $30,000 today?

The simple answer is: take the money and run.

Like the proverbial "bird in the hand that is worth two in the bush," a dollar you get today is worth more than a promise of one tomorrow. With the examples, above, the retirement plan may be riskier than you think, the Mercedes will eventually depreciate and could be full of hidden problems, and

your spouse might never make good on the promised payments.

But besides recognizing potential practical problems, it is more important that you understand two basic financial concepts to truly appreciate the fact that cash is king: inflation and the time value of money.

*Inflation.* This is the rise in the prices of goods and services. In other words, your dollar may not be capable of buying as much tomorrow as it will today. Suppose you currently have $1,000. With an inflation rate as small as 5% per year, your $1,000 would only have the power to buy $377 in goods in 20 years.

What if you and your spouse agree that you will be paid $10,000 as part of your settlement? If you're paid upon the divorce, you'd get $10,000 in today's dollars. If you have to wait three years for your money, that $10,000 will be worth much less. Consequently, if you are offered a divorce settlement payment in the future, you must account for inflation.

*Time value of money.* Quite simply, if your money is working for you today—through investing in a quality mutual fund, producing profits in your business, or even earning interest in a bank account—you are getting more value than if you have to wait until tomorrow to put that money to work. Why should you have to wait, and give your spouse the use of your money for months or years to come? Better to get your payments in cash at the time of the divorce than to miss the opportunity of using your money to best advantage.

## E. You're Playing for Keeps

In the rush to reach a settlement, divorcing couples seek the quickest way out— regardless of the cost in the future. They literally sell off tomorrow for today.

To manage money effectively, you need alternatives to help solve unexpected problems and to meet your goals. When you trade away long-term options for short-term needs, you're forcing yourself into a corner. You literally take future choices away from yourself. Accepting property—without considering maintenance costs and your future lifestyle—can strap you with debt for years to come. Agreeing to pay your spouse's bills just to hasten the divorce process may take care of some emotional needs, but it probably does not make sense financially.

**Example:** *Marla was divorcing and calculating her cost of living. During the divorce, Marla's mother provided free child care and Marla assumed that care would continue indefinitely. She did not stop to think of what would happen should her mother become unable to babysit. After Marla's divorce was final, her mother found a new part-time job and was unable to care for her grandson. Marla spent a great deal of time and money renegotiating her alimony payments to reflect her true cost of living.*

When you are in the middle of a divorce crisis, however, obvious problems may be overlooked unless you apply long-term thinking to your divorce decisions. Anytime you feel rushed or pressured, either by your spouse or the legal calendar of your divorce proceedings, take a moment to step back and look at your divorce from a future-oriented perspective. That view should help you withstand the pressures and make more informed decisions.

---

### Money Is Not Math

Anxieties and phobias about math might hamper your ability to make financial decisions when a marriage ends. Do not feel embarrassed if you are intimidated by columns of numbers and fine-print paperwork. We have purposely simplified the formulas in this book so that everyone can understand the financial information needed at divorce.

Don't worry about mastering math. You need only gather current and accurate information about your financial situation. Getting the right numbers to plug into the formulas is much more important that learning how to make complicated tax or other calculations.

Years ago, computer scientists used the jargon term "GIGO" which stood for "Garbage In/Garbage Out." If they fed the computer the wrong data (garbage in), they would get the wrong answers (garbage out). Likewise, if you try to calculate your cost of living or the value of your property using outdated information or guesswork, you will end up with "garbage" in your final settlement. So gather the correct data; if you don't want to plug the numbers into the formulas yourself, you can hire a bookkeeper, accountant or financial planner to work with you.

# 3

# Emotional Divorce: Managing the "Money Crazies"

*To make the best financial decisions divorce, you must be aware of the emotional sabotage that can wreck your settlement negotiations.*

Be on guard if you find yourself attempting to:

- get even
- get it over
- get back together

These three "gets"—plotting revenge, rushing through the divorce or pushing for a reconciliation—will hamper your ability to think clearly and act in your own best interest.

Check your attitude. Do any of the following sound like you?

*"I'm going to get even no matter what it takes. You're going to pay for what you did to me. Just you wait. I'll see you in court."*

It's normal to be angry during divorce, but if you're using the "get-even" approach, you'll probably never be satisfied. A settlement may be totally equal according to the numbers on paper, but people with this attitude continue to complain years later. Not only will you harbor bitter feelings, but it's likely you will use poor judgment on important financial questions if you are motivated by revenge. And your attorney's fees will soar.

Realize too, that if you insist on getting even, a court trial will likely cost you three times as much as an out-of-court settlement. Besides that, there is no guarantee that an ex-spouse will comply with court orders, or that the court will give you what you want. While you should certainly pursue your legal rights, the judicial system is no place to get satisfaction for your emotional demands—a well-fashioned settlement is always the best approach.

*"I don't care what happens.
I just want to get it over with."*

Stop right here. This is a major blind spot. The decisions you make during your divorce will affect you (and any children you have) for the rest of your life. It's no time to rush. While you may feel uncomfortable, your financial survival depends on participating in each step of your divorce settlement—regardless of how long it takes. And if you try too many short cuts, you could find yourself paying for them because of unresolved resentments or unexpected money problems. In a year or two, your emotional life will be different. The financial agreements you make during divorce, however, affect you permanently.

*"Maybe if I don't cause problems financially, we can work it out. I won't make waves. I'll just give in so we can get back together."*

This is one of the most damaging misconceptions during divorce. Certainly you want to work things out if it's appropriate and if *both* of you are committed to a fair and equitable settlement. But it's futile to think that if you surrender your financial leverage you can save the relationship. If you've allowed your spouse to take the dominant role, you give up even more power when you "don't make waves." Why should someone come back into a faltering relationship if you are giving the person everything he or she wants anyway? In any event, if you and your partner do get back together, your relationship will be much healthier if you are on an equal level financially and emotionally.

You may agree with all of the advice you have just read. But in reality, how do you deal with money when you are so involved emotionally with your spouse?

That is the central question you must answer for yourself and that is what we will help you do throughout this book.

Basically, the better you manage your emotions, the better you will be able to manage your money during divorce. It's a difficult task. The emotional toll of divorce is so high that therapists and counselors use the label of "crazy time" to describe it.

Ironically, you are being asked to make calm and rational financial decisions that will affect the rest of your life at a point when you are under some of the heaviest emotional pressures you are ever likely to experience. Those two tasks—the logical and linear management of money and the release of emotional tension—pull you in opposite directions. Attempting to balance these poles is an insane proposition. No wonder divorce produces "crazy time." No wonder you feel like you have the "money crazies."

Your best approach to managing these "money crazies" is to understand the divorce process in emotional terms and then take action to avoid some of the common pitfalls. Forewarned is forearmed.

## A. Reduce Stress Whenever You Can

You can begin to resolve the financial-emotional struggle of divorce by recognizing just how stressful it is. Research has shown that divorce is second only to the death of a spouse in terms of the amount of stress it produces. Some counselors contend that when other factors such as separation anxiety, moving from a long-term residence and loss of status are added to the equation, divorce becomes the most stressful event in life.

On top of all this, money is a difficult—sometimes taboo—subject, and even happily married couples experience anxiety when discussing it. You may also feel pressure because you now have to take on tasks and responsibilities that were shared or handled exclusively by your spouse. And you certainly can no longer "talk things over" with your mate.

Here are some of the ways stress affects you during divorce:

- sleeplessness
- fatigue
- loss of appetite
- inability to cope with routine tasks
- disruption in work patterns
- emotional explosions
- frustrations over any challenge, large or small

You can help combat these conditions by nurturing yourself. Do whatever is necessary for you to take care of yourself. If you have children, good self-care becomes even more important. Your frustrations are less likely to spill over onto the children if you are not ignoring your own needs.

Have a massage, go out to dinner or a movie, stroll through a museum—those are a few quick fixes that can see you through a rough period. Do not fall back on the excuse that you have little money or time to take care of yourself. Sitting under a tree or watching a sunset costs nothing, and can work wonders on your bruised emotions.

Even if you don't feel like it, try to keep your eating patterns close to normal. Good nutrition can be good medicine for your nerves. Also, exercising is one of the smartest things to do while divorcing. Besides working out physical tension and helping to fight fatigue, vigorous workouts often improve your mental state.

These stress reduction techniques sound simple on paper—but simple or not, they are crucial to practice. The stress of your divorce will last for a while—you have to learn to live with it and manage it.

## B.  Safeguard Your Sanity

During a divorce, it is important to safeguard your emotional well-being. Spend more time with people who can give you positive reinforcement and less with those who may be critical of you or your divorce. Join a support group or see a therapist if necessary. In the long run, any money you spend on your mental health will be less than you'd lose if you got fired from your job or went on a shopping spree to deal with the "money crazies."

If you don't already have one, buy a phone answering machine. Not only can you screen nuisance calls if your spouse is hostile, but also you can let others know that you are unreachable when you need to be alone.

There will be days when you feel like talking and other days when it is the last thing you want to do. You may have just calmed down, and then, when you run into a friend and re-tell your story, emotions rise again—the catch in the throat, the anger, the frustration. That may be a healthy experience, but if you're feeling like it's "too much," limit your personal conversations just as you would your phone calls.

Take control of your home environment. Clean a closet, paint a room or move the furniture. There's an almost universal tendency during divorce to think about the past—obsessively and excessively. Most people find it is simply easier to put away the family pictures, the mementos, and the visual cues that can trigger feelings of loss and depression.

You are not only affected by what you see, but also by what you hear. Instead of sitting back and passively allowing a favorite old song to make you sad, reach over and snap off the radio. The same goes for those heart-tugging commercials on television featuring happy couples—change the channel or turn off the TV. You'll be amazed at how good it can feel to exert control over something when so much of your life seems to be out of control.

## C.  Watch Out for Sore Spots

Probably, you already know which financial issues are likely to get you upset. All couples have sore spots—resentments about an unpaid bill, spending sprees, bounced checks, interfering in-laws or loans to relatives.

If you know that you will be dealing with an issue that's been a particular long-term aggravation, prepare yourself for it instead of merely reacting to the inevitable pressure. Get a good night's sleep before tackling such a problem, or postpone a confrontation until you feel strong enough to be at your best. Taking these basic steps can go a long way toward reducing the tension in your life. Remember, reducing stress means increasing your ability to make sound financial decisions.

---

### "No, We Can't Afford It Now"

Few parents enjoy denying their children toys, gifts or other pleasures. During divorce, you may find yourself repeating the phrase, "No! We can't afford it now!" more times than you care to count. Disappointing your children can only add to your level of frustration. But while you may want to protect them from harsh realties, you must also be honest and help your family adjust to the new circumstances.

Your children may be too young to understand the concept of money, much less the lack of it, so you may need an extra supply of parental patience. You can take heart in the fact that millions of couples have divorced and millions of children have survived it. Teaching children to live on a tight budget may be more valuable in the future than giving in to their every whim today.

---

## D. Be Prepared for Bad Scenes

Some emotional problems of divorce offer no easy solutions: When people are under stress, they tend to revert to their base, survival behaviors. That can lead to over-drinking, shouting matches and other bad scenes. If someone tends to be absent-minded, selfish or nagging, those tendencies will be even more exaggerated when a marriage is ending.

During divorce, couples are facing the psychological task of separating, and consciously or unconsciously look for ways to break their connection to each other. During courtship, partners do everything possible to build the relationship, while in divorce, energy goes into destroying it. The stress, coupled with these "relationship-destroying" behaviors, create many of the horror stories of divorce. The sweet irrational gestures of romance are reversed by the equally ridiculous acts of "vengeance" during separation.

Maybe that will help you understand why your spouse is behaving so badly toward you—even if you thought you'd have a "civilized divorce."

Being prepared for the actions of someone who is determined to cut off any connection to you—by wiping out the checking account, running off to another state or ruining the family's credit—can help you short circuit potential damage. Seeing bizarre behavior within the framework of the separation process may help you take it less personally. You may even find you are more detached from the short-term drama of divorce and therefore better able to concentrate on the long-term money questions that are important to you.

## E. Develop a Financially Focused Mental Attitude

To combat a devious spouse during divorce, you must develop a strong mental attitude and legal strategy. Certainly you are entitled to feelings of outrage and betrayal. You can utter the cry "How can you do this to me?!?" as much as you want to. In fact, that phrase is a common chorus in divorce cases. Yes, many things that happen in divorce *are* unfair.

But the fact remains that you will have to keep going and keep fighting for your financial life regardless of the injustices which may be perpetrated by your spouse and/or your spouse's attorney. You are the only one who can stand up for yourself. If you stay focused on the future and the financial realities of your life, you will be in a much stronger position as your divorce progresses.

## F. Avoid the "All at Once" Syndrome

Most likely, you will experience a wide gamut of feelings and moods: anger, hatred, elation, excitement, sadness, loss, depression, bitterness, rejection, loneliness, guilt and hostility. Sometimes it will feel as though you're experiencing those feelings "all at once." In fact, the "all at once" phenomenon seems to be part of the "money crazies" of divorce.

You may also feel that everything is coming apart "all at once." Just as soon as you get the car fixed, the washer or the stove breaks down. One explanation is that you simply notice problems more because of your stressful state. Moreover, by the time most people separate, a great deal of their energy has been focused on the relationship—not on the normal chores that can keep a household running. You may not be in the mood to defrost the refrigerator or check the oil in the car as usual. That lack of maintenance can catch up with you as the machinery in your life begins breaking down.

The "all at once" approach to divorce can manifest itself in other ways as well. Some people decide that since they are changing a mate, they should change everything else in their lives as well. They try to lose weight, quit smoking, get a new job and redecorate the house, all at the same time. Give yourself time. Go slowly. You will have your hands full just getting through the divorce.

## G. Manage the Ebb and Flow of Emotions

Keep in mind that emotions tend to be experienced in waves. One day you may feel fine, the next day, life is awful. Such fluctuations are common to divorce, and eventually the wave action subsides. Do not attempt to handle important money tasks on the bad days—wait until the storm calms.

Because the level of tension in a divorce is often compared to the stress that accompanies the death of a loved one, some psychologists' claim the grief processes are similar. Elizabeth Kubler-Ross' ground-breaking work on death and dying pinpointed five stages of grief: denial, anger, bargaining, letting go and acceptance. These stages, however, do not necessarily occur in this order. How you go through these stages is unique to you, but it is important that you experience them.

Marriage counselors note that people who avoid grieving by jumping into a new relationship too quickly are only prolonging the process. Those who do allow themselves to grieve for the marriages they had (or the marriages they wished they had) actually get through their divorces more quickly—and carry less psychological baggage when the marriage is over. As a consequence, they are often able to manage their financial lives better too.

While the grief processes are admittedly similar in death or divorce, some important differences do exist. Social attitudes have changed greatly, but widows and widowers still get more sympathy than those who have divorced. With divorce, too, the door to your relationship does not close with the same finality. You may still have contact with your former spouse for years and go through the grieving process many times as you make contact and separate.

The ambivalence—the love-hate relationship with your former spouse—is common when marriages end. Actually, the push and pull in and out of the relationship characterizes the separation process which began before the actual divorce. Commonly, one person in the relationship becomes discontented before the other, and this "initiator" is usually the one to ask for the divorce.

If your partner was the initiator, don't be surprised if he or she seems to have already moved on; because in fact, that person had a head start on the psychological work needed to separate. Just don't let yourself lag behind financially, or get pushed into doing something you're not ready for.

The initiator may already be out the door and pressuring you to "get on with it"—to sign over the condo, to sell the house, to separate the silverware. Meanwhile, you may still be at the "starting gate," emotionally shocked and dazed, unable to walk much less run at the pace your partner is demanding.

If you initiated the divorce, realize that it is probably in your best financial and family interests to be sensitive to your partner's rate of accepting the separation. Your negotiations are likely to be more successful if you present your financial proposals to someone who has had a chance to assimilate what is happening in the relationship on a personal level.

Psychologists have found that the hardest part of the divorce process tends to be the time just before the actual physical separation. Tensions often mount dramatically until the real break occurs. Some couples separate and re-connect several times in an attempt to save the marriage. Whatever is happening to you emotionally, continue taking steps to put your financial life in order. Should you and your partner ultimately re-unite, your relationship will be stronger if you have not used money as a weapon against each other.

## H. Don't Let Financial Tasks Overwhelm You

As you move through your divorce, it will be easy to become overwhelmed with the financial details. You may suffer from math anxiety or money phobias. Or perhaps you and your partner shared a complicated financial life.

Whatever form your feelings take, you can get some relief by breaking down your tasks into small steps. Reward yourself for completing an item. Hire a math whiz to help you when necessary. If you are upset, do not hesitate to see a counselor or join a therapy group. That strategy makes much more sense, and is less costly, than using your attorney as a therapist or asking your friends to help you understand a situation that calls for expert analysis.

Anything you can do to build your self-esteem is important now because divorce tends to make you feel worse about yourself and it is easy to confuse money issues with your sense of self-worth. Besides the stress-management techniques already described, you may also find it helpful to keep a journal. Having a notebook handy to jot down feelings throughout the day helps dissipate tense moments. This record can serve as an "invisible calculator" to tally the emotional costs of financial decisions. Tracking feelings and reactions in this way can make it easier to reach those bottom line decisions.

While it may seem as though the inner turmoil from your divorce will never end, it is a finite process which only takes time. For some people, the process lasts one or two years, while for others, recovery from a divorce may take longer. You are very likely to become a different person in that time, with different needs and attitudes. Keep that in mind as you manage the "money crazies" of your divorce—and make sure the financial choices you make today will work for you tomorrow.

---

### Divorce—On a Spiritual Level

For some people, divorce stress is more than emotional. It becomes a religious or spiritual crisis. We cannot attempt to address such a crisis in this book. You can, however, contact local churches or clergy members for referrals to divorce ministries.

One note of caution: No matter how you feel about your divorce from the spiritual point of view, you cannot ignore its legal and financial consequences.

For example, one client insisted on working exclusively with attorneys and other professionals who shared her faith. While there is nothing inherently wrong with this, it didn't work in her case. She didn't judge the professionals she hired on their competence or abilities. In the end, she had to go through the costly process of finding a new attorney and accountant to help her complete the divorce.

For more information on selecting professionals, see Chapter 9.

# 4

# Decisions To Make in the First 30 Days

*Whether you've just begun to think about divorce or you've already packed to leave, the first stage of separation is financially crucial. Any action—from moving assets to moving out of your home—must be reviewed carefully because the decisions you make now will affect your final settlement and your future.*

Use this section as a guide to help you maneuver through the most common rough spots you may face when your marriage is ending, even if you're not officially in "the first 30 days."

To make sure you do not overlook details which could lead to costly problems, read all of this chapter. Then you can decide which of the next eight chapters you should read and which you can skip.

## Chapter 5:  The Hardest Part—Is My Marriage Really Over?

If you act as though you are still a married partner while your spouse behaves otherwise, you can seriously jeopardize your financial position. Regardless of your feelings about your spouse, you must be honest with yourself in answering this question and then respond to your situation appropriately.

## Chapter 6:  The Separation— Who Must Move Out, and By When?

The date of separation can affect your debts, the value of your retirement benefits, the income taxes you may pay and possibly other financial matters.

The way in which you separate, legally, may also affect child custody and alimony. Even if you or your spouse has already moved out, you still need to document the date of the separation because your spouse may dispute it during the divorce.

## Chapter 7:  Closing the Books—What To Do With Joint Accounts

Remember the financial truism of divorce: When you're connected to someone else financially, you're at risk. Now is the time to reduce any risks you are exposed to by closing or removing names from joint credit card accounts, shared bank accounts, loans, equity lines of credit and other mutual accounts.

## Chapter 8:  Financial Fact Finding— What Must I Know and When Must I Know It?

Divorce in the "information age" means that the person with the most information wins. Gather as much financial information as you can yourself and then use the legal system to find out what you cannot. The "Financial Facts Checklist" in the chapter will guide you in your information gathering.

## Chapter 9: Getting Help—Who Can I Turn To?

Not every divorce requires a full roster of lawyers, appraisers, therapists or other professionals to complete the settlement. But at the least, you may need some help from one of them, and you need to find out whose services are most suited to you.

## Chapter 10: Reducing Risks and Protecting Property

In the upheaval of divorce, the things you take for granted can easily be overlooked. You must make sure you retain proper insurance coverage and that your business, health, income and other essentials are protected.

## Chapter 11: Avoiding Tax Troubles

Throughout divorce, you must be on the lookout for the hidden tax consequences of your decisions. Initially, you should make a binding agreement with your spouse about filing your taxes. You must also guard against the possibility that you will be held liable for any problems your spouse has with the IRS.

## Chapter 12: Going From "We" to "Me"

Setting goals may be difficult when you can only think about getting through each day. Outlining a basic plan of action, however, can help your emotional (and financial) state when a divorce begins. You also need to consider how bills will be paid. You may be entitled to receive or be required to pay temporary alimony or child support. You can make short-term agreements with your spouse, but keep an eye on the long-term impact   most notably tax consequences—before you exchange funds.

# 5

# The First 30 Days: The Hardest Part—
# Is My Marriage Really Over?

*Emotionally, it may be years before you feel complete peace of mind about the end of your marriage. Legally, a final decree from the court marks the termination of your married life.*

From a strictly financial standpoint, however, the marriage ends when you or your spouse begins to take unilateral actions, regardless of the effect on the other person. It's that moment when one spouse stops acting like a trusted friend or partner and starts putting the other spouse in economic jeopardy. One spouse might empty a bank account, leaving the other with nothing to pay the bills or hire an attorney. Or a soon-to-be "ex" might run up debts unbeknownst to the other.

A great deal of financial damage can take place in the early stages of divorce. You must protect your interests whether or not you feel the marriage is over.

Couples often go through several phases of splitting up and getting back together before the final break. While you are going through this push and pull of separation, you may find yourself walking a tightrope between conflicting demands and emotions—watching out for your personal property without antagonizing your spouse, or taking care of your individual needs while not letting your spouse off the hook for joint responsibilities.

Eventually, you will recognize when the marriage has reached a point of no return. Even then, you may hold out hope for a reconciliation. There's nothing wrong with hope—as long as you continue taking care of business. That means knowing precisely where your financial risks lie, and what to do about them. The following stories illuminate the dilemma you are in at this stage of divorce—and the danger of ignoring its consequences.

| *A Happy Ending* | *An Unhappy Ending* |
|---|---|
| It may be hard to believe when you're in the midst of a crumbling relationship, but handling money problems can sometimes help clear up other troubling issues in a marriage. Alice came in for a financial planning consultation and announced that she was considering a divorce. Although she had always worked outside the home, her husband managed the family finances and kept Alice in the dark about money. Unwilling to tolerate the situation any longer, Alice began educating herself and learning about the couple's cash flow, taxes and investments. She also consulted an attorney to assess her legal rights. Secure with her knowledge, she confronted her husband and demanded a greater financial role in the marriage. They argued bitterly and almost divorced at several points along the way. Through patience and counseling, however, they resolved their differences and kept the marriage intact. | The infamous Palm Beach divorce of Roxanne and Peter Pulitzer demonstrates what can happen if both parties are not equally committed to a reconciliation. Roxanne claims that in trying to save her marriage, she lost her financial power and leverage as a mother. Upon receiving divorce papers concerning hearings and proceedings, she says she followed her husband's instructions to throw them in the garbage because he did not intend to end the marriage. Doing just that placed Roxanne at a great disadvantage when her husband did, in fact, continue the divorce proceedings. "I lost the case before it even started," she said once it was over. Instead of focusing on the reality of her situation, she put her energy into reconciliation—and lost on all counts, including the custody of her children. |

No one can really predict which marriages will come apart or stay together, because every couple, and the dynamic between them, is unique. If you are still questioning whether you have a viable marriage or not, some options available to you are:

*Counseling*. Now is the time to find out if your marriage is worth saving. Some people cannot—and perhaps should not—let go until they have explored every avenue of reconciliation. But if your spouse refuses to cooperate, you may have little choice but to accept the inevitable and move on with the divorce.

*Temporary separation*. For some couples, time apart becomes a time for healing. Make a list of your joint obligations and expenses. Through mediation or counseling, you and your spouse may be able to reach agreements about dealing with the practical demands of life while you work on your emotional relationship.

 **Decision Time . . .**

After you give yourself some time to consider this information and your options, you must confront the main decision presented in this chapter: Is your marriage really over? This question is not meant to rush you toward divorce, but rather to help you clarify your position. You can afford to leave some questions open in life—but this isn't one of them. Once you've made this decision it will be significantly easier for you to tackle the hard tasks ahead. But if you're unclear on this, all decisions that follow become much harder to make.

Okay—take a deep breath. Write out your answer below, or speak it out loud to someone you trust. Either way, the time has come to make the decision which only you can.

*Is my marriage really over?*

---

**Whatever Stage You're In, Don't Ignore Legal or Financial Realities**

Whether you attempt counseling, a trial separation or some other form of resolving conflicts in your marriage, you cannot ignore your financial responsibilities and potential liabilities. Just as you would regard legal notices or documents as important matters at any other time in your life, so too must you recognize the serious implications of any legal actions in the early stages of divorce—even if your spouse tries to convince you otherwise. Do not ignore court orders or papers. And, if you have any reason to suspect your spouse is moving assets or taking funds from your joint accounts, you should quickly read Chapter 7 for information on how to protect your interests.

# 6

# The First 30 Days: The Separation— Who Must Move Out, and By When?

*"I told him I wanted him out by the end of the month."*

*"I can't stand it another minute—I'm getting out of here."*

*"It's over and it would be easier on all of us if you would just go."*

Don't be surprised if you find yourself saying—or hearing—any of these statements before you separate. Feelings run high and emotions seem to dictate the schedule of events in your life. Old arguments and long-held resentments commonly surface in this most difficult period, just before or during the actual physical separation. Power plays may become more troublesome as one of you may try to "force" the other out.

But no matter how you feel about your spouse, the truth is that neither of you "has to" move, except if you or your children would be in danger if your spouse stayed. In such cases, you could get a court restraining order to prohibit your spouse from remaining in the family home. In many states, you may be able to find a kit for a layperson to use without a lawyer's assistance. Also, many women's clinics provide help for victims of domestic violence. (See the Appendix.)

In the midst of ending a marriage, you may resist the idea of seeing your situation in the cold, harsh light of financial reality. But that denial could ultimately cost you thousands of dollars. Before you insist on leaving or having your spouse move out, take a little time to consider the financial consequences of the separation date.

---

**Protect Your Rights in Relations to Your Children If You Plan to Move Out**

If you have children, the primary caretaker might want to stay in the family home while the other spouse rents an apartment, housesits for someone else, or moves in with a friend. Realize, however, that by moving out of the family home, you could jeopardize your chances for getting physical custody of your children. This is because few judges like to change the status quo when it comes to kids. So before you move out, be sure to make arrangements with your spouse as to the conditions under which you will each see the children. Consider driving them to school a few mornings a week. Or take them to and from softball practice, ballet lessons or church or synagogue.

If you have any question or doubt about your potential position as a parent, or feel that you are being pushed away from your children by moving out of the house, be sure to consult an attorney familiar with local practices.

## A. The Separation Date

After thinking about who will move, the second question becomes even more crucial: by when? The date on which you formally separate can affect your credit, pension benefits, or other assets. Think of that date as a legal benchmark.

Before that date, you and your spouse are obviously still married and are subject to the same laws you've been living under since you first wed. After that date, however, you enter a gray area of financial and legal reality which is not totally clarified until the divorce becomes final. You have no control over the actions of your spouse in this time period, yet you are still tenuously connected—which means you could potentially be responsible for your spouse's bills. The value of a retirement plan, too, can go up or down by thousands of dollars depending on when you officially separate.

The separation date is a legal mechanism which works differently in different states. In a few states, the separation date is the date you or your spouse physically moves out of your joint residence. Other states consider that the separation begins the day you or your spouse files divorce papers. And in other states, the day on which you formally tell your spouse that you intend to get a divorce is the date on which you are considered separated. In either of the latter two situations, couples may continue living together after the separation date, perhaps because neither can afford to move. This, no doubt, may be very uncomfortable. (Use Section B, "Questions to Ask Your Attorney," to find out about the separation date in your state.)

Either party can try to make a case for their choice of the actual date of separation depending on the financial advantages of picking one day over another. If you are going to be responsible for the credit card charges your spouse incurred during the marriage, for instance, you'd want the date of separation to be prior to your spouse's shopping spree. Or, if your company adds a tidy sum to your pension plan each May, you might want to move out in April.

Granted, it's difficult to see the value of this date before you separate. In six months to a year, however, you will have the advantage of hindsight and a different perspective. Instead of having regrets later, take a little time right now to think about how the separation will affect you.

Below is an overview of how the separation date affects the following financial issues:

- Debts and credit
- Retirement plans and pension benefits
- Income and income taxes
- Investments and business assets
- Alimony

## If You Must Move

Although you may not like the idea, it's possible that you will have to move from your home. You can make life easier by preparing for the pressures you will face. Moving is stressful at any time; divorce only compounds the stress. Not only are you losing a mate, but you're letting go of a home and all it's been to you.

Feelings of separation and abandonment can be exaggerated by anxiety about where you will live next. To cope with your emotional reactions, look at your situation in practical terms, which helps separate real concerns from unfounded fears.

For example, movers often charge a premium for their hectic summer season, while offering lower prices between October and April. The first and last days of the month are also busy times for mover, so you may be able to save money by moving mid-month. The American Movers Conference suggests that you question a mover carefully about rates, liability, pickup and delivery, and claims protection. To move locally, you'll probably be charged an hourly rate or flat fee. Long-distance movers usually charge by the weight and mileage.

In addition to the cost of the move itself, you'll need money to hook up utilities, phones and other services. You'll have other "new house" costs like buying kitchen basics, such as salt, pepper, sugar and flour and replacing cleansers that you left behind. Count on eating out a lot, too, before you restock your kitchen or unpack your dishes and pots and pans.

*If you plan to move your children out of state.* If you move out of state and take your children with you without your spouse's consent, a judge may later deny you custody. Judges do not look favorably on parents who move their children away from their other parent, school, friends and other community ties. Before making such a move, consult an attorney to make sure you do not jeopardize your rights as a parent.

## 1. Debts and Credit

Bill collectors do not suddenly stop sending their statements just because you are going through a divorce. When you enter the limbo of separation, pay particular attention to its impact on your debts and credit standing.

### a. Debts

In general, both spouses are responsible for paying debts generated during the marriage. At the same time, once the divorce is final, neither is responsible for the debts created by the other. Debts incurred during separation, however, can be tricky. The general rule is that debts incurred after the separation date but before the divorce is final are the responsibility of the spouse who incurred them and must be paid by that person.

One exception is for "family necessities." For example, if, during the period of separation, one spouse incurs a debt for food, clothing, shelter or medical care, the other spouse is probably obligated to pay that bill. Children's expenses, too, usually fall into this category.

The general rule—that debts generated during separation must be paid by the person who incurred them—however, does not always protect you. If your partner defaults or simply refuses to pay, the creditors no doubt will come after you for payment. And because you were still married when the debts were created, the creditor will assert a right to collect from you. Your only remedy may be to try and get reimbursed from your ex-spouse.

**Example:** *Janet's husband Jim had dental work done after he moved out of their apartment, but he never paid the bill. Janet did not know anything about his dental work, and Jim left town as soon as the divorce was final. The dentist turned the bill over to a collection agency which then went after Janet for the money. Eventually she settled the bill, but not without spending her time, energy and money to resolve the problem.*

### b. Credit

Remember the warning given in the last chapter: When you're financially connected to someone else, you're at risk. You are responsible for any use of a credit or charge card by either card holder on a joint account. Also, while you are not technically responsible for charges your spouse runs up on your credit card without your knowledge, you'll have a hard time convincing the creditor that you didn't authorize the charges.

But before angrily closing all joint credit accounts, check first to see how your individual credit will be affected by such an action. If you do not have credit in your own name, be sure to establish it before you separate. Generally it is best to close joint credit accounts because you cannot control your spouse's use of them.

There may be certain circumstances in which you'll need joint credit. For instance, if you'll both be buying maintenance items for your house, rental property or children, it may be convenient to have a joint checking account to which both you and your spouse contribute. You can make a formal, written agreement as to how the account will be used and even require that all checks written on the account must have both spouses' signatures. Keep in mind, however, that though you may need to retain joint accounts, do not start any new joint financial ventures.

Extensive information on debts, creditors, establishing credit in your own name and other issues can be found in *Money Troubles: Legal Strategies To Cope With Your Debts*, by Robin Leonard (Nolo Press).

## 2.   Retirement Plans and Pension Benefits

In most situations, your retirement benefits are valued as of the date of separation. Suppose your partner's employer will make a contribution to his or her pension on a particular date—such as October 15. If you move out before that date, even if it's on October 14, then you may not be entitled to a share of the amount the employer contributes to the plan.

In addition, many companies provide an accounting of retirement benefits only on an annual basis. The amount in a pension fund, profit sharing plan or other type of benefit program could significantly differ from one part of a year to the next. By the time your divorce becomes final, a year or two could have passed from when you separated and the retirement fund may have grown by thousands of dollars. If it's your spouse's fund, you won't be entitled to any of that growth. If it's your fund, you won't be required to share with your spouse the portion attributed to the growth.

To safeguard your interest, obtain a copy of the benefit brochure issued by your own or your spouse's employer if possible. It's also helpful to have copies of the actual retirement plan itself or a summary of it. (Chapter 15 covers retirement plans in detail.) Because so many factors affect your retirement benefits, it is best to consult an attorney, financial advisor, pension plan expert or actuary who can analyze your particular situation. (See Chapter 9.)

## 3.   Income and Income Taxes

The income that you earn after the date of separation is yours and yours alone. Therefore, you are solely responsible for the taxes due on this income. Also, when you separate may influence your decision to file your income taxes jointly or separately. (See Chapter 11.)

## 4.   Investments and Businesses Assets

Many states value assets at the date of the divorce, not the separation. This means that if one spouse moves out of the house and it appreciates between that time and the time the divorce becomes final, the spouses will share in the appreciation. The valuation of investments and business assets should be double checked, however, as the rules do vary from state to state.

## 5.   Alimony

You may not realize it, but your separation date could have an effect on alimony. In many states, long-term marriages—usually marriages of ten years or more—are carefully scrutinized. In a number of states, a nonworking, dependent or lower wage-earning spouse is presumed to be in need of alimony when a long-term marriage ends. If you're a few months shy of the 10-year (or whatever length your state requires) presumptive period for alimony, you may want to stay around to not jeopardize those future payments.

## B.  Questions To Ask Your Attorney

As you can see, you'll need to carefully calculate your legal and financial positions before separating. Because the legal definition of the separation date varies from state to state, however, we cannot explain the nuances of your state's law. We can provide you with a list of important questions for you to ask your attorney or research at your local law library.

1. What constitutes the date of separation in this state? Is it the date:
   - one spouse moves out?
   - files for divorce?
   - or declares the marriage over?

2. Which debts—incurred after the date of separation but before the divorce becomes final—is each spouse responsible for?

3. What date is used—separation date, date of final negotiations or date closest to the final divorce— to calculate value of the following assets?
   - house
   - retirement benefits or pension plans
   - business assets and investments

4. Does my state have a long-term marriage law; that is, is a supported spouse from a long-term marriage presumed to be in need of alimony? If so, what period constitutes "long-term"?

5. What other legal or financial ramifications of the date of separation should I know about?

---

**Before You Move**

Before you move out of the family home, be sure to make copies of bookkeeping files, tax returns, bills, bank accounts, receipts and the like—in short, any scrap of financial information that you think could possibly be important during your divorce. Even if you don't have your spouse's cooperation in this project, it is important that you get the copies. If you must resort to the legal process of discovery (see Chapter 13), your legal bill may run sky high—and there is no guarantee that you will get all the information you may ultimately need.

You should also take an inventory of all shared or individual property. Take photographs or make a videotape to document the condition of property at stake in your divorce. (For more information on dealing with property, see Chapter 7, Section A.6, Shared Property and Special Collections.)

---

**Social Security and Divorce**

If you plan to collect Social Security benefits based on your status as a spouse, and not from your own employment, you may not be entitled to Social Security spousal benefits unless your marriage has lasted ten years. If your marriage is nearing ten years duration, it may be to your advantage to stay—or move out—before that date.

Because each worker's Social Security files are confidential, you may not be able to find out about the status of your spouse's benefits. You can try by asking your mate, visiting your local Social Security office or calling the agency at 1-800-234-5772. If you contact the agency, ask for a "Request For Earnings And Benefits Estimate Statement"—form SSA 7004. Complete it and send it back. If these methods fail, you will probably need your lawyer's help in getting the information. (See Chapter 13.)

# 7

# The First 30 Days: Closing the Books—
# What To Do with Joint Accounts

*When you and your mate are in the midst
of splitting up, you come face to face with one
of the important financial truisms of divorce:
Wherever you are connected to another person
financially you are at risk. Does that mean you
need to rush out in a panic and close all your
joint accounts? Not necessarily—it is never wise
to act in a panic, and only in a handful of
divorces do spouses deliberately destroy the
other financially.*

But even if your spouse doesn't purposefully ruin your
financial life, he or she can do things that leave you
vulnerable. One way to gauge how much financial
damage your spouse could inflict is to measure the
level of hostility between you. For example, if you're
no longer on speaking terms—or you speak only
about the children—you will probably want to act
quickly to separate your financial lives.

Even if your divorce is friendly, don't count on
that good will to determine what you should do
about joint accounts. Look at your situation objectively. Apply your own common sense and instincts.
If you can't, take friends' advice. You should be moving toward eliminating the financial obligations you
share with the person you are divorcing. Because income is often reduced—and expenses increased—by
a divorce it may not be possible to cut all connections. Nevertheless, you can still reduce your risks.

## A. Joint Account Checklist

Use the checklist that follows to alert yourself to
common trouble spots.

## 1. Credit Cards

Before closing joint credit card accounts, be sure you
have established credit in your own name. You can
apply for credit, based on your own income.[1]
Department stores, for instance, may open an individual account for you when you close a joint one. If
you don't qualify, you can apply for a secured credit
card. Many banks will give you a credit card if you
secure it by opening a passbook savings account and
returning the passbook to the bank. Your credit limit
equals a percentage (around 75) of the amount you
deposit into your account. Depending on the bank,
you'll be required to deposit as little as a few hundred
dollars or as much as a few thousand. Many secured
credit cards have a conversion option. This option
lets you convert the secured card into a regular credit
card (one not tied to a savings account) after a certain time period, if you use the card responsibly.[2]

To close joint accounts, write to creditors (look
for the "account information" address on the back of
a billing statement), inform them of your impending
divorce and ask them to close the account and cancel
all cards. Request that the company advise you of any
outstanding charges, and be sure to let them know
that you refuse to be responsible for any charges
made after the date of your letter. While such a letter
may not fully protect you, it is better than doing
nothing, and you put the burden on the creditor.

Most of the time you will have little trouble
terminating joint accounts. On occasion, however, a
creditor may demand that you pay off the balance
first. If you can afford to pay the bill, do so. That's
better than leaving the account open and allowing
your spouse to run up more debts.

---

[1] You may be tempted to apply for separate credit, listing your
soon-to-be ex-spouse's income as well as your own. Because you
don't intend to use your ex's income to repay your bills, this
practice probably borders on fraud.

[2] To find the names of banks issuing secured credit cards, call local
banks or send $3 to Bankcard Holders of America, 560 Herndon
Parkway, Suite 120, Herndon, VA 22070 and request their list of
lending institutions issuing secured credit cards. Whatever you do,
don't call a "900" number service that claims "instant credit—no
questions asked."

If you can't pay off the entire balance, you can still ask that the account be made inactive while you make payments. This strategy prohibits further charges from being made on the account. Once the balance is paid, the creditor should close the account completely. Most customer service representatives will take care of your request. If you can't make satisfactory arrangements through a customer service representative, however, ask to speak to a supervisor and continue up the chain of command. Explain that you are going through a divorce and that you are closing out your joint accounts. Remember to put all communications with credit card companies in writing, keep copies and document your payments.[3]

## 2. Equity Credit Lines

A frequently overlooked area of joint financial liability involves equity lines of credit. An equity credit line is an open-ended loan made by a lending institution—usually a bank, savings and loan or thrift company—against the equity in your home. The lender gets a secured interest in your home, and if you don't repay the loan, the lending institution can force the sale of your house.

You and your spouse may have applied for a home equity line of credit at a bank that you may have forgotten about. Equity credit lines which supply a checkbook can be used just like a joint checking account. Whichever spouse has the checkbook has access to the money. Be sure to pay a visit to your banker. Take a letter with you requesting that the account be closed or frozen because of your divorce. By leaving an equity line of credit open during the divorce, you risk losing your home.

Similar to an equity line of credit is a margin account, offered by stock brokerage firms. To close the account, follow the same procedure as with your

bank, asking in writing—and possibly in person—that the account be frozen. Your goal is to keep your spouse from withdrawing money, trading stocks or taking profits. While you may want to shut down the account now, you'll probably have to wait until you are closer to a settlement before closing it completely.

⚠️ **Beware of unknown loans**

Just as you may be unaware of money taken from a joint equity line of credit, so too may your spouse have "unknown loans." Beware of a spouse who suddenly starts talking about paying back a loan to his or her mother, uncle or best friend. The "loan" may be repaid with your joint money. The relative or friend may simply hold this money for your spouse and hand it over once the divorce is final.

## 3. Joint Checking, Saving and Other Deposit Accounts

As with joint credit cards, you will not want to close joint checking or saving accounts unless you have an account in your own name, or will open one immediately. If you don't close a joint account you run the risk that your spouse could come in and empty it without your knowledge.

You have a few options:

- Ask the bank to freeze the account and not allow either you or your spouse to move money in or out without both of your signatures.

- Take out half the money in the account and place it into your individual account.

- Freeze or close the accounts and place all the money into a neutral account. You'll probably need an agreement with your spouse to use this option.

---

[3]If, during your separation, your spouse uses a joint credit card account (before you get a chance to close it) and charges items such as food or clothes, you might be responsible for the payments because these expenses are considered to be common necessities of life. See Chapter 6, Section A.1.a.

## Using an Escrow Account To Deposit Joint Funds

If a divorcing couple can't agree about what to do with the proceeds of a closed joint account, they can open an escrow account. Escrow accounts, usually opened at banks, are essentially safe "holding places" for money, normally used while a house sale—or lawsuit—is pending.

Money from the joint account, or other joint liquid assets, can be put into the escrow account until the property settlement is complete. Both spouses can deposit money into the account, but neither can withdraw anything from it without the approval of the other spouse and the escrow agent—the person who oversees the account.

 **Caution—delays can hurt**

If your spouse takes all the money from your joint accounts, your settlement—or a court—will probably provide for you being reimbursed. That, however, could be months or years away. Until then, you have to deal with losing your share of a joint account. If you have nothing in a personal savings or checking account, you may have to borrow money to cover the short-fall.

## If You Are Broke

If you are out of money, you are probably safe in withdrawing one-half of the cash in your joint accounts. (If you have any doubts, ask your attorney.) Of course, there's also the old standby methods of holding a garage sale or calling your Mom and Dad. You could also ask for temporary alimony. (See Chapter 12.)

## 4.  Safe Deposit Boxes

Just as one spouse can remove all money from a joint checking account, so too can that spouse take all of the items out of a joint safe deposit box.

Unfortunately, safe deposit boxes are one of those items in which "whoever gets there first" is the operative rule. Try to take possession of both keys to the safe deposit box if at all possible. If your spouse empties the box before you do, you may have little chance of re-claiming the contents. If you at least have an inventory—and an estimate of values—you can ask the judge for reimbursement.

You might possibly protect yourself if you can get to the box prior to the divorce and write an inventory of the contents and take photos of the items. Then have the bank officer sign the list documenting your inventory. If your spouse removes anything later, you'll have some proof of what was taken.

One of the only ways to legally protect yourself is to get a restraining order from the court. The order would prevent either spouse from having access to the box until you reach a settlement or the court removes the restraining order. (See Chapter 1.)

## 5.  Joint Investments and Other Holdings

Make a list of any investments or other assets you can think of. Immediately call your broker and any of the financial institutions involved. Tell them that no stocks or other holdings should be moved, transferred or liquidated without the knowledge and approval of both you and your spouse. Be sure to follow up the call with a letter.

When it comes to joint investments, you will have to move quickly. Most stock transactions are handled over the phone. Your spouse may be the one who normally deals with the broker. He or she could make one phone call, and, in a matter of minutes have all of your joint holdings sold.

On the other hand, if you call first to freeze the accounts before your spouse can transfer investments, you stand a good chance of protecting your interests. Call your broker and then send a follow-up letter. Be sure to tell the broker to make a note to the "on line" file on the computer if the firm uses them. That way, when your spouse speaks to anyone else at the firm, the computer will show that the account has been frozen. Also, if the account has check writing or credit card privileges, specify whether or not the freeze applies to those transactions.

### Sample Letter to Broker

```
Rodney Washington
Bull and Bear Investment Company
3400 Financial Square, Suite 1740
Boston, MA 02000

November 27, 1992

Dear Mr. Washington:

This letter is to inform you that my spouse
and I are in the process of divorce. Please
freeze our account, #12345-67890, so that
no transactions occur until further notice.
Please make a note to this effect on the
firm's "on line" file on the computer. This
freeze is to be effective immediately and
this letter confirms my instructions to you
by telephone on November 24, 1992.

These instructions apply to the assets in
our account [except for or including] the
check writing and/or the credit card privi-
leges we currently have with this account.

Yours truly,


Lenore Kwong
```

## 6. Shared Property and Special Collections

While your furniture, appliances and knickknacks around the house may not be as valuable as other assets and investments, this property can cause more aggravation and antagonism than almost anything else. Emotions flare up when you reach for a favorite tool only to find it missing, or look for your mother's antique brooch and discover it is gone.

To avoid future problems, do an inventory of your home and possessions similar to the kind you would conduct for insurance purposes. Obviously, it will be simpler to do such an inventory while you are still living in the family home and have access to your property—so do it before you move out.

List the contents of each room and photograph or videotape the area as documentation. Your ultimate goal as part of your divorce is to divide these items as fairly as possible. Few couples split the small items exactly 50-50, but you still want to get appraisals of the property so your division is not horribly one-sided. You can get simple appraisals of household property by asking furniture or appliance dealers and auctioneers to visit your home and give you written estimates. Any coin, gold or other collection should be appraised by a reputable dealer. Realize that these items will be appraised at the amount the dealer is willing to pay—not the retail value.

While these appraisals are useful as a starting point, in reality, collections and property are only worth what you can sell them for. If you are valuing property on your own, use "garage sale" values—that is, if you saw your furniture, microwave or other property at a garage sale, how much would you really pay for it. The person who will not be getting the household items may only remember the original price tag, not the current value, so you have to insist on using the garage sale price.

In the mean time, jointly owned household property should not be disposed of unless both spouses agree, as neither one owns an item outright until the settlement. You only own your personal, separate property. Your children's property, such as furniture or toys, should be given to the children and not divided in the divorce settlement.

## 7.  Joint Tenancy

Many couples hold property, especially real property, in joint tenancy. Joint tenancy's major advantage is that when one joint owner dies, the remaining owners automatically inherit the deceased's portion of the property without having to go through the long, expensive probate process. Property held in joint tenancy can easily be divided as part of your divorce settlement, and usually doesn't have to be dealt with until settlement time. If you fear dying while your divorce is pending, however, and don't want your spouse to automatically inherit your share, you can change your joint tenancy ownership to tenancy in common. With tenancy in common, you own equal shares, but upon your death your share goes to whomever you've named in your will or other estate planning document.

The best way to convert property from joint tenancy to tenancy in common is to obtain your spouse's agreement and then together execute a deed in which you make this change. For example, a couple could transfer their house "from Herbert and Donna Walker as joint tenants to Herbert and Donna Walker as tenants in common." You can obtain a blank deed from a title insurance or real estate office.[4]

If you cannot find a blank deed, you could simply draft a statement saying "Herbert and Donna Walker hereby transfer their real property located at 4555 Ellison Boulevard, Fargo, North Dakota, from Herbert and Donna Walker as joint tenants to Herbert and Donna Walker as tenants in common." Be sure you both sign the statement before a notary public. Then record the deed or statement in the office where your original house deed is recorded.

If your spouse will not consent to the change, you can complete the deed or statement yourself. Write "Donna Walker hereby transfers her interest in the real property located at 4555 Ellison Boulevard, Fargo, North Dakota from Donna Walker joint tenant to Donna Walker tenant in common."[5] Again, sign it before a notary and record in the office where your original house deed is recorded.

---

### Financial First Aid for Divorce Emergencies

If a stranger stole your wallet with all the credit cards inside, you'd probably have more protection than if your spouse wipes out your joint accounts. Almost nothing can stop one spouse from closing a joint account without the knowledge of the other. During a divorce it can come down to who gets there first—to the bank account, the brokerage office or the safe deposit box.

If you need to take severe action against your spouse, you might immediately ask the court for a restraining order to freeze all accounts and joint holdings while the divorce is pending. (See Chapter 1, Section C.) Remember, however, this freeze denies both you and your spouse access to the account.

---

 **You could increase hostility**

By closing accounts, or serving your spouse with a restraining order, recognize that you are "upping the ante" and increasing the degree of conflict in your divorce. You (and any professional advisors you use) must assess the risks and the consequences, because sooner or later, you will meet your spouse at the negotiating table.

---

[4]In California, homeowners can use Nolo's *Deeds Book*, by Mary Randolph.

[5]In some states, a spouse cannot unilaterally change property from joint tenancy to tenancy in common—he or she must have the other spouse's consent. To find out if that's the case in your state, ask your lawyer. If it is, and your spouse won't consent, you'll have to wait until the final settlement to transfer ownership.

## B. Questions To Ask Your Attorney

Closing accounts isn't always a straight-forward procedure, and can vary from state to state. Below is a list of important questions for you to ask your attorney or research at your local law library.

1. Do any state laws prohibit you from withdrawing one-half of the cash in your joint accounts?

2. Can a spouse unilaterally change property from joint tenancy to tenancy in common or must he or she have the other spouse's consent?

# 8

## The First 30 Days: Financial Fact Finding—What Must I Know and When Must I Know It?

*Most often in marriage, one partner takes care of the paperwork and possibly the financial decision making. This is a practical arrangement when you're still together, but a potential disaster during divorce.*

No one can make proper financial decisions without adequate information. How can you tell whether to keep the family home if you do not know what it costs to maintain it? On what will you base requests for alimony or child support if you are in the dark about living expenses? Both you and your spouse will need to document your financial life as you go through the divorce and now, in the early stages, is the best time to start.

If you left the bookkeeping up to your partner, you may feel as though you are starting from scratch. It's important not to panic. Take control by finding out as much as you can about the finances of your marriage. And realize that you *will* live through this part of your divorce.

Linda, a 35-year-old mother of two, recalled that when she first separated from her husband she was petrified at the thought of confronting her financial life. As she kept at it, however, the job became easier. "Now I can look at all of these complicated papers and forms and not feel scared," she reports.

If you were the family bookkeeper, you will be in much better shape than the spouse who did not participate in managing the paperwork. You can move on to Section C, below and begin verifying the financial information you will need during your divorce.

Whatever role you played previously, by the time the divorce is over, you will probably know more about the details of your financial life than you ever cared to. You will go through three phases during your divorce:

1. *Information gathering.* This is the step in which you find information and sort files, receipts, bill statements and other papers.
2. *Information analysis.* After sorting your papers, you'll want to review your files, appraisals and valuations. It's also important to calculate taxes and other costs either by yourself or with an accountant or financial adviser.
3. *Decision making.* Once you analyze what you own and owe, and what it costs to live, you can begin to decide what to do with your property in the divorce.

Start investigating your financial position now. Do not wait until you are at the bargaining table for the final settlement to figure out what your house is worth, or the value of your spouse's retirement benefits. When you enter the negotiations, you want to have as much up-to-date information as you can.

At this stage of the divorce process (the First 30 Days), you should focus on information gathering only. Even if you do not understand all of it, do not get sidetracked from your financial fact-finding mission. Later on, you can concentrate on decision making. For now, your time is best spent on documenting your economic situation. Staying focused may seem hard, but it gets easier as you go along. Besides, it will help you:

- save time and money, especially once you hire an attorney
- distinguish your separate property from the marital assets
- negotiate a settlement from a position of strength
- begin building a foundation for a secure financial future.

## A. Advice to the Terminally Disorganized

Ideally, your books and accounts are up-to-date, and in order. More likely, however, you will have to hunt for records and receipts. You are not alone. Almost no one is as on top of their personal finances as they would like to be—or pretend to be.

Tax returns are gold mines of information in a divorce. If you do not currently have access to your tax returns of the past three to five years, you can get copies from the IRS. Your first step is to request the copies. Call the IRS (1-800-829-1040) and ask for Form #4506. Complete the form and send it back. You should get copies of your returns within about 45 days.

The IRS generally sends your tax information to the "Address of Record" on your previous return. If you've moved, or are concerned about arousing your spouse's anger or suspicion, ask that the forms be sent to your office, your attorney, a friend or a post office box. Once you have copies of the tax returns, you can review them with a trusted accountant or financial planner who can show you how to find basic information on the forms.

Copies of credit or loan applications, cancelled checks and bank, brokerage and credit union statements also provide a great deal of financial information.

If you know you'll have trouble staying organized once you begin getting your paperwork together, you can hire a local bookkeeping service. You might also consider the services of a professional organizer. Modern life has gotten so complicated that there is a national association of professional organizers. Local groups may be listed in the phone book yellow pages or classified advertisements in the newspaper. If you can't find a referral through those sources, you can write to the National Association of Professional Organizers at 1163 Sherman Road, Northbrook, IL 60062. Before hiring a professional organizer, make sure the person listens to you and asks what you want—not tells you what you need.

No matter what approach you take in organizing your documents, keep it simple. You can buy an inexpensive three-ring binder to hold your various papers. As your stack of information grows, create categories of documents by using the divider tabs that come with the binder. The Net Worth and Cash

Flow statements in Chapter 9 will give you an idea of the kinds of divisions you can make.

When you begin to feel overwhelmed, remember that you are not just shuffling papers to get through your divorce. You are doing the groundwork for your financial decision making and security for many years to come. And that is worth the effort it takes to become informed and organized about your paperwork.

## B. If You Think Your Spouse May Be Hiding Assets

Unfortunately, divorce can be the occasion for a game of financial "cat and mouse" in which one spouse hides assets or makes other unethical moves. In some cases, the gaps in the financial information you get from your spouse occur because of honest mistakes. Many people are not detail-oriented when it comes to personal finances, and in the stress of divorce, may forget some specifics.

On the other hand, some spouses purposely conceal the value of a business or switch funds into secret accounts. If the judge finds out, he may declare that the spouse who hides assets is guilty of "economic misconduct." This misconduct is likely to affect the final settlement—the misbehaving spouse will probably get less than his or her full share.

If you have any reason to believe your spouse is being less than candid with you about income or other assets, you will have to do a little detective work on your own. You may need to examine old income tax returns to spot discrepancies.

If you're still not convinced, consider hiring a special type of Certified Public Accountant (CPA), often called a forensic accountant. These specialists will comb through your records and can usually create an accurate picture of your spouse's financial position. Their services, however, can be expensive. You must weigh the cost of hiring a forensic accountant against the dollar amount at stake in your divorce.

The legal process of "discovery" can be used to force a reluctant spouse to turn over records and statements. Discovery is a formal information gathering process used in lawsuits. Parties (usually through lawyers) send papers to each other asking that questions be answered or documents turned over.

Another procedure used in discovery is taking depositions—that is, orally asking questions. Be warned, however, that discovery is usually time consuming and costly, and may ultimately turn up nothing of importance. Therefore, gather information informally if possible.

---

### Searching for Hidden Assets

This checklist was adapted from one created by Ginita Wall, a CPA and Certified Financial Planner in San Diego, California. This list includes common ways in which a spouse may undervalue or disguise marital assets. Be advised, however, that you may have difficulty finding some items or getting the proof you need to show they exist. As mentioned, a forensic accountant, or formal discovery procedures, may help.

- Collusion with an employer to delay bonuses, stock options or raises until after the divorce. You might find this information by taking the deposition of your spouse's boss or payroll supervisor, but more likely you'll need a forensic accountant.

- Salary paid to a non-existent employee. The checks will be voided after divorce. Again, you might find this information by taking the deposition of your spouse's boss or payroll supervisor, but you'll probably need a forensic accountant.•

- Money paid from the business to someone close—such as a father, mother, girlfriend or boyfriend—for services never rendered. The money will no doubt be given back to your spouse after the divorce is final.

- Delay in signing long-term business contracts until after the divorce. Although this may seem like smart planning, if the intent is to lower the value of the business it is considered hiding assets.

- Skimming cash from a business he or she owns.

- Antiques, artwork, hobby equipment, gun collections and tools that are overlooked or undervalued. Look for lush furnishings, paintings or collector-level carpets at the office.Income that is unreported on tax returns and financial statements. Lifestyle costs will exceed income, so document any of the cash expenses you know your spouse has incurred.

- A custodial account set up in the name of a child, using the child's Social Security number.

- Debt repayment to a friend for a phony debt.

- Expenses paid for a girlfriend or boyfriend such as gifts, travel, rent or tuition for college or special classes.

- Investment in certificate "bearer" municipal bonds or Series EE Savings Bonds do not appear on account statements because they are not registered with the IRS. The government is phasing out these bonds, realizing that it is losing a lot of money.

- Cash kept in the form of traveler's checks. You may be able to find these by tracing bank account deposits and withdrawals.

## C. Financial Facts Checklist

The following list contains most of the items you will want to gather, whether you are doing your divorce yourself or working with an attorney or other legal or financial professionals. We recommend doing it yourself—you'll save time and money, and gain a sense of control over your divorce.

Most of this information should be in your files at home or your office, or possibly in a safety deposit box. If you don't have a clue about where to find a particular item, watch the mail as it arrives. You may be able to glean the names of insurance companies, banks, brokerage houses and other institutions which you may need to contact to get information. As noted in Section A, above, you can get copies of past tax returns from the IRS. Your insurance agent should be able to answer questions on policies, and the personnel or benefits office of your (or your spouse's) employer can shed some light regarding retirement benefits. For information on real estate, contact the agent who sold you the house or the company that loaned you the money for the house.

Put a check (√) in the blanks corresponding to items you have. Enter an X for items you and your spouse don't have. You'll probably have to leave some spaces blank and enter a √ or X as you conduct additional financial fact finding. Some of the terms in the chart may be unfamiliar to you. Don't worry. We'll cover them later in the book. For now, use the list to jog your memory—or your accountants—about what documents to look for.

## Financial Facts Checklist

| | |
|---|---|
| *Tax returns—state and federal—past 5 years* | |
| *Previous divorce documents including property settlement* | |
| *Pre- and post-marital (nuptial) agreements* | |
| *Wills and trust documents* | |
| *Written agreements with employer, partners or employees* | |
| *Pay stubs—both spouses—past 3 months* | |
| *Statements or documents from:* | |

| | |
|---|---|
| Savings accounts | Margin accounts with brokerage firm |
| Checking accounts | Credit union accounts |
| Certificates of deposit | Credit card accounts |
| Mutual funds | Commodities |
| Cash management accounts | Collections—gold, coins, stamps, etc. |

*Insurance policies—both spouses:*

| | |
|---|---|
| Life | Liability |
| Automobile | Disability |
| Homeowner's | Renter's |
| Personal umbrella | Health (for parents and/or children) |

*Employee/group insurance benefits—both spouses:*

| | |
|---|---|
| Medical | Disability |
| Life | |

*Other employee benefits:*

| | |
|---|---|
| Auto allowances | Bonuses |
| Cafeteria plans | Deferred compensation |
| Expense account | Military |
| Sick pay | Severance pay |
| Stock options | Vacation pay |
| Travel benefits | |

*Retirement plans:*

| | |
|---|---|
| Money purchase plans | Profit sharing plans |
| 401K salary saving | Thrift |
| ESOPs | Defined benefit plans |
| TSAs | IRAs or Sep IRAs |
| Keoghs | |

*Financial statements:*

| |
|---|
| Net worth—balance sheet or list of assets and liabilities |
| Cash flow or income and expense statement |
| Statements or documents regarding |
| Separate property—inheritances, gifts and others |
| Personal injury awards |

*Real estate records:*

| | |
|---|---|
| Current value | Monthly payments |
| Original mortgage | Original purchase price |

CHAPTER

# 9

## The First 30 Days: Getting Help—Who Can I Turn To?

*During divorce, you're going through a time of transition unlike any other in your life. Everything is changing. No matter how capable you are, you'll need help to get through this transition. Besides gathering emotional support, you may have to consult with legal professionals and others trained to deal with issues unique to the divorce process. In some cases, you may seek help through counseling with a therapist, a member of the clergy or a spiritual group.*

Even if you have little money and few resources, it's important to get support. Check with local libraries, community organizations, law schools, colleges or government agencies for low-cost services. In some areas, divorce specialists and centers can advise you for a small fee.

The kind of help you seek will depend on what you need. For some, a personal counselor or therapist is crucial; others want only a temporary advisor to handle technical financial details. As your divorce progresses, you may also need to call on a variety of specialists ranging from attorneys to real estate agents, credit counselors to appraisers. Because your future is at stake, don't cheat yourself; get the best you can afford. Comparison shop and check references before signing contracts for outside services.

## A. Questions to Consider When Seeking Outside Help

While you need to ask different, specific questions for each service provider you consult, the following for questions are useful for dealing with professionals in general. Even if your income is minimal, review these questions before deciding whether or not to work with advisors.

### 1. Is the Person Competent and Suited To Handle My Specific Case?

Obviously, you want to work with someone who can do a good job and be trusted. Beyond those basic qualities, it's essential to determine if the person's training and services match your needs. In other words, you don't want to hire a bookkeeper if your situation calls for an accountant to take care of complex calculations or taxes. By the same token, an experienced divorce attorney is a better bet than a lawyer who specializes in business transactions. Interview potential consultants on the phone or use introductory sessions to outline your case and find out exactly what to expect before you hire anyone.

> **⚠ Beware of pressures to hire the first person you consult**
>
> If you accept a complimentary session with a lawyer or other professional, realize that you may be pressured into hiring that person. You may be sold a service that you do not want or need. To avoid such problems, clearly state that you are only gathering information in the initial session and do not intend to make a hiring decision until after you have had a chance to sort through the information you receive. Remember, too, the old adage that if something sounds too good to be true, it probably is. Be wary of any lawyer who seems to promise you the world, making guarantees that you can get anything you want in your divorce. There are no guarantees.

### 2. How Are Professionals Paid?

How a professional is paid—by the hour, on a retainer or through commissions—inevitably affects you. This is a statement of fact, not a matter of philosophy or morals. If you'll be paying by the hour, you must understand how that time will be billed. Does the professional bill in 10-minute, 15-minute or longer intervals? Are you going to be charged for time on the phone? Does the clock begin to "run" the minute you walk in the door? Find out.

When people work on commission, their livelihood depends on selling you something. Again, there's nothing wrong with that —you just need to recognize that reality and act accordingly. For instance, when you call for information about insurance coverage, the agent may try to sell you a new policy or different kind of coverage. Only you can decide whether or not it's appropriate to make such a purchase. Because of the emotional strain of divorce, take extra time to make decisions or insist on getting a second opinion before you buy anything.

### 3. What's the Best Use of this Professional's Services?

Like many people going through a divorce, you may sometimes feel that you don't know where to turn. As personal and financial pressures mount, you could go to the wrong people for the wrong services. Trying to use your lawyer as a therapist or your banker as a tax consultant is an exercise in frustration. Think about your needs first and be sure you are using each professional's expertise appropriately. Recognize the limits of each advisor you contact. Your local real estate agent, for example, may not be able to appraise the value of commercial property or a vacation house located in a different city. If necessary, ask for referrals to specialists and keep asking questions until you find the right person to answer them.

## B. Selecting Professionals To Assist You

Besides providing quality service, a good professional should explain potential risks in your situation and offer realistic appraisals of results and consequences. (Of course, the more risks the professional finds, the more money he or she stands to earn.) Keep that in mind as you review these descriptions of professionals who can help you during divorce.

### 1. Lawyers

*Fees and Payment.* For assisting during a divorce, lawyers charge hourly rates—anywhere from $125 to $250 per hour. Be sure to find one that fits your wallet.[1] Be aware, too, that many lawyers will require that you pay an up-front retainer before they do any work, sometimes amounting to thousands of dollars. As the lawyer does work for you, the bill is paid out of your retainer.

When the lawyer uses up the retainer, she'll either bill you directly or ask for another lump sum from which to draw. If you hire a lawyer who requests a retainer, be sure that you get monthly statements showing the work done, the amount billed, the amount deducted from your retainer and the amount left over. If there's a balance remaining at the end of the case (or if you change lawyers), you're entitled to get that money back.

There is no sure fire way of finding an attorney. Friends and relatives may be able to suggest lawyers, but check out their recommendations carefully to see if you will work well with the person. Also remember

---

[1] If it's at all possible, you should pay your own attorney's fees. Financial negotiations and lines of authority remain clear when each party pays for his or her own legal representative. If there is no way for you to afford an attorney, in some states, a judge can order that the spouse who is significantly wealthier must pay all or part of the other spouse's attorney's fees during the divorce. If you can't afford a lawyer, be sure to ask if there's any possibility of your spouse paying the bill.

that friends and relatives may have been happy with a particular lawyer, but they may not be able to judge if they really received the best representation.[2]

When you meet with an attorney, ask specific questions about fees and services. Be sure you feel comfortable communicating with your potential lawyer and check on how often this person will be available to you. Ask about fees and billing practices, too.

In some states, such as California, consider hiring a certified family law attorney. These specialists must pass an examination that tests their specific knowledge of divorce law. Most keep current on developments in divorce law by attending continuing legal education programs. They may know more about divorce law—including support, custody and property division questions—than non-specialists, but they may charge more as well.

### Don't Just Turn Your Case Over to a Lawyer

Jill and Sam[3] had been married four years when Jill first consulted a lawyer. Aside from personal problems with Sam, Jill was concerned because he refused to file income tax returns and the IRS had begun actions against the couple.

Jill saw Barbara Smith, a partner in the law firm of Brown, Smith & Jones. Barbara explained that a divorce would best protect Jill. She said that if Jill decided on a divorce, the case could be handled by Jonas Falk, a new attorney at the firm whose billing rate was less than half of Barbara's. Jill was assured that Jonas could handle the case under Barbara's supervision because it was routine—the couple had no children, owned little property except a house and alimony wasn't an issue. Jill agreed, signed an agreement and paid a $2,500 retainer fee.

Sam and Jill sold their house before the divorce papers were filed, netting a profit of $50,000. Pending completion of the divorce, Sam and Jill placed the money in a bank account.

During the first quarter of the year, Jonas charged Jill about $3,000 for two routine legal tasks. The first was getting a court order allowing Jill a $10,000 advance from the account—which went to pay the law firm's bills. He also got a court order preventing removal of the remaining $40,000 from the account until the divorce was final.

Then in early April, the firm told Jill that Barbara—who supposedly had been supervising Jonas—had left the firm. When Jill expressed concern that she hadn't been told earlier, another partner, Elaine, agreed to supervise Jonas. Elaine also implied that Jill's position would suffer if Jill fired the firm. Feeling somewhat wronged but persuaded by Elaine's recommendation, Jill agreed to remain with the firm.

---

[2]For further help on finding a lawyer, see the Appendix Section, *Resources Beyond this Book*.

[3]All the names in this story have been changed.

Elaine asked Jill to let the firm start a legal process of "discovery," to find out whether Sam was concealing any jointly owned assets. Elaine estimated the cost of discovery at $2,500.

Jill didn't see the need for this. Sam didn't have a job, and as far as Jill knew, all his money came from an inheritance that was clearly his alone. But Elaine cautioned that Jill would never forgive herself if she later found that Sam had hidden assets to which Jill was entitled. Feeling overwhelmed, confused and under pressure to make a decision that day, Jill consented.

Discovery ended up costing $8,000 and never established that Sam had hidden property. One reason for the high cost was that Jonas, who was unfamiliar with local court rules, made several procedural mistakes that required additional appearances and new papers. His inexperience also meant that tasks took him many more hours than a more experienced lawyer.

As Jill began to realize that Jonas was learning to practice law at her expense, she became angry. She complained about his lack of knowledge and got $1,000 knocked off a bill. She noted that his work wasn't being overseen, and was told that Elaine would increase her supervision.

A year and a half after Jill had hired the firm, she'd paid almost $13,000 in legal fees and costs, and neither the divorce nor the tax problems were any closer to resolution. Panicked, Jill tracked down Barbara Smith, now in practice on her own. For a fee, Barbara consented to supervise Jonas again, and everyone agreed to the arrangement.

Although neither Sam nor Jill thought there was much to fight about, their lawyers disagreed. Settlement proposals flew back and forth at an average cost of $150 an hour. The lawyers took a number of extreme positions, supposedly in the name of negotiating strategy, and negotiations, paperwork and court appearances dragged on for months.

Finally, a court judgment was entered based on a settlement agreement signed by Jill and Sam. Jill received her share of the profit from the house, her car and her half of the joint bank accounts. This was exactly what it always appeared she was entitled to receive—and what she and Sam had agreed to at the beginning of the case almost two years earlier. These final negotiations cost Jill another $17,000 in legal fees.

But all was still not well. The judgment left open the question of who was responsible for any potential tax liability. In addition, Jill and Sam were each made responsible for half of the capital gains taxes owed on the house sale, including interest and penalties that had mounted considerably during the divorce case. In short, the law firm failed to help Jill with the very tax problems that originally led her to seek legal help—and even made them worse.

Furthermore, after the divorce was final Jill received a letter pointing out that she received a $15,000 cash settlement from her divorce and had a balance on her account of $14,043.53. The firm asked for immediate payment.

Including the amount Jill had already paid, this brought the bill for what should have been a routine divorce to $32,000. Jill refused to pay the last bill, and the firm threatened to sue. Jill requested that the fee dispute be decided by three arbitrators. At the last minute, the law firm agreed to drop the last $14,043.53 fee request. Jill could have proceeded with the arbitration and possibly obtained a partial refund of fees paid, but she'd had enough.

Jill's case didn't have to progress as it did. She knew clearly what property she and her husband owned—and they had agreed on how to divide it. But many people aren't in Jill's shoes. They need to gather financial information in order to understand their position and obtain a fair settlement of the marital property. They needed to take charge of their case and question their attorneys regarding legal strategies and costs of services versus benefits received.

## 2.  Mediators

*Fees and Payment.* Mediators charge hourly or daily rates. Mediators who are also lawyers usually charge what lawyers charge—$125 + per hour. Mediators who are therapists, psychologists, social workers or clergy members charge less—usually beginning around $75 an hour. Some mediators have sliding scales based on the parties' income. In most cases, the parties share the cost equally.

If you have little property to divide or if you and your spouse are in general agreement but for perhaps one or two issues about the divorce, you may contact a mediator to work with you on your divorce settlement. To find a mediator, look in the phone book, ask friends for referrals or contact law offices or divorce centers for leads.

A mediator acts as an *impartial third party* to help you and your spouse resolve conflicts. By contrast, lawyers are *advocates* for their client's position. Consequently, your individual interests may not be represented in the same manner as if you had someone advocating your position. Mediators represent the *marital* interest, not that of either spouse. Do not expect a mediator to take sides.

When working with a mediator, you must be precise about what you want to achieve in the sessions. Ask for a private caucus session with the mediator if necessary to clarify your personal goals.

Used properly, mediation can be less costly than a prolonged legal battle. To finalize your settlement, however, you may still need to hire a lawyer or typing service. Often, a mediator will draw up a "memorandum of understanding" which outlines your agreement. Then, you could spend a short amount of time with a lawyer or typing service who can file the papers to make the agreements legally binding.

## 3.  Financial Planners

*Fees and Payment.* Financial planners may charge hourly or work on commission. Fee-based financial planners generally charge you for the hours spent on creating a financial plan or consulting with you on your investments, usually at a rate of $80-$200 per hour. Commission-based planners, on the other hand, earn money on the stocks or investments they sell you. The planners deduct their commissions—anywhere from 2% to 8.5%—from the amount of money you initially invest. A commission-based planner should disclose the amount of commission he or she stands to make on a sale.

A financial planner can be useful at this time as you are preparing for your financial future as a single person. A planner should be able to help you identify potential risks in your settlement agreement and the tax consequences of decisions you are contemplating. Planners can also review your net worth and cash flow statements as well as your retirement benefits, investment portfolio and business holdings.

To find a financial planner, ask for a referral from an accountant, banker or attorney you trust. You can also call the International Association for Financial Planning (IAFP) at 404-395-1605. Ask for members of its Registry of Financial Planning Practitioners in your area. To be admitted to the Registry, a financial planner must pass an exam, submit a comprehensive financial plan for review by an IAFP committee, submit several recommendations and evaluations from clients and take annual continuing education courses.

To be certain you are dealing with a reputable professional, check references and credentials. Planners who have undergone a rigorous program offered through Denver's College for Financial Planning earn the title of Certified Financial Planner (CFP). Chartered Financial Consultant (ChFC) is another credential to look for. It's given to financial planners who pass a series of courses at The American College, located in Bryn Mawr, Pennsylvania.

### When To Use—Or Not Use—Mediation

Whether mediation is appropriate is a critical question to ask at the start of any mediation. It also needs to be asked throughout the entire process, by both the parties and the mediator.

"Is each party able to stand up for himself or herself?"

Is each person in the process there under his or her own steam?"

"Is the intensity of the emotional charge between the parties so strong that one or both are disabled by it?"

Is each person able to track the progress of the mediation?"

The following was written by Gary Friedman, Director of The Center For Mediation In Law and author of the forthcoming book, *Sitting in the Middle* (Workman Press).

Central to determining mediation's appropriateness is whether or not the parties can deal fairly with one another. Differences in the parties' openness to the process, the tendency of one party to dominate the other, inequalities in ability (or willingness) to deal with the subject matter must all be examined. Before jumping into mediation, ask yourself several questions:

"Is each party open to reaching a result that is fair to the other?"

"Are the parties able to communicate clearly with each other? Can they express themselves *and* hear the other?"

"Is each party able to identify his or her own sense of what is important as a realistic and solid base for making choices? Is each able to express and assert that sense?"

"Is either person unwilling to seek outside support or unable to use it effectively when it is needed?"

The decision whether or not to mediate should be an informed one, and one capable of reconsideration. Either party's hesitation should be taken seriously; both must be willing for the process to be meaningful. A decision not to mediate or to stop the mediation does not mean that adversary litigation is the sole choice. You can bring in a co-mediator, use a type of mediation more protective of the parties or work with lawyers committed to collaborating with their clients.

---

In hiring a financial planner, look for someone who can analyze your case and the financial impact of divorce—not someone whose primary focus is on selling investments. You also want someone who can communicate with your attorney because the financial implications of your divorce will no doubt have an impact on the legal consequences. Your planner should help you identify and assess risks so you can protect yourself. Few of us manage our finances as well as we could, but you will find it to your benefit if you choose a planner who is willing to tell you what you would rather not hear.

## 4. Stockbrokers and Money Managers

*Fees and Payment.* Stockbrokers are paid commissions by the client—usually 1% to 8.5% of the amount of money invested. Money managers receive a percentage—usually 1% to 3% of the money they manage.

Stockbrokers tend to focus on individual stock, bond, mutual fund and insurance transactions. Money managers look at the overall performance of an investment portfolio and evaluate how it meets your short-term and long-term needs for growth, income and safety.

In gathering information on your financial condition, you may have to contact your stockbroker for copies of brokerage accounts or other items. Again, as with other professionals who work on commission, recognize that your stockbroker may try to sell you products when you call for financial information.

## 5.    Accountants

*Fees and Payment.* Accountants charge by the hour or per project, usually between $80 and $125 per hour or several hundred dollars per project.

Accountants can provide a variety of services ranging from auditing a business to assessing employee benefits packages. A Certified Public Accountant (CPA) can work as a tax consultant—but don't assume that all CPAs can provide personal tax services. If you have income tax concerns, you may want to start by consulting an Enrolled Agent (EA), a tax specialist qualified to practice before the IRS.[4] If you think a spouse is hiding assets or covering up essential financial facts, you may want to hire a forensic accountant. These specialists can trace marital property and evaluate financial reports, among other services.

---

[4]To find out about enrolled agents, and to find one in your area, you can call the National Association of Enrolled Agents at 800-424-4339 or 301-984-6232.

## 6.    Bankers

*Fees and Payment.* Bankers are paid a salary by the bank that employees them.

Your bank and banker can prove quite useful in helping you with various financial issues of divorce, such as cancelling or opening lines of credit, establishing new accounts or getting a loan. Do not expect a banker, however, to advise you on investments or other complex issues outside his or her realm of expertise. Also, while bankers work on salaries, they often function as sales people for their own institutions and they promote their own products. Your banker may advise you to park your money in a Certificate of Deposit even though your long-term goals might be better served by investing in stocks or mutual funds. Get information from several different sources or consult with your financial planner before making a long-term decision.

## 7.    Insurance Agents

*Fees and Payment.* Insurance agents are paid commissions. The commissions are paid by the insurance company, but the company prices its policies to include the commission. Ultimately, the customer pays the commission, but you will not see this charge on your bill.

Insurance is one way to protect yourself from risks, and during divorce it's important to review your coverage. Contact your insurance agent to double check your policies for life, health, disability, property and business. Also check the cash value of the policy—it may be different than the amount stated in your contract because the actual rate of interest paid may differ from the rate of interest assumed when the policy was originally bought. Divorce is a good time to check the cash value of policies because this value represents marital property to be divided. Also, cashing in the policy can provide emergency cash if necessary. When you divide the family cars, be sure to check your auto insurance to make sure you are paying only to insure yourself (and perhaps your driving-age children) on the car(s) you keep.

If you do not have an insurance agent, shop around and talk to several to find one you can work with. Be aware that insurance agents hold sales positions and may ask you to buy a new policy or expand an old one when you call for information. Resist their pressures and be sure you absolutely need any new insurance you purchase.

## 8.   Real Estate Agents

*Fees and Payment.* When a real estate agent is involved in the sale of a home, that agent usually receives a commission from the money the seller receives for the house, even if the agent has been working with the buyer. An agent who simply appraises a house usually will do so for free, in the hope of getting your business later when you sell.

Because your house may be the most valuable asset in your divorce settlement, you will want to get an accurate appraisal of its current market value. Try to get estimates from several real estate agents or from a certified appraiser so you can negotiate from a knowledgeable position.[5] The best agents to ask are those familiar with the neighborhood. If you used an agent when you bought the house, that person is often one of the best suited to appraise the property now.

## 9.   Therapists

*Fees and Payment.* Therapists charge by the hour (the "50-minute" hour), usually between $50 and $100 per session. Keep in mind, especially if money is tight, that your medical insurance may reimburse you for all or part of your therapy sessions.

In the stress of divorce, a therapist or counselor can be a valuable ally and resource for helping resolve personal issues. To find someone, ask friends

---

[5]Certified appraisers are covered in Chapter 14. You can get some referrals from real estate agents, escrow companies and lending institutions.

for referrals, contact a local mental health association or call family service agencies. As with any professional, it's important to check credentials, but also make sure the therapist's approach feels appropriate to you. Don't hire a Freudian who does long-term psychoanalysis if you want short-term counseling to help you get through the divorce process. If you can't afford one-to-one therapy, you may be able to find support and encouragement through a self-help group, community services or program sponsored by a religious group.

## 10.   Credit Counselors

*Fees and Payment.* Use the services of credit counselors who are affiliated with non-profit organizations such as the United Way, a local "Y", or a church- or synagogue-run association. The National Foundation for Consumer Credit, the sponsors of Consumer Credit Counseling (CCC) also has offices nationwide. As non-profits, these organizations should charge you no more than a nominal fee.

Credit counselors can help you negotiate with your creditors and set up systems to manage your finances. The best known credit counselors are CCC, an organization set up and sponsored by major creditors such as department stores, credit card companies and banks, and overseen by volunteer creditors and consumer advocates.

To use CCC to help you pay your debts, you must either have some disposable income or be willing to sell some of your property. A CCC counselor contacts your creditors to let them know that you've sought CCC assistance and need more time to pay. Based on your income and debts, the counselor, with your creditors, decides on how much you pay. You then make one or two direct payments each month to CCC, which in turn pays your creditors. A CCC counselor can often get wage garnishments revoked and interest and late charges dropped.

CCC may, if allowed by state law, charge you a monthly fee of about $20 for setting up a repayment plan. CCC also helps people make monthly budgets, and if allowed by state law, charges a one-time fee of about $20. If you can't afford the fee, CCC will waive it.

CCC has several hundred offices, located in every state except Wisconsin. Look in the phone book to find the one nearest you or contact the main office at 8611 2nd Avenue, Suite 100, Silver Springs, Maryland 20910, 800-388-2227.

## 11. Typing Services and Consumer Advocates

*Fees and Payment.* Typing services and consumer advocates charge per project (for typing forms) or by the hour, when helping you work with your creditors.

Typing services and consumer advocates cannot give legal advice or represent you on legal matters, but they can offer several services at low cost. If you need to rebuild your credit or work with your creditors during your divorce, or you want help in preparing your divorce papers, typing services and consumer advocates may be able to help you with the following:

- explain how to work with the credit bureaus in your area

- assist you in negotiating with your creditors

- help you in getting incorrect, outdated and ambiguous information removed from your credit file

- assist you in writing letters to creditors, collection agencies and government agencies

- help you prepare your own divorce papers.

In selecting a consumer advocate or typing service, you must weed out the good (honest and competent) from the bad (dishonest and/or incompetent). Good consumer advocates or typing services will provide you with a written contract that describes the services they plan to provide, state the total price you will be charged and explain their complaint procedure and refund policy.

Here are some things to look for when choosing a consumer advocate or typing service:

- *An established or recommended service.* Few consumer advocates or typing services stay in business unless they provide honest and competent services. A recommendation from a social service agency, friend, court clerk or lawyer is probably a good bet.

- *Reasonable fees.* The fee should be based on the amount of work a task requires, the specialized nature of the task and reasonable overhead. For example, if the task is straightforward and takes just 30 minutes of typing, the fee should reflect the rate charged by basic typing services with similar overhead—about $10 a page or $20 an hour.

- *Reliance on quality self-help publications.* Good consumer advocates or typing services provide ready access to reliable self-help materials, either for free or at a reasonable price.

- *Trained staff.* One indication of whether or not people are committed to providing good service is whether or not they have undertaken skills training. Appropriate training is available through independent paralegal associations and continuing education seminars for financial planners and consumer advocates.

To locate a consumer advocate or typing service in your area, call the National Association for Independent Paralegals (NAIP) at 800-542-0034.

## 12.  Actuaries

If a pension or retirement plan is at stake in your divorce, you may need the services of an actuary, a specialized financial professional. For details, including fees charged, see Chapter 15, Section B.3.c.

## 13.  Business Appraisers

To determine the financial value of any business—including a sole proprietorship or professional practice—a business appraiser conducts a detailed analysis. A full discussion of the work of business appraisers, including the fee normally charged to evaluate an enterprise, is found in Chapter 17, Section C.1.

### Are Fees Paid to Professionals Tax Deductible?

You can deduct from your income taxes certain fees paid to professionals. Not many fees are deductible, but especially during times of divorce, every bit can help. Here are the rules:

- If you receive alimony, you can deduct all attorney fees you pay to secure or collect that alimony. If your spouse is paying your legal fees, the fees are not deductible. Nor are fees paid to lawyers by the alimony payor.

- All fees paid to any professional—including attorneys, accountants, financial planners and stockbrokers—for advice on tax consequences arising during a divorce, are deductible from your income taxes.

To deduct the fees, your adviser must itemize your billing showing exactly how much you were charged for the advice regarding alimony collection or tax issues. Be sure to get this breakdown.

# 10

# The First 30 Days: Reducing Risks and Protecting Property

*If you have no choice but to drive through a snowstorm on a curvy road, you would no doubt put chains on your tires and check the antifreeze. In navigating through your divorce, you must also take precautions so that you can survive financially.*

Use this chapter to "check the anti-freeze"—that is, to make sure you are doing what you can to reduce risks and protect yourself and your property.

## A. Insurance

Insurance is designed to protect you from financial disaster. But when you divorce, your coverage itself may be at risk. Because policies can make for boring reading, and almost no one thinks about this subject until it's too late, insurance needs are commonly forgotten during divorce.

To demonstrate the importance of insurance in your life, ask yourself:

"If I were in an accident or suddenly became ill, how would I pay my medical expenses?"

Of course, being aware of what can happen without insurance—and doing something about your situation—are two different things. Begin to take action by reviewing the steps below and then following up on these items.

### 1. Health Insurance

Find copies of your current policy. Check with your insurance agent to be certain that you and/or your children are still covered according to the policy terms. Find out how long your current policy will remain in effect and what the costs will be for the next six months to one year.

If you are covered under a company policy, you may need to speak to the personnel office or a special agent who handles the firm's health care. If your family is covered by your spouse's insurance, you may still be able to retain protection even if your spouse tries to remove you.

### 2. Life Insurance

When you divorce, you need to reconsider who should be named the beneficiary of any life insurance policies. Often, divorcing people forget to change the beneficiary. Then, years later, when one spouse dies, the *ex*-spouse gets all the benefits—even if there is a second spouse or if the deceased spouse wanted someone else, such as the children of the marriage, to be the beneficiaries. Whoever is named in the policy is the person who will receive the benefits.[1]

Don't automatically remove your spouse from your policy, however. You probably want to keep your soon-to-be ex-spouse as the beneficiary of your policy if your spouse will need a lump sum of cash to rear your minor-age children if you die before they reach adulthood. Also, your spouse may insist on being the beneficiary of a life insurance policy if you are paying alimony. That way, your ex-spouse won't lose the stream of income you provide if you die prematurely.

Sometimes in divorce, one spouse may want to name the children as beneficiaries rather than have any money go to the children's other parent. Think carefully before you make such a move. If the children are under 18 when you die, the probate court that oversees the distribution of your assets will require that a guardian be appointed to manage the in-

---

[1] In some divorce settlement agreements, the spouses may name who the beneficiaries of their life insurance policies will be. In some cases that go before a judge, the judge might make a similar order. If your settlement agreement or divorce decree says who the beneficiary will be, but you forget to change the policy, the beneficiaries named in the agreement or decree *may* be protected when you die. But they may also end up in a messy fight with the insurance company. Don't rely on the settlement agreement or divorce decree to name the beneficiary.

surance proceeds—usually in a bank account—until the children reach 18. If the guardian wants to remove money from the account, called a blocked or suspended account, the guardian will need court approval—an expensive, time-consuming and cumbersome procedure. And even when the money is distributed to the children at age 18, keep in mind that young adults who receive a vast amount of money may not be mature enough to handle it and could spend these funds on cars instead of college.

### 3. Disability Insurance

Another risk to your income is that you may become disabled—or the ex-spouse who is paying your support may become disabled. Check to see what type of disability coverage is available. Talk to the benefits department at the company at which you or your spouse are employed. Or contact your insurance agent to determine the cost of getting your own coverage for disability.

*If you're a single parent.* You may hesitate to buy disability insurance due to the expense and your perceived lack of need. Consider the harsher reality your children would face, however, if you became disabled and unable to work.

### 4. Business Coverage

Do you or your spouse own your own business? Check to see if you have insurance which is referred to as "key man" coverage. (Yes, that's "key man" not "key person" coverage.) This coverage is designed so that the business can cover its costs of running in the event of the death of the business owner or another "key" person.

---

### Keeping Health Care Coverage Through Your Spouse's Employer

If your health insurance is through a plan offered by your spouse's employer, and 20 or more people work for that employer, you can continue the health care coverage after the divorce. Under the federal COBRA (Consolidated Omnibus Budget Reform Act) law, divorced spouses of employed medical plan participants can pay for their own coverage for up to 36 months after the divorce. Your spouse's employer must inform you of your right to continue the coverage when your divorce becomes final. Don't leave it to your ex-spouse to notify the employer of that date. You should contact your ex-spouse's employer (probably the personnel department) and request the continued health care coverage as soon as your divorce is final.

Remember—the maximum length of time you can continue the coverage is 36 months. Thirty six months is not very long. As soon as your continued coverage begins, you should start looking for individual coverage, which may be less than the continued group coverage if you are healthy. (Ask if the provider of your continued coverage offers conversion to individual coverage. If it does, study the plan carefully. Individual conversion plans are usually expensive and limited in the benefits given.) Also, if you obtain a new job that includes group health insurance, or you remarry and your spouse's employer offers group coverage, your continued coverage will usually be terminated.

Keep in mind that if you don't obtain new insurance before the end of the 36-month period, you risk getting ill and becoming uninsurable.

---

## B. Property and Estate Protection

While the ultimate fate of your property may be unknown at the moment, you should nevertheless protect your interests by double checking title documents and reviewing your will, trusts and other materials which dispose of your property at death.

## 1.   Title Documents

In order to divide assets and negotiate your divorce settlement, you must know how title (history of ownership) to those assets is legally recorded, regardless of whether that property is ultimately considered your separate property or part of the marital assets. For real estate, title documents (deeds) should be recorded at the local county records office. You should take a look at all recorded deeds to make sure your spouse has not unilaterally removed your name from property held jointly. For example, either spouse can change title held in joint tenancy into tenancy in common.[2] If you can't find the deeds at the recorder's office, a title company can help you.

With other types of property, title documents are not as obvious—for example, car registration forms and bank account and investment statements. To protect yourself from having your spouse unilaterally change title, you may need to write to the department of motor vehicles, bank or stockbroker to ask that no transactions involving your property take place until the divorce is settled.

## 2.   Wills, Trusts and Other Estate Planning Documents

If you've ever made a will or living trust, or taken other measures to determine what will happen to your property after your death, your divorce may drastically alter your plans.

---

[2]Joint tenancy property has "a right of survivorship." This means that if either joint tenant dies, the other owner automatically inherits the deceased's portion, even if a will or other document states otherwise. Joint tenancy property is owned equally by the joint tenants. To sell joint tenancy property, all owners must agree or the owner who wants to sell must change title from joint tenancy to tenancy in common and then sell his share. Tenancy in common does not have the right of survivorship. Either owner can leave—or sell—his share to whomever he wants.

If you die before your divorce is final, your spouse may be entitled to a share of your property—even if your will leaves everything to other beneficiaries. To obtain a share, your spouse would have to go to court after your death and make a claim.

In many states, divorce automatically revokes part or all of your will. It's common for divorce to cancel all parts of your will that leave property to your ex-spouse; in some states, the entire will is wiped out. In any case, you should make a new will.

If you don't have a will and haven't arranged to transfer your property by other means (for example, joint tenancy or a living trust), at your death your property will be distributed according to state law. Usually this means your spouse and children will get your property. If you're divorced and have no children, your property will probably go to your parents, siblings and siblings' children.

---

**Planning for Your Children**

If you have children, it's especially important to also have an estate plan. At the least, you should consider:

• who will take care of your children if you can't

• how they will be supported if you're not around

• who will manage the property you leave them

In your will, you can name someone to be the personal guardian of your children—the person who would have physical custody. And you can name the same person, or someone else, to manage the property your children inherit from you. As for figuring out how to support the children after your death, you may want to consider term life insurance—it's a relatively cheap way to provide quick cash for beneficiaries.

### Nolo's Estate Planning Tools

Nolo Press publishes several books and software programs to help you make a will or otherwise plan your estate. If you want to draft a simple will, including one that lets you put property in trust for your children, you can use either *Nolo's Simple Will Book*, by Denis Clifford or *WillMaker* software (good on IBM, IBM compatible and Macintosh computers). For more extensive estate planning, we recommend *Plan Your Estate with a Living Trust*, also by Denis Clifford or *Nolo's Living Trust* software (Macintosh) by Mary Randolph. Ordering information is in the back of the book.

# 11

# The First 30 Days: Avoiding Tax Troubles

*You may be in the habit of procrastinating about taxes until the eve of April 15. But when you're divorcing that's far too late. While you do not have to confront every small detail in your tax papers when you're in the midst of a separation, you can take basic precautions that will save you money and prevent hassles later.*

For instance, suppose you assume that you and the spouse you are divorcing will file your income taxes jointly. At tax time, however, you discover your spouse has already filed separately. How will you pay the IRS for taxes you did not expect to owe? Better to grapple with the filing question now than to make costly assumptions that can easily be wrong.

*Assume you will file separately.* You can always amend your return and file jointly. But once you file jointly, you cannot amend it to file separately.

The following guidelines will help you address the income tax questions that are most important at this stage of your divorce. As you move through the rest of the divorce process (and this book), you will face more complicated tax issues regarding your property. For now, stick to the basics.

## A. Figure Your Tax Bill Jointly and Separately

You're not going to want any nasty surprises next April 15. To avoid problems, make a rough calculation of your federal and state taxes or ask your accountant or tax preparer to help you. Figure the amounts you would pay if you filed separately or with your spouse. Even if you haven't done all the paperwork necessary to find the exact amount of your final taxes, it's useful to get an estimate. With estimates you will at least have an objective guide for deciding how to file. You'll also be able to use the information

if you eventually try to convince your spouse to file jointly.

If possible, try to discuss the decision on tax filing with your spouse, lawyer, accountant or tax advisor. Your goal is to reach an agreement about filing and then document that agreement in writing.

*If you don't have access to tax information.* One spouse often does most of the bookkeeping for a family. If your spouse played that role and does not want to give you financial information, you may have to get a court order or use legal discovery (evidence gathering) techniques. For either, you'll probably need the help of an attorney. (See Chapter 9.) Consult the Appendix for resources. Before obtaining legal help, however, be sure to point out to your spouse that both of your legal bills will rise because of his or her attempts to withhold information. You can also contact your accountant for copies of previous returns or write to the Internal Revenue Service and request form #4506. By completing and returning this form to the IRS, you should be able to get the tax information you need. (You might also request form #503 and #504, which are IRS publications for separated and divorced people.)

If you have to wait for copies of previous returns and financial information, you can work with a tax accountant to estimate the amount you will owe the IRS. You can find out about deductions in several ways. Banks and lenders can tell you how much interest has been paid on a mortgage and charities can give you the dollar amount you or your spouse may have donated. Call your spouse's employer to verify his or her salary. In Chapter 13, you will prepare Net Worth and Cash Flow statements which can help clarify your tax situation.

*Preparing for the divorce.* If you will pay or receive temporary alimony, calculate how taxes will be affected by those payments. (See Chapter 12.) Furthermore, if you and your spouse anticipate receiving a tax refund, recognize that this money is likely to be considered marital property and will be divided or assigned as a part of your property division.

## B. When in Doubt, File Separately

If you and your spouse are unable to agree on how to handle your taxes, file separately. As we've noted, you can amend two separate returns (yours and your spouse's) and file jointly; you cannot, however, amend a joint return later so that each of you can file separately. If you initially file separately, you have only three years to amend your returns and file jointly. Although filing separately may actually cost more in dollars, it could save you a great deal of grief.

You especially want to file separately if your spouse misrepresents income or expenses, or takes an extremely aggressive posture toward the IRS. If you file jointly, you could be liable for back taxes, interest and penalties on a joint return. By filing separately, you will lessen your risk and keep your options open.

## C. Obtain a Court Order Outlining Temporary Alimony and Child Support

Often in divorce, spouses reach informal, private agreements about temporary alimony or support payments. But they neglect to get the agreements in writing or to get a court order outlining the agreement. This is a mistake. If you're paying alimony, you may resent it—but at least there is one bright spot. Alimony, including temporary alimony, is deductible to the payor, and taxable as income to the recipient. In order for alimony payments to be tax deductible (or taxable), however, they must be court ordered or in writing and signed by both parties.[1] If you are paying (or receiving) alimony based on an informal, oral agreement, you cannot deduct those payments (or need not report them as income) on your tax return.

---

[1] Money paid to an attorney in an effort to reduce the amount of alimony the payor must pay is also deductible from income taxes. Be sure to have your attorney itemize your bill so you can deduct that portion.

### Are You Liable for Your Spouse's Tax Debts?

If your spouse owed taxes when you entered the marriage, only your spouse is liable for the bill. All of your spouse's separately owned property can be used to pay the bill, as well as his or her share of the marital property. In community property states, this means that all community property—*including the wages of the spouse who does not owe money to the IRS*—can be taken.

Once you split up, you and your spouse can protect yourselves against each other's later liability by filing your tax returns separately.

But if taxes are owed for years you were married or separated—even if the tax bill comes after the divorce is final—both spouses are liable. You may be able to reduce or minimize your liability (this is called the "innocent spouse" rule), however, if:

- the bill is for unreported income in excess of 25% of the amount originally reported, you didn't know, or had no reason to know of the underreporting, and you did not significantly benefit from the omitted income; or

- the bill is for omitted income or an illegal deduction, you didn't know, or had no reason to know that there was an understatement of your tax liability, and it would be unfair to hold you liable for the taxes owed.

It's important to note that the IRS is reluctant to give a spouse this break. If you need to rely on it, gather substantial documentation of your innocence, such as paperwork showing your spouse had a separate bank account to which you had no access. You may also need testimony from accountants, tax preparers, stockbrokers and financial planners who can state that they dealt only with your spouse and had no reason to believe you were involved in the underreporting.

If the IRS has not declared you "an innocent spouse," but your ex-spouse agrees to pay a back tax bill, you are still liable for it. If your ex does not pay, the IRS can and will come after you for money.[2]

---

[2] For information on dealing with the IRS, see *Winning the IRS Game: Secrets of a Tax Attorney*, by Fred Daily (Dropzone Press).

Child support is neither deductible for the payor parent nor taxable as income to the recipient parent. Regardless of whether or not you and your spouse are physically living apart, you will want to make arrangements for child support so that your children are adequately cared for.

Getting a court order is not difficult. If you and your spouse agree to the amount of temporary alimony and child support, you can put your agreement into writing as a "stipulation." Your attorney can then take the simple steps to get that stipulation turned into a court order. It involves asking the judge to sign the stipulation,. You and your spouse should not have to appear in court.

## D. Get Your Tax Agreement in Writing

Whatever you and your partner decide to do about taxes, be sure to get the agreement in writing. Have it notarized or possibly even have it reviewed by an attorney.

# 12

The First Thirty Days:
Going From "We" to "Me"

*If you're thinking about a divorce or beginning one, the last place you may want to look is to the future. At this stage, you might see only problems ahead. Nevertheless, you need to begin changing your outlook from "we" to "me"—from being part of a couple to being on your own.*

To do that, it's helpful to set basic goals for yourself. In most goal-setting exercises, you're asked to think about where you'd like to be in a few years—an effective approach for some people. In counseling divorcing clients, however, we've found it helpful to turn the question around. If you have trouble looking at the future, answer this:

*Where don't you want to be in the next five years?*

Speaking financially, few of us want to be in debt, burdened with property we can't sell or working two jobs just to survive. Yet that could happen to you if you drift through a divorce without planning ahead. By thinking about the kinds of financial problems you'd like to avoid, you can narrow your focus

and clear the way for what you *do* want to accomplish.

As an initial planning exercise, use the columns below to jot down the immediate problems and goals you foresee. (Use the examples in italics to give you ideas about your own needs.)

Once you have a basic idea of where you'd like to go in the future, take a few moments to re-examine where you are now. Use these questions to help you think about your own situation.

## A. Major Upcoming Life Events

These events affect what you will and will *not* be able to do with money. For instance, if your teenagers are beginning college in a year, you may need a smaller house and a larger paycheck. You may be completing your own education and will need to budget time and money for a career change or job search. Perhaps you're reaching retirement age and must prepare for living on a reduced income. Whatever your situation, it's better to anticipate major events and prepare for them financially instead of getting caught off guard when it's time to take care of a major expense.

## Where I Do/Don't Want To Be in the Next Five Years

|  | Financial Problems To Avoid | Financial Goals To Meet |
|---|---|---|
| In the next six months | Letting bills become overdue<br><br>Paying interest only on credit cards<br><br>Using credit cards for all purchases<br><br>Not tracking my expenses | Pay off credit cards, or at least reduce balances by 50%<br><br>Create a monthly budget calendar listing to avoid overdue bills<br><br>Save 5% of income each month in emergency reserve<br><br>Research and start monthly investing into XYZ mutual fund |
| In the next year | Not enough money to pay mortgage<br><br>Being late on mortgage<br><br>No medical insurance<br><br>Borrowing from friends and Mom | Sell house and prepare to buy my own—set aside $20,000 toward down payment<br><br>Obtain disability insurance policy |

## B. Anticipated Financial Commitments

To whom are you committed and for how long? Have you agreed to support aging parents or another family member? Is that an indefinite agreement or does it last for a specific number of years? Will you need to have money available for a business investment? Do you have an upcoming balloon payment? Again, the answers to questions such as these determine what's possible for your financial future.

Now think about what's happening in your life and make a list of Major Upcoming Life Events and Anticipated Financial Commitments. By getting this information down on paper, you will not only clarify your financial needs but also reduce fears about the future. (Again, use the italicized examples to get you started).

### What's Happening in My Life

| Major Upcoming Life Events | Anticipated Financial Commitments |
|---|---|
| *Daughter beginning college in 2 years* | *Pay for mother's health care* |
| *Move to new home in 3 years* | *Pay Mom's retirement home mortgage of $800/month* |
| *Job change in spring because of recent layoffs* | *New car—$300 month* |
| *Son's wedding next June* | *Remodel kitchen—$15,000* |

Finally, review the list you just made and mark your top three priorities in order from one to three. You can write this list below. The items you selected will answer the question "Where Do I Go From Here?" because these are the next major issues which will demand your attention and time. We recommend tackling only three items at a time, because once you begin to work on these, your financial condition is likely to change and you may have new priorities. You can repeat this exercise any time you feel stuck about deciding "what to do next" in your divorce.

*What Do I Do Next?*

1.

2.

3.

## C. Where Does the Money Come From?

You've taken a look at what you absolutely *must do* and what you'd *like to do* next in your life. But how are you going to pay for it? Where will the money come from?

During your separation, you can get money in the same ways you did while married. Funds are available to you through:

- a job (salary) or business (income)
- borrowing/credit
- selling property or assets
- your spouse—in the form of temporary alimony

But in this time period—between today and the final settlement—you are in a unique situation. You are setting the stage for the settlement and you do not want to make financial mistakes that could work against you.

For instance, a woman who had never worked during her marriage went out and got a low-paying job in a retail store and left her children in the care of her parents when her husband filed for divorce. In the final settlement, she received no alimony because she was already working to support herself—even though she had wanted to go back to school to get training for a better job. Had she borrowed money to live on instead of getting the retail job, she might have been able to make a strong case for alimony.

In another case, the husband dutifully paid the household bills and temporary alimony for the two years that elapsed between the separation and the final settlement. Problems arose, however, because he had made the payments based on an informal arrangement with his spouse and not based on a court order or even written agreement. In his final settlement, he received no credit (and ultimately, no tax deduction) for the alimony he paid out. (See below.)

As these cases illustrate, you must not only figure out where the money is coming from, but also keep track of where it is going. The following tips address both concerns.

*If you borrow or use credit cards.* Under normal circumstances, financial planners would not recommend that you go into debt. During divorce, however, you may need to borrow money simply to survive. If you must use credit cards, try to find those with the lowest interest rate possible. If you borrow from family or friends, see if they will let you start paying them back when you're back on your feet.

It's crucial for you to document any money spent to support yourself and your children . If you use joint marital credit cards for "common necessaries of life"—food, shelter, clothing or medical care—you may be able to obtain a reimbursement for half of the costs. (See Chapter 6, Section A.1.a.)

*If you sell property or assets.* Before selling any jointly owned property without your spouse's knowledge or consent, ask your attorney if you are legally permitted to do so. You will not be able to sell real estate, motor vehicles or other assets with title documents that need both spouse's signatures. If you do sell any joint assets, be sure to set aside one-half of the proceeds for your spouse, or keep clear records of the money you received so that your spouse gets similarly valued property in the settlement.

*If you need temporary alimony.* If you need help paying the bills while the divorce is pending, you can request that your spouse pay temporary alimony. If your spouse is unwilling to do so voluntarily, you will need to request a hearing before the judge to have the issue resolved.

The judge looks at the needs of the requesting party—particularly that spouse's ability to support himself or herself—and the other spouse's ability to pay the temporary alimony. In a few counties, court officials have issued guidelines for judges to use in setting alimony. (For more information on alimony, see Chapter 19.)

If you will be paying alimony, be sure to get your agreement either ordered by a court, or in writing. If you don't, you cannot deduct the payments from your income tax. If you will be receiving al-

imony pursuant to a court order or written agreement, you must report that alimony as income on your tax return. (See Chapter 11, Section C.)

### Enforcing—and Making Permanent—Temporary Support Agreements

If your temporary alimony agreement is in writing, but has not been ordered by the court, you may want to take that extra step to obtain a court order. Without a court order, you probably won't be able to enforce the agreement if your spouse doesn't pay.

As explained in Chapter 11, getting a court order is not difficult. If you and your spouse agree to the amount of temporary alimony, you can put your agreement into writing as a "stipulation." Your attorney can then take the simple steps to get that stipulation turned into a court order. It involves asking the judge to sign the stipulation. You and your spouse should not have to appear in court.

CHAPTER

# 13

# Getting a Handle on
# Your Property and Expenses

*What—exactly—is at stake in your divorce? To answer that question, you must "get a handle" on your property and living expenses.*

In this chapter, you define which property is legally yours and which assets you may have to struggle for in the tug of war of divorce. You will also develop a much-needed picture of your cash flow. And you will learn how to use legal discovery procedures if you have any trouble getting the information you need.

By completing the tasks which follow, you will lay the foundation for the analysis and decision making that must be done to reach your final settlement. Think of this stage as developing your data base or stocking your pantry with the items you will need throughout the divorce process.

The four basic issues you must address at this point are:

- Who owns what—marital property and the laws of your state
- Who knows what—using legal discovery
- Net Worth—what do you own and what do you owe?
- Cash Flow—where does the money go?

## A. Who Owns What—Marital Property and the Laws of Your State

You must know what property is owned by you alone—as opposed to property owned separately by your spouse or by the two of you together before you begin to approach your property settlement. Keep in mind that the rules which follow are generals. To get the specifics on the property laws of your state, you will have to consult your lawyer or do some legal research.

Read this section for an overview of ownership. Once you have determined which of your property is separate and which is marital, you will list this information in the Net Worth statement in Section C, below.

### 1. Jointly Owned Property

During marriage, couples accumulate property, called marital property. Depending on which state you live in, however, marital property will take different forms.

*Common Law Property: Mississippi.* Only Mississippi follows traditional common law principles, which developed in England and came to the United States in the 18th Century. Under this system, marital property is divided at divorce according to who has legal *title* to the property—that is, who owns it. Only property jointly owned by a couple can be divided by the court. Common law property division can also be referred to as "title division."

*Community Property: Arizona, California, Idaho, Louisiana, Nevada, New Mexico, Texas, Washington and Wisconsin.* Community property, which comes from Spain, defines all earnings during marriage and all property acquired with those earnings as community property. At divorce, community property is divided equally (in half) between the spouses. A spouse who contributed separate money to an item bought with community funds may be entitled to reimbursement for that contribution. Conversely, a spouse who added community property money to a separate property item belonging to the other may be reimbursed.

In most community property states, a court has the discretion to divide the property equitably (fairly), if dividing the property in half would result in unfairness to one party. Additionally, in some community property states, a spouse deemed at fault in ending the marriage may be awarded less than 50% of the community property.[1]

*Equitable Distribution of Property: All Other States.* In the 40 states that follow equitable distribution principles, assets and earnings accumulated during marriage are divided equitably (fairly) at divorce. In theory, equitable means equal, or nearly so. In practice, however, equitable often means that as much as 2/3 of the property goes to the higher wage earner and as little as 1/3 goes to the lower (or non) wage earner—unless the court believes it is fairer to award one or the other spouse more. In some equitable distribution states, if a spouse obtains a fault divorce, the "guilty" spouse may receive less than a full share of the marital property upon divorce.

## 2. Separately Owned Property

In all states, a married person can treat certain types of earnings and assets as separate property. This means that at divorce, this separate property is not divided under the state's property distribution laws, but rather is kept by the spouse who owns it.

In community property states, the following is considered separate property:

- property accumulated before marriage;
- property accumulated during marriage with pre-marital earnings (such as income from a pension that vested before marriage) or with the proceeds of the sale of pre-marital property;
- gifts directed to only one spouse;
- inheritances; and
- property acquired after permanent separation.

In the equitable distribution states, separate property includes:

- property accumulated by a spouse before marriage;

---

[1]These exceptions do not apply in California.

- gifts directed to only one spouse; and
- inheritances.

In Mississippi, all property is the separate property of the acquiring spouse unless a document showing title to the property indicates otherwise. Earnings are considered a spouse's separate property, and assets acquired with those earnings are not divided at divorce unless they've been mixed (commingled) with jointly owned property or the property of the other spouse.

---

### Separate Is Separate Unless It's Mixed

In community property and equitable distribution states, the separate property of a spouse remains separate property unless it is mixed ("commingled") with marital property or the other spouse's separate property.

---

## B. Who Knows What—Using Legal Discovery

As described in Chapter 8, there are several ways to gather financial information. Doing it yourself will not only keep your lawyer's bill down, but it will also educate you about your family's finances and give you the strength to negotiate from a position of knowledge.

If you can't find the information yourself, however, and all efforts to collect it informally fail, you can have your lawyer conduct "discovery." Discovery is the term for formal procedures used to obtain information during a lawsuit. As with all matters in your divorce, remember that the attorney works for you and you should make the decisions about how extensive discovery procedures should be. If you've never seen the checkbook and signed the tax return for years without reviewing the papers or participating in their completion, then your lawyer may have to do a lot of digging to create a picture of your financial life.

Likewise, if you have participated in budgeting and bookkeeping, but your spouse owns a cash-and-carry grocery store and you feel that the business is being used to hide assets, discovery may be worth every penny you spend.

On the other hand, if you and your spouse have few assets and you have a pretty good idea of what you're both worth, then you may simply waste time and money using discovery to ferret out information on assets that you know are non-existent.

Think financially and act legally—remember that truism in divorce. Apply that maxim to discovery procedures and you should be fine.

In a divorce, the common discovery devices likely to be used include:

*Deposition (or examination before trial)*. A deposition is a proceeding in which a witness or party is asked to answer questions orally under oath before a court reporter. In divorces, many lawyers want to "take the deposition" of the other spouse in order to ask about potential hidden assets.

*Interrogatories*. Interrogatories are written questions sent by one party to the other for the latter to answer in writing under oath. Interrogatories are often used to ask a spouse to list all bank accounts, investment accounts and other assets ever held by that spouse.

*Request (or notice) for production of documents*. This is a request to a party to hand over certain defined documents. In divorce cases, parties often request from each other bank statements, pay stubs and other documents showing earnings, assets and debts.

*Request (or notice) for inspection*. This is a request by a party to look at tangible items (other than writings) in the possession or control of the other party. Items commonly inspected are houses and cars. In divorces, the request often comes up regarding house appraisals. For example, Bill and Bernice are divorcing. The court ordered Bill out of the family home to allow Bernice to stay with the children. Bill and Bernice have decided to sell the house, but don't

agree on the value. Bernice won't give Bill's appraiser access to the house. Bill must request an inspection.

*Bill of particulars*. A request for more information about allegation in a complaint (or petition) or answer (response).

*Subpoena and subpoena duces tecum*. An order telling a witness to appear at a deposition or to provide certain documents to a specific party. It's commonly used to get documents directly from banks, insurance companies, stockbrokers and the like.

## C. Net Worth—What Do You Own and What Do You Owe?

Subtracting what you owe from what you own reveals your net worth. During divorce, your Net Worth statement can serve as your touchstone for the information you will need when you analyze assets and prepare for negotiating your settlement. Doing this work now will put you ahead when reach Chapters 14 through 20.

In the past, you may have calculated your net worth for loans or business purposes. Now, you need to figure your net worth to get an overview of your current financial situation and to begin to determine which assets you want to keep in your divorce settlement. Although your net worth won't tell you what assets to keep, it can help you look at the "big picture" of your financial life. You may find that you are worth much more—or much less—than you thought you were.

Debts incurred during a marriage are usually considered joint debts—that is, during the marriage, both spouses are legally responsible for them. When a couple divorces, however, responsibility for marital debts is allocated in accordance with the property division laws of the state.

This usually means that the debts are divided equally or equitably, especially when they were incurred for food, shelter, clothing and medical care (called necessaries). The court also considers who is better able to pay the debts (the spouse with the higher income and/or lower living expenses). If a couple has many debts but also has much property, a common result is for the spouse better able to pay the debts to assume their payment and also to receive a larger share of the property to even up the division.

To find your net worth, use the worksheets on the following pages. If you can't fill in everything on each statement, don't worry. Gather as much information as you can. If you eventually hire someone to help you, you'll be far ahead and will save money by gathering this information yourself.

---

### Do You Hate Filling Out Forms?

Almost no one enjoys the task of writing information into small blanks on financial forms. In your divorce, however, you must get your financial facts straight. Any attorney or other professional you consult is probably going to want the information you are documenting in your Net Worth and Cash Flow statements. Most important, you will be organizing the information you must have to make the decisions in your divorce.

Get help or meet with others who are dealing with the same issues so you can help each other when the work gets tedious. You are not completing these forms as a mere exercise—you are using them to lay the groundwork for your new financial life.

# NET WORTH: ASSETS & LIABILITIES
## Assets

| | Title or Owner | Source of Asset | Date of Purchase | Tax Basis | Location Or Bank | Account Number | Interest Rate | Current Balance or Market Value |
|---|---|---|---|---|---|---|---|---|
| **CASH & CASH EQUIVALENTS** | | | | | | | | |
| Cash | | | | | | | | |
| Checking | | | | | | | | |
| Checking | | | | | | | | |
| Savings | | | | | | | | |
| Savings | | | | | | | | |
| Credit Union | | | | | | | | |
| Money Market Funds | | | | | | | | |
| Money Market Funds | | | | | | | | |
| Money Market Funds | | | | | | | | |
| Other Liquid Assets | | | | | | | | |
| **SUBTOTAL: CASH & CASH EQUIVALENTS** | | | | | | | | |
| **MARKETABLE ASSETS & INVESTMENTS** | | | | | | | | |
| Life Insurance | | | | | | | | |
| Life Insurance | | | | | | | | |
| Stocks | | | | | | | | |
| Bonds | | | | | | | | |
| Mutual Funds | | | | | | | | |
| Mutual Funds | | | | | | | | |
| Loans/Accounts Receivable (due within one year) | | | | | | | | |
| General Partnerships | | | | | | | | |
| Limited Partnerships | | | | | | | | |
| **SUBTOTAL, MARKETABLE ASSETS & INVESTMENTS** | | | | | | | | |

# NET WORTH: ASSETS & LIABILITIES
## Assets

| | Title or Owner | Source of Asset | Date of Purchase | Tax Basis | Location Or Bank | Account Number | Interest Rate | Current Balance or Market Value |
|---|---|---|---|---|---|---|---|---|
| **RETIREMENT PLAN ASSETS** | | | | | | | | |
| Keogh | | | | | | | | |
| IRA | | | | | | | | |
| IRA | | | | | | | | |
| Pension/Profit Sharing - 401(K) | | | | | | | | |
| *SUBTOTAL, RETIREMENT PLAN ASSETS* | | | | | | | | |
| **REAL ESTATE ASSETS** | | | | | | | | |
| Residence | | | | | | | | |
| Vacation Home | | | | | | | | |
| Income Property | | | | | | | | |
| Unimproved Real Property | | | | | | | | |
| *SUBTOTAL, REAL ESTATE ASSETS* | | | | | | | | |
| **BUSINESS INTERESTS/ASSETS** | | | | | | | | |
| Closely Held Stock (Private) | | | | | | | | |
| Sole Proprietor | | | | | | | | |
| Other Business Assets | | | | | | | | |
| *SUBTOTAL, BUSINESS INTERESTS/ASSETS* | | | | | | | | |
| **PERSONAL PROPERTY** | | | | | | | | |
| Automobile | | | | | | | | |
| Automobile | | | | | | | | |
| Home Furnishings | | | | | | | | |
| Jewelry/Furs | | | | | | | | |
| Collections/Coins/Stamps | | | | | | | | |
| Motorcycle/Motorhome | | | | | | | | |
| Boat/Plane | | | | | | | | |
| *SUBTOTAL, PERSONAL PROPERTY* | | | | | | | | |

## INSTRUCTIONS FOR NET WORTH:
## ASSETS AND LIABILITIES—ASSETS

To determine your net worth, you need to estimate the current value (last column) of each asset you own. Complete the remaining columns if the information is available. List all marital property—not just the property in which you have an interest. These columns aren't necessary in determining net worth, but will help you understand as much as possible about your assets so you can make informed decisions when it comes time to divide your marital property.

*Title or owner.* Title is a legal term that simply means ownership. Several types of property—such as houses, cars and stocks—come with title documents (the house deed, car registration and stock certificate). When property is owned jointly, these title documents specify exactly how "title is held"— meaning how the property is owned. In this column, list the owner of an item of property, and how ownership is listed on any title document. The possible ways to hold title to property are:

- *Joint tenancy.* Co-owners of joint tenancy property own the property in equal shares. When two or more persons own property as joint tenants, and one owner dies, the remaining owner(s) automatically inherit the share owned by the deceased person. This is termed the right of survivorship. For example, if a husband and wife own their house as joint tenants and one dies, the other person ends up owning the entire house, even if the deceased person attempted to give away her half of the house in her will.

At any time, a joint tenant can terminate a joint tenancy and change title to tenancy in common. (See below.) The consequence is the destruction of the right to survivorship.

- *Tenancy by the entirety.* Tenancy by the entirety is a way married couples can hold title to property in some non-community property states. Tenancy by the entirety is very similar to joint tenancy; upon the death of one of the spouses, the property automatically passes to the surviving spouse, regardless of contrary provisions in the will. Unlike joint tenancy, however, one person cannot unilaterally sever the tenancy by the entirety. After divorce, jointly owned property cannot be held as tenancy by the entirety. Instead, it changes to tenancy in common (below) unless you specify joint tenancy.

- *Tenancy in common.* Tenancy in common is a way for any two or more people to hold title to property together. Each co-owner has an "undivided interest" in the property which means that no owner holds a particular part of the property and all co-owners have the right to use all the property. Each owner is free to sell or give away his interest. On his death, his interest passes through his will or by intestate succession if he had no will. Divorcing spouses who plan to own property after the split usually hold the property in tenancy in common. Occasionally, ex-spouses will continue to hold property in joint tenancy.

- *Community property.* Couples in community property states can take title as community property. Community property is divided equally at the end of their marriage. Property owned jointly after divorce cannot be held in community property.

- *Separate title.* Sometimes title will be in only one person's name, even if both spouses own the property. In community property and equitable distribution states, the property will be divided between the spouses if the spouse whose name is not on the title document can otherwise prove an ownership interest. For example, if the house is in the wife's name only, but the cancelled checks for the mortgage payments are written on the husband's separate account, the property will be divided. In Mississippi, a spouse with an ownership share whose name is not on the title document will need the help of a lawyer to obtain his interest.

*Source.* Specify where the money to purchase the asset came from. Be sure to note whether the source is separate or marital property.

*Date obtained or received.* Put the date you bought items or received a gift or inheritance. For items bought over time—such as shares of the same stock—list all dates and the number of shares bought each time.

*Tax basis.* Tax basis is an important concept that will come up later in this book. Essentially, it's an amount from which the IRS figures out how much profit (called gain) you've made on an asset and therefore how much you owe in taxes. In Chapter 14, we provide detailed instructions for determining an asset's tax basis. For now, just total up what you paid, the cost of any improvements, tax benefits (such as rollover of gains from prior house sales or depreciation taken on rental property) and, in some cases, reinvested dividends. Keep in mind that if you receive valuable gifts or inheritances, the tax basis is figured from the time of the original purchase, not from the time you receive it.

*Location or bank.* Enter where the asset is located or held.

*Account number.* List, if applicable.

*Interest rate.* If this asset earns interest, list the rate here. To find this information, check your bank account or brokerage statement. Because interest rates change frequently, you may have to call the deposit institution directly. When rates are in flux, use 6%-8%.

*Current balance or market value.* For deposit accounts and similar investments, list the balance from your last statement. For other assets, list the market value from the most recent appraisal.

# NET WORTH: ASSETS & LIABILITIES
## Liabilities

| | Original Loan Amt. | Date Made Mo/Yr | Secured By (collateral) | Interest Rates on Loan | Term of Loan | Monthly Payment | Balloon Payment Date Due | Balloon Payment Amt Due | Balance Due |
|---|---|---|---|---|---|---|---|---|---|
| Housing: Mortgage | | | | | | | | | |
| Housing: Mortgage | | | | | | | | | |
| Trust Deed(s) | | | | | | | | | |
| Other: Equity Loans, Liens, etc. | | | | | | | | | |
| *SUBTOTAL, MORTGAGE/LOANS* | | | | | | | | | |
| Auto Loan | | | | | | | | | |
| Auto Loan | | | | | | | | | |
| *SUBTOTAL, AUTO LOAN* | | | | | | | | | |
| Bank Loan | | | | | | | | | |
| Bank Loan | | | | | | | | | |
| Finance or Credit Loans | | | | | | | | | |
| *SUBTOTAL, BANK LOANS* | | | | | | | | | |
| Private Loan | | | | | | | | | |
| Private Loan | | | | | | | | | |
| *SUBTOTAL, PRIVATE LOANS* | | | | | | | | | |
| Other Loans | | | | | | | | | |
| Other Loans | | | | | | | | | |
| *SUBTOTAL, OTHER LOANS* | | | | | | | | | |
| Credit/Charge Account | | | | | | | | | |
| Credit/Charge Account | | | | | | | | | |
| Credit/Charge Account | | | | | | | | | |
| *SUBTOTAL, CREDIT ACCOUNTS* | | | | | | | | | |
| Unsettled Damages | | | | | | | | | |
| Claims | | | | | | | | | |
| *SUBTOTAL, DAMAGES/CLAIMS* | | | | | | | | | |
| Student Loan | | | | | | | | | |
| Student Loan | | | | | | | | | |
| *SUBTOTAL, STUDENT LOANS* | | | | | | | | | |

**INSTRUCTIONS FOR NET WORTH:**
**ASSETS & LIABILITIES—LIABILITIES**

The other half of figuring out your net worth is listing your liabilities, that is, what you owe. Use the worksheet provided.

*Original loan amount.* Enter the amount you originally borrowed. Don't include interest. On your credit cards, put the amount of your purchase or cash advance.

*Date made.* Put the date the debt was incurred. For credit cards, note the various dates you charged items.

*Secured by.* A secured debt is linked to specific items of property, called collateral, which guarantees payment of the debt. List the collateral here. Common examples of secured debts are mortgages, home equity loans, second mortgages (the house is collateral) and car or other vehicle loans (the motor vehicle is the collateral). On occasion, a department store charge is a secured debt. The store would have made you sign a "security agreement" when you charged your purchase. Be sure to check.

*Interest rates on loans.* List all interest rates. If the rate is variable (as many mortgages and credit cards are), list the present rate and note that it is variable.

*Term of loan.* How many years do you have to repay the loan or debt?

*Monthly payment.* List the amount you actually pay each month.

*Balloon payment.* Many borrowers can't afford the monthly payments when they apply for loans to be repaid in equal monthly payments for a set period. To help them qualify, lenders lower the monthly payments and collect the difference at the end of the loan in one large payment called a balloon payment. If any of your loans come with balloon payments—they often accompany privately offered second mortgages. List the due date for any balloon payments and the amount of the payment in columns 7 and 8.

*Balance due.* Enter how much it would cost to pay off the loan in full. Check with the lender or creditor to determine the loan payoff amount.

# NET WORTH: BALANCE SHEET SUMMARY

*Refer to the Net Worth Assets and Liabilities worksheets for subtotals for each category. Write the subtotals in the appropriate blanks on this Balance Sheet Summary. Add sub-totals of Assets for sum of Total Assets; and sub-totals of Liabilities for Total Liabilities. To find your Net Worth, subtract Total Liabilities from Total Assets.*

## Assets Summary:

SUBTOTAL, CASH & CASH EQUIVALENTS    $ _____

SUBTOTAL, MARKETABLE ASSETS & INVESTMENTS    _____

SUBTOTAL, RETIREMENT PLAN ASSETS    _____

SUBTOTAL, REAL ESTATE ASSETS    _____

SUBTOTAL, BUSINESS INTERESTS/ASSETS    _____

SUBTOTAL, PERSONAL PROPERTY    _____

### <u>Sum of Total Assets:</u>    $ _____

## Liabilities Summary:

SUBTOTAL, MORTGAGE/LOANS    $ _____

SUBTOTAL, AUTO LOAN    _____

SUBTOTAL, PRIVATE LOANS    _____

SUBTOTAL, OTHER LOANS    _____

SUBTOTAL, CREDIT ACCOUNTS    _____

SUBTOTAL, DAMAGES/CLAIMS    _____

SUBTOTAL, STUDENT LOANS    _____

### <u>Sum of Total Liabilities</u>    $ _____

# NET WORTH:    $ _____

**INSTRUCTIONS FOR NET WORTH:**
**BALANCE SHEET SUMMARY**

Finally, to determine your net worth, you must subtract your liabilities from your assets. Copy the subtotals from the Assets and Liabilities statements. Sum up each subtotal. Then subtract the liabilities from the assets.

## D. Cash Flow—Where Does the Money Go?

The income and outgo of money is called your cash flow. Regardless of how your settlement winds up, you must realize that initially, a divorce forces *two* households to exist on the same income that had previously supported only *one*. So you need to know, as precisely as possible, what it costs you to live. If you have children, you must take their needs and expenses into account.

The cash flow worksheets below outline the income and outgo of money in your life—day-to-day living expenses and sources of income. While filling out the worksheets, be realistic. And do not worry if you do not have the information for every line. Do the best you can.

# CASH FLOW: INCOME AND EXPENSES

## Income

| | Self | | Spouse | |
|---|---|---|---|---|
| | Per Pay Period | Per Month | Per Pay Period | Per Month |
| **A. SALARY & WAGES** — Pay period is: [ ] weekly [ ] biweekly [ ] monthly | | | | |
| Gross income (including commissions, allowances and overtime): | | | | |
| Subtract:      **Federal & State Taxes** | | | | |
|          **FICA-Social Security** | | | | |
|          **Other (medical or other insurance,** | | | | |
|          **pension, stock plans, union dues...** | | | | |
| | | | | |
| **B. SELF EMPLOYMENT** | | | | |
| Gross Income | | | | |
| Subtract:      **Federal & State Taxes** | | | | |
|          **Self Employment taxes** | | | | |
| *NET INCOME FROM SELF-EMPLOYMENT* | | | | |
| **C. OTHER SOURCES** | | | | |
| Bonuses | | | | |
| Commissions | | | | |
| Dividends | | | | |
| Interest Income | | | | |
| Rental property | | | | |
| Royalties | | | | |
| Notes and trust deeds | | | | |
| Annuities, pensions/401(K) | | | | |
| Alimony | | | | |
| Child Support | | | | |
| Social Security | | | | |
| Other (Misc.) * | | | | |
| Subtract: Any Deductions | | | | |
| *NET INCOME FROM OTHER SOURCES* | | | | |
| **TOTAL NET MONTHLY INCOME FROM ALL SOURCES** | | | | |
| **ESTIMATED NET ANNUAL INCOME (net monthly income x 12)** | | | | |

\* include income from disability, unemployment insurance, AFDC and other public assistance, etc.

## INSTRUCTIONS FOR CASH FLOW: INCOME & EXPENSES—INCOME

Income generally comes from three sources:

- earned salary or wages from your job as an employee;

- earnings from your own business as a self-employed individual; or

- miscellaneous other sources, such as job bonuses, interest earned from investments and income from a disability insurance policy.

Record all sources of income for you and your spouse, completing only those categories that apply. For investments from marital property such as interest income, rental property and notes and trust deeds, divide the monthly income by two and enter half in your column and half in your spouse's column.[2] If either you or your spouse holds more than one job or owns a self-run business, total your income on a separate sheet and enter the total on this worksheet.

---

[2]If this investment or asset is not owned 50-50—for example, your second house that produces rental income was bought partially with one spouse's separate property and partially with marital property (that is, income earned during marriage)—enter the appropriate percentages.

# CASH FLOW: INCOME AND EXPENSES
## Expenses

| Category | Month | Month | Month | Month | Monthly Average | Annual Monthly x 12 | Allocated for Children |
|---|---|---|---|---|---|---|---|
| *RESIDENCE EXPENSES* | | | | | | | |
| Rent (if applicable) | | | | | | | |
| House Payment — 1st Trust Deed (principal + interest) | | | | | | | |
| 2nd Trust Deed (principal + interest) | | | | | | | |
| Equity Loan/Loans | | | | | | | |
| Utilities: | | | | | | | |
| Phone | | | | | | | |
| Gas, Heating Oil | | | | | | | |
| Electricity | | | | | | | |
| Water | | | | | | | |
| Cable | | | | | | | |
| Other (specify) | | | | | | | |
| Maintenance: | | | | | | | |
| Gardening | | | | | | | |
| Pool Service | | | | | | | |
| House Cleaning | | | | | | | |
| Periodic Repairs | | | | | | | |
| Domestic Help ( ___ days @ $ ___ /day) | | | | | | | |
| Furniture Replacement | | | | | | | |
| Appliances Replacement | | | | | | | |
| Other (specify) | | | | | | | |
| Fees and/or Taxes: | | | | | | | |
| Condo/Homeowners assn. | | | | | | | |
| Property Taxes | | | | | | | |
| Insurance: | | | | | | | |
| Homeowners/renters | | | | | | | |
| Other (specify) | | | | | | | |
| *SUBTOTAL, RESIDENCE EXPENSES* | | | | | | | |

# CASH FLOW: INCOME AND EXPENSES

## Expenses

| Category | Month | Month | Month | Month | Monthly Average | Annual Monthly x 12 | Allocated for Children |
|---|---|---|---|---|---|---|---|
| *PERSONAL EXPENSES* | | | | | | | |
| Food:   Supermarket | | | | | | | |
|   Restaurant | | | | | | | |
| Clothing:   Personal | | | | | | | |
|   Work | | | | | | | |
|   Dry Cleaning/Laundry | | | | | | | |
| Medical:   Doctor (unreimbursed charges) | | | | | | | |
|   Dentist | | | | | | | |
|   Eye Doctor | | | | | | | |
|   Medicines/Prescriptions | | | | | | | |
| Variable monthly expenses | | | | | | | |
|   Entertainment | | | | | | | |
|   Cultural/recreational | | | | | | | |
|   Gifts (birthdays, wedding, etc.) | | | | | | | |
|   Drug/variety store items | | | | | | | |
|   Books, magazines, newspapers | | | | | | | |
|   Periodical subscriptions | | | | | | | |
| Membership dues | | | | | | | |
| Education:   Tuition (self & others) | | | | | | | |
|   Books & Fees | | | | | | | |
|   Other | | | | | | | |
| *SUBTOTAL, PERSONAL EXPENSES* | | | | | | | |
| *CHILDREN'S EXPENSES* | | | | | | | |
| Allowances | | | | | | | |
| Child Care | | | | | | | |
| Education: Tuition, Books, etc. | | | | | | | |
| Other | | | | | | | |
| *SUBTOTAL, CHILDREN'S EXPENSES* | | | | | | | |

# CASH FLOW: INCOME AND EXPENSES

## Expenses

| Category | Month | Month | Month | Month | Monthly Average | Annual Monthly x 12 | Allocated for Children |
|---|---|---|---|---|---|---|---|
| *INSTALLMENT DEBT* | | | | | | | |
|    Loan Payment (specify loan) | | | | | | | |
|    Loan Payment (specify loan) | | | | | | | |
|    Credit Cards (if carried month to month) | | | | | | | |
|    Student Loans | | | | | | | |
|    Other * | | | | | | | |
| *SUBTOTAL, INSTALLMENT DEBT* | | | | | | | |
| *TRANSPORTATION* | | | | | | | |
|   Car expenses:  Car payments | | | | | | | |
|    Gas (include gas cards) | | | | | | | |
|    Tolls & Parking | | | | | | | |
|    Auto Insurance | | | | | | | |
|    Maintenance | | | | | | | |
|    Registration Fees | | | | | | | |
|   Vacations:  Plane fares | | | | | | | |
|    Hotel costs | | | | | | | |
|    Extra expenses | | | | | | | |
|   Public Transportation: (bus, cab, etc.) | | | | | | | |
|   Other (boat, plane, RV, etc.) | | | | | | | |
| *SUBTOTAL, TRANSPORTATION* | | | | | | | |
| *INSURANCE EXPENSES* (specify amounts) | | | | | | | |
|   Individual:  Life | | | | | | | |
|    Medical | | | | | | | |
|    Disability | | | | | | | |
|   Group:  Life | | | | | | | |
|    Medical | | | | | | | |
|    Disability | | | | | | | |
| *SUBTOTAL, INSURANCE EXPENSES* | | | | | | | |

* (include personal loans, loans from finance or credit company, debt-consolidation loans, back taxes or IRS penalties, if repaying on installment program, and any other loans or installment payments you make which are not included elsewhere.)

# CASH FLOW: INCOME AND EXPENSES

## Expenses

| Category | Month | Month | Month | Monthly Average | Annual Monthly x 12 | Allocated for Children |
|---|---|---|---|---|---|---|
| **OTHER EXPENSES** | | | | | | |
| Alimony | | | | | | |
| Support for dependents | | | | | | |
| Legal/Accounting (non-business) | | | | | | |
| Contributions (church, charity, etc.) | | | | | | |
| Misc. | | | | | | |
| *SUBTOTAL, OTHER EXPENSES* | | | | | | |
| **List and add Subtotals of all Expenses:** | | | | | | |
| *RESIDENCE EXPENSES* | | | | | | |
| *PERSONAL EXPENSES* | | | | | | |
| *CHILDREN'S EXPENSES* | | | | | | |
| *INSTALLMENT DEBT* | | | | | | |
| *TRANSPORTATION* | | | | | | |
| *INSURANCE EXPENSES* | | | | | | |
| *OTHER EXPENSES* | | | | | | |
| **TOTAL EXPENSES** | | | | | | |

### INSTRUCTIONS FOR CASH FLOW: INCOME & EXPENSES—EXPENSES

Designed to create a realistic picture of your cash flow, this worksheet is divided into seven categories—residence, personal, children, installment debt, transportation, insurance and other.

To determine your current expenses, record your actual expenditures for the three past months for each item that applies. For regular expenses, such as rent, mortgage or car payment, list the monthly amount in the Monthly Average column. For irregular expenses, such as utility bills, meals out or vacations, list the Monthly Average by totaling the first three columns and dividing by three. Multiply the Monthly Average by 12 and enter the amount in the Annual column. Finally, estimate how much of each expense is allocated for your children and enter it in the last column.

Be aware that certain payments can be listed under more than one category. For example, car payments fall under installment debt and transportation. To help develop a picture of where your money actually goes, we specify items whenever possible—the car payment is under transportation. When you complete the worksheet, double-check it to be sure you have not listed the same expenses under more than one category.

Income and expenses must be considered together. If you're spending too much, you've got to reduce those expenses or increase your income. Otherwise, you'll find yourself facing serious debt problems.

---

### Listing Credit Card Expenses

To get a clear picture of your spending, list your various credit card expenditures under appropriate categories. For example, if your Visa bill is $198 with $120 spent for clothes and $78 for meals out and you pay the bill off in full each month, enter the $120 under clothes and $78 under food expenses. If, however, you carry a balance on your credit card bill—for example the bill totals $4,000 now and you make monthly payments of $300—enter the amount of the monthly payment under installment debt.

# 14

# What Will Happen to the House?

*The house.*

*Who gets it?*

*Who pays for it?*

*Who gets how much out of it?*

*And who put what into it?*

Wrangling over the house is practically a universal pastime among divorcing couples. Not only is a house the largest asset you are likely to have, but it's also loaded with symbolic meanings and emotional attachments. A home can represent the commitment to partnership between husband and wife, a place where the children grew up or a refuge from the demands of life. Perhaps it stands for a connection to the community—or to the future generations of your family to whom you hoped to give the house.

Whatever a house has meant to you, you're threatened with its loss during divorce.

But rather than thinking you will "lose" your house during divorce, consider at least five basic options available to you:

*Option A: Sell the house together and split the proceeds with your spouse*

*Option B: Buy out your spouse's share and keep the house for life*

*Option C: Buy out your spouse's share and sell the house in the future*

*Option D: Sell your share of the house to your spouse*

*Option E: Own the house jointly with your spouse and sell it in the future*

To ease your anxieties, it helps to look at the numbers to find the true value of your home so you can make an informed choice. In the following sections, we explain the financial factors you need to consider before choosing the best option.

**Understand your state's laws**

Keep in mind that your options regarding the house may be limited by the laws in your state and the particular circumstances of your case. For example, in some states, judges may presume that a custodial parent and children will stay in the family home until the children reach maturity.

## A. Financial Versus Legal Realities

To understand your options better, consider home ownership from both the legal and the financial perspective.

## B. The House—Keep It or Sell It— Now or Later?

If you've been in a house any length of time, you're probably accustomed to paying a set amount each month on your mortgage. Too often, people going through divorce focus on that monthly payment, which looks lower than anything they would have to pay if they moved out and bought another home.

But looks are deceiving. A low or moderate monthly payment can keep you from seeing many of the other costs of owning a home. Suppose you *do* keep the house. Will you be able to cover the upkeep costs—repairs, cleaning, painting, gardeners and the like? What if you decide to sell it in a few years? Are you prepared to cover the costs of sale—and taxes owed on any profit you make in the sale—alone? Can you afford to buy out your partner's share of the house and still have money to live on? Unless you know the true costs of keeping a home, you can't answer these questions.

| *Legal Reality* | *Financial Reality* |
|---|---|
| In some states, if a couple has minor children, a court will not allow the family home to be sold and the proceeds split, or bought by the non-custodial parent, at divorce. The rationale is to minimize the disruption in the lives of children whose parents are divorcing. Instead, the parent with physical custody of the children is given the chance to buy out the other parent. If that parent can't afford to buy the other out, the custodial parent is given the home temporarily. Only when the children leave the home or the custodial parent remarries or moves is the house sold and the proceeds divided. | If you are a custodial parent who can't afford to buy the other out but must keep a house, recognize what the true costs are. You and your spouse must agree—or have a court order—concerning who will pay the monthly mortgage and maintenance costs, who will pay for major repairs and who will take the tax deductions. Be prepared to bear these costs alone, in the event your spouse reneges on any agreement you make. |

| *Legal Reality* | *Financial Reality* |
|---|---|
| During the marriage, you and your spouse purchased a house from income earned during your marriage. You've assumed that if you sell the house, the proceeds will be split 50-50. In the 40 states that follow equitable distribution principles, however, the split may be different.[1] That is because in those states, judges are supposed to divide property fairly. In reality, fair often means that the higher wage earning spouse receives 2/3 of the proceeds; the other spouse pockets only 1/3. | If you and your spouse can reach your own settlement without going to court, you can each negotiate the best deal for yourself, rather than have a judge impose one on you. Rarely is anyone happy with the settlement carved out by a judge, who won't factor in most financial consequences of keeping or giving up certain assets. A negotiated settlement, though not perfect, is usually more palatable. |

---

[1] The 40 equitable distribution states are all except Arizona, California, Idaho, Louisiana, Nevada, New Mexico, Texas, Washington (community property states), Wisconsin (a modified community property state), and Mississippi (common law property state).
See Chapter 13 for a full discussion.

## C. Steps Toward Settling the House

Finding the true value of your house will take several calculations. Follow the steps below:

1. What is your total housing cost per month?

2. What is the current fair market value of your house?

3. How much will it cost to sell the house?

4. What is the equity value of your house?

5. What is your share of the house?

6. What is the tax basis for your house?

7. What would the after-tax/after-sale value of your house be if you sold it with your spouse?

8. What would the after-tax/after-sale value of your house be if you keep it now and sell in the future?

9. What is your best option regarding the house?

10. How do you feel about this decision?

### Don't skip vital steps

You may be tempted to skip certain steps, knowing that you favor one option over the others. Nevertheless, we strongly advise you to work through each step before making a decision. Having all of the calculations will give you the most comprehensive picture of your financial choices—and can alert you to costs you may have overlooked.

If you are absolutely certain about your plan of action, however, complete steps 9 and 10, and those listed for each option.

### Option A:  Sell the house together and split the proceeds with your spouse

Complete steps 1-7. You need to know not only your current housing costs and equity value, but also the costs of selling the house and the amount of profit you will realize after the taxes are paid.

### Option B:  Buy out your spouse's share and keep the house for life

Complete steps 1, 2, 4, 5, 9 and 10. If you are absolutely certain you are not going to move from your house before you die, then you do not have to worry about paying the taxes on the possible profit or the costs generated by a sale. But you do need to know the true monthly costs of housing to decide if you can afford to stay put and you should figure out if you can afford to buy out your spouse.

### Option C:  Buy out your spouse's share and sell the house in the future

Complete steps 1-6, 9 and 10. As this option can hold the most unforeseen financial risks, you'll want to take into consideration as many known factors as possible. As with Option B, you must determine if you can afford your monthly housing costs. You also want to approximate how much you stand to make if you sell the house. Most importantly, you must recognize the tax implications of a future sale.

### Option D:  Sell your share of the house to your spouse

Complete steps 1-7, 9 and 10. To determine whether or not your spouse is making a good offer for your share of the house, you must understand its true market value after taxes are deducted. If your spouse offers to purchase the house for its equity value, you'll want to take this offer because you'll be receiving an amount which greatly exceeds the economic value of the house.

### Option E:  Own the house jointly with your spouse and sell it in the future

Complete steps 1-6 and 8-10. The information gathered in the first six steps will enable you to make the more difficult calculations about the future as outlined in step 8. When a divorcing couple holds on to their house, it's usually because either a custodial parent is staying with the children or the housing market is so weak that the couple doesn't want to sell the house yet. Keep in mind, however, that owning the house together can be tricky emotionally.

## 1.  What Is Your Total Housing Cost Per Month?

Your mortgage does not represent the entire amount you spend on housing. You must also consider costs like your utilities and maintenance to get a true picture of expenses. Use these steps to find your Net Monthly Housing Cost:

a.  List your Gross Monthly Housing Cost.

b.  Total your Gross Monthly Housing Cost.

c.  Find your Net Monthly Housing Cost by subtracting Tax Savings from your Gross Monthly Housing Cost.

An example and formula for your own use follow these explanations.

### a.  List Your Gross Monthly Housing Cost

List the amount you pay each month for the items below. You may already have this information on the Cash Flow Statement you completed in Chapter 13. If you don't know the monthly cost of an item, or if you don't incur an expense every month, estimate the amount you spend per year and divide by 12. To estimate what you'll spend on significant repairs and maintenance needs, look around the house and note any major work that needs to be done. Check previous invoices to get an idea of what you'd normally spend on these expenses—or call a plumber, electrician or whomever else you may need for an estimate.

| Item | Example | Your Monthly Cost |
|---|---|---|
| Mortgage payment | $1,200 | $ |
| Second mortgage (or equity credit) payment | 272 | $ |
| Property tax | 188 | $ |
| Insurance | 42 | $ |
| Utilities | 100 | $ |
| Yard maintenance | 50 | $ |
| Pool maintenance | 50 | $ |
| Other maintenance (painting, plumbing) | 50 | $ |
| Major repairs (roof, siding) | 500 | $ |
| Major appliances (refrigerator) | 50 | $ |
| Gross Housing Cost Per Month | $2,502 | $ |

### b.  Total Your Gross Monthly Housing Cost

The price of owning and maintaining your house is higher than your monthly mortgage alone. Even if certain expenses aren't being incurred now—or haven't been for a while—do not be lulled into thinking they no longer exist. This list includes the cost of repairs because if you keep the house, those repairs will be your sole responsibility. You may be able to get your spouse to split repair costs with you when you negotiate the settlement, but because that possibility is still unknown, figure that you will have to come up with the money yourself.

For instance, Julie knew she'd have to pay $6,000 to fix her roof if she stayed in the marital house. In her settlement negotiations, she insisted that her husband Ron knock $3,000 off the amount she would pay him for his share of the house. Ron hesitated, arguing that by fixing the roof Julie was improving the potential sale value of a house she was keeping. Julie pointed out that the damage to the roof occurred during the marriage, and further that renovation and major repair expenses do *not* increase the value of the home on a dollar for dollar basis. Ron reluctantly agreed to reduce his share by $3,000.

### c.  Find Your Net Monthly Housing Cost by Subtracting Tax Savings From Your Gross Monthly Housing Cost

In considering your monthly housing costs, you should not overlook the tax benefits of home ownership. Under current tax laws, you can deduct your mortgage interest payment and the property taxes you've paid, so your housing costs may be *lower* than the sum of your Gross Housing Cost. You can use federal tax form 1099 to calculate the amount of your mortgage interest for the year.

In addition, you may be able to deduct points and closing costs included in your mortgage. When you purchase a house, you can deduct points and closing costs in the year of purchase. If you refinance the mortgage on your house, your deductions for the points are spread out over the life of the new loan. Points on loans for home improvements are deductible in the year in which the loan is taken out.

To calculate your tax savings, add the total amount of interest paid on your mortgage during the year to the amount you paid in property taxes. Multiply that number by your tax bracket—we assume a 28% federal tax bracket. Divide this calculation by 12 to get a monthly average. Subtract the monthly average from your Gross Housing Cost to get your Net Housing Cost. Although the result may not be the exact amount you can deduct, you'll get a pretty close estimate for your housing costs. For precise figures, consult your accountant or tax advisor.

**Example:** *Mitch and Candy's house is worth $150,000. Their mortgage is $1,200 per month ($14,400 per year) and they pay $272 a month ($3,264 per year) on a second mortgage. Their annual mortgage payments are $17,664 ($14,400 + $3,264). $14,000 of those payments is interest. They pay property taxes of $2,250 a year. Their federal tax bracket is 28%, giving them an annual Tax Savings of $4,550 or $379 a month. Assume their Gross Monthly Housing Cost is $2,502.*

| | | |
|---|---|---|
| Mortgage Interest | | $14,000 |
| Property Taxes | + | 2,250 |
| Deduction | = | 16,250 |
| Tax Bracket | x | .28 |
| Tax Savings | = | 4,550 |
| Monthly Tax Savings | ·/· 12 = | $   379 |
| | | |
| Gross Monthly Housing Cost | | $ 2,502 |
| Monthly Tax Savings | - | 379 |
| Net Monthly Housing Cost | = | $ 2,123 |

To apply this formula to *your* situation, fill in the blanks below. You will need to know your annual mortgage interest, annual property taxes and tax bracket.

$ _____    **Annual mortgage interest**

To find your mortgage interest, contact your lender and request a calculation of the annual mortgage interest on your loan. Or, ask the lender for an amortization statement. On this statement, you will see a monthly listing of how much of the mortgage payment repays principal (your debt or balance due) and how much pays interest on the loan.

$ _____    **Annual property taxes**

To find your property taxes, refer to your state tax returns or call the county tax assessor.

_____ %  **Tax bracket**

To find your tax bracket, check the income tax schedules contained in the IRS tax packet or ask a tax advisor to verify your current tax bracket. Or, use 28%, the bracket into which most people fall.

Now use those numbers in the formula below and write in the Net Monthly Housing Cost in the blank below. You will refer to this number later when making a decision on the house.

| | | |
|---|---|---|
| Mortgage Interest | = | $_____ |
| Property Taxes | + | $_____ |
| Deduction | = | $_____ |
| Tax Bracket | x | $_____ |
| Tax Savings | = | $_____ |
| Monthly Tax Savings | ·/· 12 = | $_____ |
| | | |
| Gross Monthly Housing Cost | | $_____ |
| Monthly Tax Savings | - | $_____ |
| Net Monthly Housing Cost | = | $_____ |

$ _____     **Net Monthly Housing Cost**

## 2. What Is the Current Fair Market Value of Your House?

The current "fair market value" of your house is the amount you can realistically expect to sell it for. You can obtain fair market value estimates from real estate agents free of charge. You might especially want to ask the agent who helped you buy the house originally.

You can also get estimates of fair market value from a certified appraiser, but be prepared to pay. For a referral to a certified appraiser, ask a banker, your lender or contact the Appraisal Institute at 875 N. Michigan Ave., Suite 2400, Chicago, IL 60611; 312-335-4100.

Agents generally look at a house from several financial angles and take an average of these values to estimate what it is worth. The two primary views they take are:

- what the market will bear—that is, the sales prices of comparable houses in the area and

- your house's replacement value (the cost of building materials and the like.)

Once you find the Fair Market Value of your house, write it here:

$ _____     **Fair Market Value**

## 3. How Much Will It Cost to Sell the House?

In calculating how much money it takes to actually sell your house, you can do a quick ballpark estimate or you can follow the steps to find as precise a figure as possible. To find a precise figure, you'll have to include not only the costs of sale, but also the amount it will take to fix up the house and prepare it for a sale.

### a. Quick Ballpark Estimate of Cost of Sale

Take the Fair Market Value figure you determined in step 2, above. To get a ballpark amount for the sales cost, multiply that amount by .08. Eight percent is an accurate reflection of what it costs to sell a house. Obviously, some sales will yield higher or lower costs of sale, but 8% will do in getting a rough estimate. Enter that number in the "Cost of Sale" blank, below.

### b.  Precise Valuation of Cost of Sale

To obtain a more accurate cost of sale figure, you need to total the following amounts:

$ _____     **Agent's commission**

The amount a real estate agent charges you for selling a house. Generally, it averages 6% of the final selling price. The fee can sometimes be negotiated down. Also, if you list your house as a "FSBO"—for sale by owner, you avoid the agent's commission altogether, but be sure to educate yourself about the process before you list your house as a FSBO.

$ _____     **Closing costs**

Included in these costs are escrow fees, recording costs, appraisal fees and miscellaneous expenses which can add up to several thousands of dollars. A lender or real estate agent can help you figure the exact amount.

$ _____     **Attorney's fees**

In a few states, you will need to hire an attorney to help you "close" the sale of your house. If you used an attorney when you bought the house, base your figure on that amount, taking into account inflation and the passage of time. Otherwise, ask a real estate agent for an estimate.

$ _____     **Fix up costs**

Estimate here the amount of money you will have to spend to prepare your house for sale. Does it need major repairs or just a paint job? Does the foundation, roof or plumbing need work? Will you need to have it inspected?[2]

$ _____     **Cost of Sale**

_____

[2] As you will see in step 6, below, sometimes the money you spend on fixing up a house for sale is tax deductible. To be deductible, however, fix up costs cannot cover permanent improvements on the property, such as installing a swimming pool or putting in an entirely new driveway. Items considered deductible include painting the house and most repairs, such as replacing damaged fixtures, fixing cracks in a driveway and redecorating a spa unit. Further, fix up costs must be paid no later than 30 days after the date the house is sold, and the work must have been completed in the three months (90 days) before the house is sold, to be deductible.

### 4.  What Is the Equity Value of Your House?

The equity value of your house is, quite simply, the Fair Market Value (the figure you obtained in step 2) minus whatever debt you have connected to your house. Remember—if a court calculates each spouse's share of a house, the court would consider only the amount of equity. That number, however, does not reflect the costs of sale or taxes—that is, the financial reality of owning or selling a house.

The debt connected to your house equals what you owe to any lenders (first mortgage, second mortgage, or home equity loan or line of credit) plus any liabilities on the house. All liabilities must be paid before any cash disbursements can be made from the sale of a house. Liabilities include income or property tax liens, child support liens, judgment liens (if someone sues you and obtains a judgment, that person can put a lien on your house), or mechanic's or materialman's liens placed by a contractor who did work on your home but who wasn't paid.

Ask your lender the balance on your mortgages and equity loans. The lender may offer you two figures—a principal balance and a payoff balance. The principal balance is simply the amount of principal remaining to be paid on your loan. The payoff balance is the principal balance plus an additional month's interest and any prepayment charges you must pay to close out the loan. Use the payoff balance in calculating the debt on your house.

You may not be aware of all liens on your property. Tax and mechanic's liens, for example, often appear without the owner's knowledge. To find out about any liens on your house, you'll have to do a title search. You can hire a title insurance company to conduct the search, or you can visit the records office in the county where your deed is recorded. A clerk in that office can show you how to search for any liens on your house.

### Find the Equity Value of Your House

| Debt against house | Balance |
|---|---|
| Mortgage balance | $ |
| Second mortgage balance | $ |
| Equity loan or line of credit balance | $ |
| Property tax lien | $ |
| Income tax lien | $ |
| Child support lien | $ |
| Judgment lien | $ |
| Mechanic's or materialman's lien | $ |
| Other lien | $ |
| **Total current debt on house** | $ |

Now subtract the debt on the house from its fair market value to obtain the equity value.

Fair Market Value (step 2)      $ _____

Current Debt on House      - $ _____

Equity Value of Your House      = $ _____

$ _____ **Equity Value of Your House**

## 5. What Is Your Share of the House?

You may have expected your marriage to be a 50-50 proposition and you might believe that your divorce will be the same—a simple division where each person gets half. When it comes to the house, however, those percentages may not hold up. For example, you may be entitled to only 25% of the house, or as much as 75%.

In this step, you must determine what share of the house belongs to you because you will use that amount in later calculations. When you determine the total value of the house under different scenarios, you need to know your share so you can divide that total value by the amount you can expect to receive. For instance, if you and your spouse have $100,000 to split on the house and you are each entitled to 50% of it, you'd get $50,000. But if you were only a one-fourth owner of that house, you'd be entitled to $25,000, not $50,000.

The laws of your state and the origin of the money used to buy your house determine the amount of your share. Refer to Chapter 13, Section A, for an overview of marital and separate property. If you entered the marriage with one spouse owning the house, the other spouse may nevertheless be entitled to a share at divorce. In community property states, improvements (such as additions, renovations and substantial upkeep) to the owner's separate property by the non-owner spouse are usually considered community property, giving the original non-owner some ownership interest.

In equitable distribution states, separate property improvements by one spouse to the other's separate property may result in the non-owner spouse acquiring a monetary interest (equal to the value contributed, or equal to any increase in the value of the property) in the improved property. In the common law state (Mississippi), the contributing party will obtain a monetary interest in the other's property generally only if title to the property was changed to reflect the contribution.

Once you have determined your ownership share, enter it here.

_____% **Your Ownership Share of the House**

## 6. What Is the Tax Basis for Your House?

The tax basis of an asset is a little-mentioned financial concept no one thinks about until it's time to sell the asset—or until a divorce.

The tax basis is simply the dollar amount the IRS uses to determine if you've made or lost money on an asset. Essentially, your tax basis is the original purchase price plus the cost of any improvements you have made, minus any tax benefits (such as depreciation for home office use) you have realized. Knowing the tax basis lets you calculate your profit to determine whether or not you'll owe taxes on that profit when your house is sold during or after divorce. If the house isn't sold until after the divorce, the person who keeps the house keeps the tax liability.

Enter the below amounts to figure your tax basis.

$ _____    **Purchase price**

The purchase price should be on the original purchase contract or closing statement—check your home bookkeeping files or a safe deposit box. A tax return for the year you bought the house should show this amount. If you still can't find it, call the escrow company that processed your purchase or your lender. If you owned a home previously and filed IRS form 2119 in the year you purchased your present home, find the number listed as the "adjusted basis of new main home" (the sales price less any gain you postponed paying taxes on). Use this number as the purchase price.

$ _____    **Improvements**

Improvements are items that add value to your house, such as adding a new bathroom or den, installing a security system or doing extensive landscaping. These costs are not fix up or repair costs. You will need to go through your files to find receipts to document the improvements made to your house.

Here is a quick checklist of common improvements:

- Adding walks, sewer lines, septic tanks, lamp posts, retaining walls, fences, gates
- Aluminum siding
- Appliances, such as washer and dryer, dishwasher, garbage disposal, refrigerator
- Built-in furniture or bookcase
- Carpeting, linoleum or other flooring

- Constructing or improving driveways, gutters, drain pipes, dry wells
- Landscaping
- New furnace, heating system, air conditioning, plumbing
- New shower, bathtub
- Permanent storm windows, storm doors
- Replacing roof
- Restoring a run-down house
- Room addition, including patio, deck, porch, garage
- Swimming pool, tennis court, sauna, hot tub

$ _____    **Tax benefits**

Tax benefits refer to the rollover of gain from prior homes or depreciation taken for something like a home office or business. (See sidebar for an explanation of rollovers.) To find your tax benefits, refer to your state tax returns or call your accountant. *For simplicity's sake, you can calculate the tax basis without including any tax benefits.*

Use the numbers you filled in above to complete this formula.

| | | |
|---|---|---|
| *Purchase Price* | $ | _____ |
| *Improvements* | + $ | _____ |
| | = $ | _____ |
| *Tax Benefits* | - $ | _____ |
| *Tax Basis* | = $ | _____ |

$ _____    **Tax Basis of Your House**

### Rollover of Profit from Prior House Sales

One of the biggest tax benefits for homeowners is that they defer (rollover) the taxes owed on the profit (gain)—the selling price minus the cost of sale and the tax basis—earned each time they sell a primary residence and buy one of equal or greater value. Rolling over the gain is mandatory. You cannot buy a higher priced house and pay taxes on the gain anyway. Taxes are paid only when you buy a less expensive house or do not purchase a new house after selling the old house at a profit.

Suppose a couple bought a house for $40,000 when they first married 25 years ago. Five years later they sold the house for $60,000. Instead of paying taxes on the $20,000 profit, they purchased a $65,000 house. They sold the $65,000 house eight years later for $90,000. Again, instead of paying taxes on the $25,000 profit from that sale, they bought a $105,000 house.

If the couple stays in that house and never sells it, they won't ever pay taxes on the profit because taxes can be assessed only after a sale. If the couple sells the house at or after their divorce, however, without buying another house, they'll owe taxes—a lot of taxes. They'll owe taxes on the $20,000 of profit from the first house, $25,000 from the profit on the second house, plus whatever profit they make when they sell the third house.

Of course, not every house sale yields a profit. Suppose Abe and Grace bought their first house three years ago for $200,000. They are divorcing, and the market has dropped dramatically. The most they can expect to get for the house is $175,000. Selling the house at a loss has no tax impact. There's no profit on which they owe taxes. At the same time, the IRS doesn't allow a taxpayer to deduct the loss suffered on a primary residence. On the other hand, if Abe and Grace had owned a prior home that sold for a profit, they would owe taxes from the profit they rolled over from the first house into the present house, even though they sold their present house at a loss.

### 7. What Would the After-Tax/After-Sale Value of Your House Be If You Sold It with Your Spouse?

People who have a profit on the sale of a house can roll that profit forward (and delay paying taxes on it) by purchasing a new house of equal or greater value within 24 months of selling the first house.[3] If they don't buy a new house, they must pay taxes on the profit. Because divorcing couples generally do not buy a new house together, you must know what taxes you would have to pay if you sell now, upon divorce. That will let you figure out the after-tax/after-sale value of your house, and it will reveal your future options concerning house purchases and tax deferrals.

To find the after-tax/after-sale value of your house, enter the following information:

_____ %  Tax Bracket (step 1)

$_____  Fair Market Value (step 2)

$_____  Cost of Sale (step 3)

$_____  Current Debt on House (step 4)

$_____  Tax Basis of Your House (step 6)

Now take the following steps:

1. Find the Adjusted Sales Price by subtracting the Cost of Sale from the Fair Market Value.

2. Find the Gain or Loss on the potential sale of your house by subtracting the Tax Basis from the Adjusted Sales Price. If you experienced a Loss, use zero as the amount of Gain.

3. Find the Taxes On The Gain by multiplying the Gain by your Tax Bracket.

4. Find the After-Tax/After-Sale Value by subtracting the Current Debt on House, Taxes on Gain and Cost of Sale from the Fair Market Value.

---

[3]A few other rules apply if you want to rollover the profit. You can use the IRS rollover provision only once in 24 months, and you can't use it if you've owned your house fewer than 24 months.

**Example:**

1. Find the Adjusted Sales Price

| Fair Market Value | | $250,000 |
|---|---|---|
| Cost of Sale | - | 20,000 |
| Adjusted Sales Price | = | $230,000 |

2. Find the Gain or Loss

| Adjusted Sales Price | | $230,000 |
|---|---|---|
| Tax Basis | - | 100,000 |
| Gain (or Loss) | = | $130,000 |

3. Find the Taxes on Gain

| Gain | | $130,000 |
|---|---|---|
| Tax Bracket | x | 28% |
| Taxes on Gains | = | $ 36,400 |

4. Find the After-Tax/After-Sale Value

| Fair Market Value | | $250,000 |
|---|---|---|
| Current Debt on House | - | 90,000 |
| Taxes on Gain | - | 36,400 |
| Cost of Sale | - | 20,000 |
| After-Tax/After Sale Value | = | $103,600 |

Now fill in the numbers for your house.

1. Find the Adjusted Sales Price

| Fair Market Value | | $_____ |
|---|---|---|
| Cost of Sale | - | $_____ |
| Adjusted Sales Price | = | $_____ |

2. Find the Gain or Loss

| Adjusted Sales Price | | $_____ |
|---|---|---|
| Tax Basis | - | $_____ |
| Gain (or Loss) | = | $_____ |

3. Find the Taxes on Gain

| Gain | = | $_____ |
|---|---|---|
| Tax Bracket | x | $_____ |
| Taxes on Gain | = | $_____ |

4. Find the After-Tax/After-Sale Value

| Fair Market Value | | $_____ |
|---|---|---|
| Current Debt on House | - | $_____ |
| Taxes on Gain | - | $_____ |
| Cost of Sale | - | $_____ |
| After-Tax/After-Sale Value | = | $_____ |

$_____    **After-Tax/After-Sale Value**

---

**A One-Time Rollover Exclusion If You're 55 or Older**

If you or your spouse are nearing age 55 or have passed that age, you can reduce or avoid paying taxes on the profit in the sale of your house through a tax benefit known as the one-time exclusion. This exclusion lets a single person or a married couple pocket, tax free, $125,000 of profit when a residence is sold. This exclusion is available only once. If a married couple uses it, *neither* spouse—*nor* their future spouses—can ever use it again. On the other hand, if you sell the house after the divorce, you can *each* take advantage of the $125,000 exclusion, as long as the house was your primary residence for three of the five years preceding the sale.

One note of caution: Keeping a house on the assumption that you'll use the one time exclusion someday is risky. Congress is in the mood to reduce the deficit. While the one time exclusion is here today, it may not be tomorrow.

## 8. What Would the After-Tax/After-Sale Value of Your House Be If You Keep It Now and Sell In the Future?

Of all the options you may pursue regarding the house, the choice of selling it in the future can be the most difficult to analyze. Take your time and get help in ascertaining values if you need it.

No one can predict what will happen in the real estate market of the future. But real estate brokers can make calculated guesses about it. Based on the assumption that you would not keep a house that is expected to decrease in value, anticipate that the house value will stay the same or, more likely, increase.

But increase by how much?

A technical aid, the Future Value Factor chart, lets you calculate changes in the value of an asset like a house. We've included a Future Value Factor chart in the Appendix. Use it, along with the formula, below, to get an idea of what your house will be worth in the future. But remember that this will be only an estimate.

To use the Future Value Factor chart, you must decide on how long you plan to stay in your house (called the Holding Period) and you must select a rate of Inflation. Financial planners often figure an annual inflation rate of 5% when estimating future values.[4]

You will see that the Future Value Chart has two lines—one for the Holding Period and one for the rate of Inflation. Follow the two lines until they intersect. That will give you the Future Value Factor.

To find the future after-tax/after-sale value, enter the following information for your house:

_____

[4] Depending on the state of the economy and your local housing market, you may be tempted to use an inflation rate higher than 5%. Certainly many houses increase in value at a rate substantially higher than the inflation rate. Nevertheless, we recommend that you be conservative when speculating on the future value of your house. It's better to expect less and get more than vice versa.

_____ %   Inflation (rate you anticipate)

_____ %   Tax Bracket (step 1)

$ _____   Fair Market Value (step 2)

$ _____   Current Debt on House (step 4)

$ _____   Tax Basis of Your House (step 6)

$ _____   Holding Period (how long you plan to keep the house)

$ _____   Future Value Factor (Appendix)

Now take the following steps:

1. Find the Future Value Factor (see chart in Appendix) by estimating the Holding Period and the rate of Inflation.

2. Find the Future Sale Value by multiplying the Fair Market Value by the Future Value Factor.

3. Find the estimated Cost of Sale by multiplying the Future Sale Value by 8%.

4. Find the potential Gain on the sale of your house by subtracting the Cost of Sale and the Tax Basis from the Future Sale Value.

5. Find the potential Taxes On the Gain by multiplying the Gain by your Tax Bracket.

6. Find the Future After-Tax/After-Sale Value by subtracting the Current Debt on House, Taxes on Gain and Cost of Sale from the Future Sale Value.

### Example:

1. Find the Future Value Factor—See Appendix.

   *For the purpose of this example, assume a Holding Period of five years and a rate of Inflation of 5%—the Future Value Factor is 1.2763.*

2. Find the Future Sale Value

   | | |
   |---|---|
   | *Fair Market Value* | $250,000 |
   | *Future Value Factor* | x   1.2763% |
   | *Future Sale Value* | = $319,075 |

3. Find the estimated Cost of Sale

| | | |
|---|---|---|
| Future Sale Value | | $319,075 |
| Estimated Costs | x | 8% |
| Cost of Sale | = | $ 25,526 |

4. Find the potential Gain on the sale of your house

| | | |
|---|---|---|
| Future Sale Value | | $319,075 |
| Cost of Sale | - | 25,526 |
| Tax Basis | - | 100,000 |
| Gain | = | $193,549 |

5. Find the potential Taxes On the Gain

| | | |
|---|---|---|
| Gain | | $193,549 |
| Tax Bracket | x | 28% |
| Taxes on Gain | = | $ 54,194 |

6. Find the Future After-Tax/After-Sale Value

| | | |
|---|---|---|
| Future Sale Value | | $319,075 |
| Current Debt on House | - | 90,000 |
| Taxes on Gain | - | 54,194 |
| Cost of Sale | - | 25,526 |
| Future After-Tax/ After-Sale Value | = | $149,355 |

Now fill in the numbers for your house.

1. Find the Future Value Factor

Enter number from Appendix: _____

2. Find the Future Sale Value

| | | |
|---|---|---|
| Fair Market Value | | $_____ |
| Future Value Factor | x | $_____ |
| Future Sale Value | = | $_____ |

3. Find the estimated Cost of Sale

| | | |
|---|---|---|
| Fair Sale Value | | $_____ |
| Estimated Costs | x | $_____ |
| Cost of Sale | = | $_____ |

4. Find the potential Gain on the sale of your house

| | | |
|---|---|---|
| Future Sale Value | | $_____ |
| Cost of Sale | - | $_____ |
| Tax Basis | - | $_____ |
| Gain | = | $_____ |

5. Find the potential Taxes on the Gain

| | | |
|---|---|---|
| Gain | | $_____ |
| Tax Bracket | x | $_____ |
| Taxes on Gain | = | $_____ |

6. Find the Future After-Tax/After-Sale Value

| | | |
|---|---|---|
| Future Sale Value | | $_____ |
| Current Debt on House | - | $_____ |
| Taxes on Gain | - | $_____ |
| Cost of Sale | - | $_____ |
| Future After-Tax/ After-Sale Value | = | $_____ |

$ _____   **Future After-Tax/After-Sale Value of Your House**

---

**If You and Your Spouse Keep the House Now and Your Spouse Buys It From You After the Divorce**

If you plan to hold onto your house now with your spouse, and then either buy out your ex-spouse or sell to your ex-spouse after the divorce, see your accountant or other tax advisor immediately. This scenario has serious tax consequences, depending on whether the sale occurs within six years of the divorce or after six years. Taxes are also affected by your continued residence in the house or your departure from it. Do not try to determine the tax consequences on your own.

---

Before moving on to step 9, look more closely at the figures in steps 7 and 8 which show how the value of one couple's house changes according to legal or financial reality.

**Example:** *Juan and Maria purchased their home 10 years ago for $50,000. They added a room for $10,000 and made no other improvements. Their tax basis, then, equals $60,000. The current fair market value of the house is $250,000. To sell it will cost $20,000 (8% of the fair market value). They refinanced the house a few months ago and have debt against it of $90,000. Maria wants to keep the house to prevent disruption of the children's lives, and then plans to sell it in five years when both children will be in college. Juan and Maria used only marital property when they purchased the house and therefore agree to split its sale proceeds 50-50.*

*Legal Reality*

| | | |
|---|---|---|
| Fair Market Value | | $250,000 |
| Current Debt on House | - | 90,000 |
| Equity Value of House | = | 160,000 |
| Each Spouse's Share (at 50-50) | = | $ 80,000 |

If Maria purchased Juan's share of the property based on its equity value only, she'd have to give him $80,000. She could not deduct the costs of sale which she will incur when she sells in five years. Nor can she factor in the taxes she will have to pay on the profit (assuming she doesn't buy a new house of equal or greater value within two years of the sale). In other words, she purchases an inherent debt which is often undisclosed or misunderstood. In a divorce, lawyers and judges don't discount the value of the house by taxes and cost of sale unless the house is actually sold.

*Financial Reality*

| | | |
|---|---|---|
| Original Purchase Price | | $ 50,000 |
| Improvements | + | 10,000 |
| Tax Basis | = | 60,000 |
| Fair Market Value | | $250,000 |
| Cost of Sale | - | 20,000 |
| Tax Basis | - | 60,000 |
| Gain | = | $170,000 |
| Tax Bracket | x | 28% |
| Taxes on Gain | = | $ 47,600 |
| Equity Value of House | | $160,000 |
| Cost of Sale | - | 20,000 |
| Taxes on Gain | - | 47,600 |
| After-Tax/After-Sale Value | = | $ 92,400 |
| Each Spouse's Share (at 50-50) | = | $ 46,200 |

If Maria purchased Juan's share of the property based on its after-tax/after-sale value, she'd have to give him only $46,200, compared to the $80,000 owed from a split of the equity value. But what if Juan insists on getting equity value? Then Maria ought to modify her plans and they should sell the house jointly. If she really wants to keep the house, and cannot get Juan to accept the after-tax/after-sale value, Maria could try a few negotiating tactics, such as:

- offer to split the difference between the after-tax/after-sale value and the equity value;

- ask Juan to pay some of the potential tax liability (such as 30%), but not 50%; or

- have Juan discount the price by the broker's fees—that is, reduce the amount Maria would have to pay him by the estimated broker's cost in the event of a sale—while not pushing the tax issue.

Maria may have to hold a hard line to get the price she wants. Even if she winds up paying the equity price, at least she'll know the costs she will bear in the future and will have a realistic expectation of what she will receive from a future sale of the house. Maria must keep in mind, however, that if she buys out Juan's share and he discounts the equity value by only the cost of sale, and Maria eventually sells the house, she may lose money (in relation to Juan) because of her tax liability.

**Tax Note—If You Borrow Money
To Keep the House**

If you have to borrow money to keep the house—either
to buy out your spouse or to keep up payments—remember this rule: To deduct the interest you pay on
your mortgage, the lender (a bank, your parents or
anyone else) must have a secured interest in the
house. That means you must give that person the right
to foreclose on the house if you miss the payments. If
the loan is unsecured—that is, the lender can't foreclose if you miss a payment—you cannot deduct the
mortgage interest you pay.

## 9. What's Your Best Option Regarding the House?

Your house can be worth different amounts under
different circumstances. Complete the chart below to
compare your housing costs, the equity value of the
house, the after-tax/after-sale value of the house and
the future after-tax/after-sale value of the house.
Then divide by the percentage that represents your
share in the house. If you want to buy your spouse
out and stay in the house, can you realistically afford
to?

### Comparative Housing Costs

| | Your Share | Spouse's Share |
|---|---|---|
| *Net Monthly Housing Cost*<br>Enter amount determined in Step 1: $ _____<br>Divide by the percentage representing each spouse's share of the house: | $ | $ |
| *Equity Value of Your House*<br>Enter amount determined in Step 4: $ _____<br>Divide by the percentage representing each spouse's share of the house: | $ | $ |
| *After-Tax/After-Sale Value of Your House*<br>Enter amount determined in Step 7: $ _____<br>Divide by the percentage representing each spouse's share of the house: | $ | $ |
| *Future After-Tax/After-Sale Value of Your House*<br>Enter amount determined in Step 8: $ _____<br>Divide by the percentage representing each spouse's share of the house: | $ | $ |

Reconsider your options in light of your calculations. The advantages and disadvantages of each option below are recapped below.

### Option A: Sell the house together and split the proceeds with your spouse

*Advantages:* You share the cost of sale and the tax liability with your spouse. Also, you can each take advantage of the IRS rollover provision that lets you defer the taxes on the profit by buying a house of equal or greater value than the one you sold within 24 months of the sale.

*Disadvantages:* You'd be selling the family home, to which you may have strong emotional ties. Further, the amount you receive from the sale of the house may not be enough for you to afford to buy another house.

*Is this a viable option for me?* _____ Yes _____ No

### Option B: Buy out your spouse's share and keep the house for life

*Advantages:* You will have an established, secure place to live. You will never have to pay taxes on any profit because you will not sell the house and realize any profit on it. Nor will you ever have to pay the cost of sale.

*Disadvantages:* Very few people live and die in one place. In fact, most people sell their homes about seven years after purchasing them. If, for any reason, your mind or circumstances change, you will have to sell your house and bear taxes and sale costs alone. In addition, homeowners often view their houses as an asset to sell at retirement. If you keep the house for life, you will not have the proceeds from its sale to use as retirement income.

*Is this a viable option for me?* _____ Yes _____ No

### Option C: Buy out your spouse's share and sell the house in the future

*Advantages:* For the sake of children, or stability in your own life, it may serve you to keep the family home. In addition, if you hold onto the house and do not sell it until you reach age 55, you can take advantage of the IRS one-time exclusion that let's you sell a house and not pay taxes on the first $125,000 of profit.

*Disadvantages:* When you eventually sell the house, you will be solely responsible for costs of sale and taxes on the profit if you sell before age 55. In addition, if Congress ever eliminates the one-time exclusion provision for people over 55, you would not be able to reduce the amount of taxes owed on your profit.

*Is this a viable option for me?* _____ Yes _____ No

### Option D: Sell your share of the house to your spouse

*Advantages:* You do not have to pay taxes on the money you receive because the IRS does not tax money received as a property buyout during a divorce. Any new house you buy after the divorce will have a new tax basis, and so you will not have to rollover the gain from the old house.

*Disadvantages:* You may not earn enough on the sale of the house to afford to buy a new one. If your income is not high enough, you may not qualify for financing. Consider, too, how you will feel if your ex-spouse is living in your old house with a new spouse.

*Is this a viable option for me?* _____ Yes _____ No

### Option E: Own the house jointly with your spouse and sell it in the future

*Advantages:* You (and your children) will continue having a familiar place in which to live. You and your spouse will jointly share the eventual costs of sale and taxes. While you're living in the house, your spouse may pay part of the mortgage (perhaps in the form of alimony or child support), repair costs or maintenance costs.

### Continued Home Ownership and Estate Planning

If you decide to hold onto your house with your spouse and sell in the future, you will need to plan your estate and possibly acquire adequate life insurance coverage in the event of the other spouse's death. You should also evaluate how title to the house is held.[5] For example, couples that held their property in tenancy by the entirety or as community property will no longer have that option after divorce. If you held your house in joint tenancy while you were married—where the other automatically inherits if one owner dies—that joint tenancy may no longer be appropriate. You might prefer tenancy in common, where you can leave your share of the house to whomever you wish when you die.

 **Decision Time . . .**
Regarding the house, the following option is the best one for me:

_____    *Option A: Sell the house together and split the proceeds with your spouse*

_____    *Option B: Buy out your spouse's share and keep the house for life*

_____    *Option C: Buy out your spouse's share and sell the house in the future*

_____    *Option D: Sell your share of the house to your spouse*

_____    *Option E: Own the house jointly with your spouse and sell it in the future*

*Disadvantages:* The spouse who leaves the house for more than two years loses the ability to roll over any profit into a new house because the family house will no longer be the primary residence.[6] In addition, major misunderstandings between divorced spouses can arise as to responsibility for repairs, maintenance, improvements, taxes and the like. Non-resident spouses often resent making payments on a house in which they are not living. Methods for handling potential conflicts must be put in writing and signed by each party.

*Is this a viable option for me?* _____ Yes _____ No

---

[5]Title to property is covered in Chapter 13, Section C.

[6]Under some circumstances, this spouse could possibly use the "one-time exclusion" of $125,000 if aged 55 or older. But that spouse must have lived in the family home for three of the last five years. See your tax advisor for the details.

## 10. How Do You Feel About Your Decision?

Even though the option you will choose may make sense in strict financial terms, you may still have some reservations about it. Take a few moments to clarify any lingering doubts or emotional reactions you have about your decision on the house.

*How am I affected by this choice emotionally?*

*Is this choice consistent with my future goals?*

*How will my children be affected?*

*My reasons for making this decision are:*

1.

2.

3.

4.

5.

# 15

# Retirement Benefits: Who Gets What?

➡️ If neither you nor your spouse has a retirement plan, skip ahead to Chapter 16.

If you can get through this chapter, you should have no trouble getting through your divorce.

Retirement plans can be complicated and hard to understand—just like the end of a marriage. But we'll try to make it as painless as possible.

Unlike home ownership—a practice that's been around a long time—retirement planning is practically brand new. Generations ago, few people had to worry about late-life security because most just didn't live that long (except perhaps for George Burns).

The 1930s, though, gave us Social Security, and by the 1960s, retirement planning had become a booming business. Then, in the 1980s, billions of retirement dollars found their way into an exploding financial scene that included new investments, IRAs and profit sharing plans. Presiding over this tempting nest egg today are insurance companies, corporate managers, investment bankers and government bureaucrats—all of whom have their own language and logic which can be hard to follow.

So take your time. Be prepared to re-read parts of this chapter. To make things easier, we've designed the information so that you need to read only the material that applies to you and your spouse. Before you get to those specifics, however, read Section A for a general explanation of the concepts you should understand to divide your retirement benefits.

## A. Retirement Benefits— Concepts To Consider

Whether you know a little or a lot about the current status of your retirement benefits, you must understand how divorce affects them. The following concepts will alert you to common misconceptions about what happens to retirement plans when a marriage ends.

### 1. Retirement Plans Are Property To Divide at Divorce

Naturally, you may be emotionally attached to the retirement benefits that you worked so hard to earn or that you feel entitled to as part of your commitment to the marriage. The idea of sharing benefits with the spouse you're divorcing probably does not thrill you.

Nevertheless, retirement plans are but one more marital asset to be divided in the courtrooms of most states—if you and your spouse cannot agree on how to split them. Take heart, however, in the fact that retirement benefits often serve as useful bargaining chips when spouses trade assets in the final property settlement.

### 2. You Don't Own Your Retirement Plan

You don't own your retirement plan—you're only its beneficiary. It's similar to buying a car and financing it through the bank. You don't own the car—the bank does. You can drive it, let your friends use it and take care of it, but until the loan is paid off, you don't technically own it.

Essentially, the bank holds title to the car for your benefit. You are entrusted with the car while making payments—but if you totally wreck it or fail to make a payment, everything changes—that is, the bank can come and take the car away from you.

Similarly, your retirement plan is owned by the organization which holds title to it. Usually, that organization is your employer or a previous employer. With a retirement plan, you trust that the funds you (or your employer) contribute to the plan will be there when it's time for you to receive the benefits of ownership—your retirement money. The organization may promise to invest your money, earn interest on it or develop further benefits for you.

As with your car loan, the promises made by you and the organization are spelled out in a trust agreement . But if you are fired, if you quit or if the company merges or goes bankrupt, everything changes—the benefits can be taken away. There are no guarantees, just promises.

### 3. Retirement Plans Are Not Created Equal

Retirement plans vary tremendously. Even if two plans look equal on paper, fine print plan provisions can make one plan intrinsically more valuable than another. For instance, one plan may allow for a lump sum payout upon retirement while another may not. Getting your retirement dollars in a lump sum may provide more flexibility than getting monthly payments in dollars whose value erodes over time—or disappears entirely if the plan becomes insolvent in later years.

While retirement plans themselves comply with federal regulations, each state may view them differently at divorce. Because divorce laws differ around the country, one state may define retirement benefits as marital property (an asset to be divided at divorce) while another may rule that benefits are earnings (an asset divided at divorce in only about eight states). Be sure to ask your lawyer how your state treats retirement benefits upon divorce. (See Section C, below.)

In the worse cases, some divorce settlements treat retirement benefits as *both* marital property and income, creating "double dipping." (See Section B.5.a.iii, below.)

### 4. Some Plans Promise Better Tax Breaks Than Others

One major attraction of many retirement plans is that you can defer paying income taxes on the money that accumulates in the plan. In some other plans, you must pay income taxes on the money before it's deposited. One task during your divorce will be to determine the tax position of your benefits. Normally, you want to defer paying the taxes until you withdraw the money from the plan and presumably are in a lower income bracket or have a lower annual income.

### 5. Divorce Leads to Division Decisions

Will you split the retirement money now or later?

A present division means you divide the value of the plan now, at divorce. A future division means the plan is divided at retirement or at the point in the plan owner's career when the benefits would normally be paid out. When and how you divide the plan depends on the type of plan you have, payout provisions, valuation methods and other factors. Your division decision at divorce has a direct impact on your future financial security so do not make this choice lightly.

## B. Steps to a Settlement

Now that you've become familiar with the general concepts involved in splitting retirement plans at divorce, carefully review these steps for analyzing your benefits and deciding what to do with them.

1. What types of retirement plans do you and your spouse have?

2. Who is the plan participant or owner?

3. What is the "legal value" of your retirement plans?

4. What is the "financial value" of your retirement plans?

5. How will you and your spouse divide your plans?

6. How do you feel about your decision?

## 1.  What Types of Retirement Plans Do You and Your Spouse Have?

If you had a nickel for every type of retirement plan there is, you could afford to travel around the world—and pay for your divorce to boot. (Attorney's fees not included.)

Don't worry, though. To get through your divorce, you'll need to understand only a few fundamental plan categories.

Little agreement exists on how retirement plans should be categorized and almost every book and expert on the subject uses a different system. Below, we categorize plans as defined contribution, defined benefit, personal annuities and IRAs. We also define three special categories of plans—Keoghs, non-qualified deferred compensation and Social Security. Once you determine which types of plans are at stake in your divorce, you can read only the sections that cover those types of plans.

### a.  Plan Types Defined

What follows are definitions of the several types of retirement plans. Read the definitions carefully. If you're sure you and your spouse have one of the plans shown on this list of definitions, put a check mark next to that plan. Put a question mark in the blank next to any plans that warrant further investigation, and then check them off if you find out that you and your spouse own one of these plans.

**Qualified Plans.** Qualified plans are retirement plans that meet the requirements of Internal Revenue Code § 401(a). Contributions by an employer to a qualified plan are tax deductible to the company.

___  *Defined Contribution Plans.* Defined contribution plans pay only the amount of money that has accumulated in your pension plan account when you retire—no more and no less. If you have $125,000 in your account, you will receive $125,000 at retirement.

___  *Money Purchase Plans.* Employer contributions to money purchase plans are based on a percentage of your salary. For example, if you earn $40,000 a year and have a 10% compensation contribution plan, your employer would put $4,000 into your retirement account. This plan requires an employer to make its agreed-upon contribution—whether or not the company is profitable. Failure to contribute subjects the company to penalty taxes. At retirement, you'll be entitled to the amount that has accumulated in your account. You can receive the benefits in a lump sum at retirement, or in monthly payments for a set number of years, depending on the terms of the plan.

___  *Profit Sharing Plans.* As the name implies, a profit sharing plan means that a company must generate in order to contribute to the employee's retirement kitty. Companies must use a fixed or discretionary formula for making contributions. The money that goes into a profit sharing plan is invested and accumulates tax free for eventual distribution (payout) to employees or their beneficiaries. The distribution takes place at retirement, after a certain number of years, or when certain events take place such as disability, death or termination of employment. As with other defined contribution plans, your benefits are based on the amount that has accumulated in your account at retirement.

___  *Salary Saving/401(k) Plans.* One of the most popular types of employee benefit options, the 401(k) plan gets its name from the section of the Internal Revenue Code (401(k)) which defines it. Under this plan, an employee can choose to delay receiving income by making pretax contributions to a profit sharing or stock bonus plan.

___ *Thrift Plans*. A thrift plan may also be called a "savings plan," because a part of the employee's salary is "saved" for retirement. The amount the employee puts into this plan directly bears on the benefits that are ultimately paid out. The amount an employer contributes is usually a match of the amount of the employee's contribution. For example, when an employee puts one dollar into the plan, the employer matches it by contributing a dollar. The employer can make additional contributions if it so chooses. A thrift plan may take the form of a money purchase pension plan or a profit sharing plan.

___ *Employee Stock Ownership Programs (ESOPs)*. The funds contributed to Employee Stock Ownership Programs are a percentage of the employee's total annual compensation. Held in trust for the employees (or their beneficiaries), the funds in these programs are used to buy stock from stockholders or the company itself. Upon retirement (or departure from the company), employees receive their vested interest in the plan in the form of employer stocks or possibly cash. The employee cannot be required to sell the stocks back to the company; however, the employer may prohibit the employee from selling the stocks to competitors of the company. Specific provisions of the plan usually define the rights of employees to exercise their stock options.

**Qualified Plans.** See above.

**Defined Benefit Plans.** Defined benefit plans promise a future stream of income when an employee stops working. For instance, your plan might provide you with 60% of your highest annual earnings as the benefit payable during retirement. Unlike defined contribution plans, the value of defined benefit plans is normally calculated by specialized financial professionals called actuaries.

___ *Government Plans/Military Pensions*. These defined benefit plans are offered to civil service workers, government employees or military personnel. Specific governmental regulations may apply.

___ *Business/Corporate Defined Benefit Plans*. Put a check mark if you work for a business or corporation and have a defined benefit plan.

**Personal Annuities.** In planning for retirement, an individual may purchase an annuity, which is a contract between that person and an insurance company. The buyer makes payments to the insurance company which invests the payments so as to provide a stream (or lump sum) of income at retirement.

___ *Deferred Annuities*. When payments are made from an annuity contract at some specific future date, it is called a deferred annuity.

___ *Tax Sheltered Annuities (TSAs)*. TSAs are tax-deferred (which means taxes are not paid until the money is paid out) annuities for teachers, public school system employees and employees of non-profit organizations, who can deposit up to 20% of their annual salary into the annuity.

**Individual Retirement Accounts (IRAs).** A popular way for many people to save for retirement, IRAs became restricted by the tax reforms of the 1980s.

___ *Individual Retirement Accounts (IRAs)*. While anyone can contribute to an Individual Retirement Account, the tax breaks offered by these plans are often not as great for employed workers offered a retirement plan through his or her job. For IRA holders with no other retirement plan, annual contributions are fully tax deductible and not paid until the plan pays out at retirement. Early withdrawal penalties are usually charged if the plan is tapped prior to retirement or the specified date of payout.

___ *Simplified Employee Pension IRAs (SEP IRAs)*. SEP IRAs are retirement benefits in the form of an IRA offered by some companies.

**Miscellaneous.** During divorce, you may also deal with Keoghs, non-qualified deferred compensation plans or Social Security. If you and/or your spouse have any of these retirement benefits, read the following section.

___ *Keoghs*. In the early 1960s, New York Congressman Eugene Keogh sponsored legislation to create retirement vehicles for self-employed people. Because of several changes in the law, self-employed people have many retirement plans to pick from, though none are technically Keogh plans. They may be money purchase plans, profit sharing plans or any other label that is found on corporate retirement plans. If you or your spouse are self-employed, review your plan—and the definitions above—to find the type of plans you have. Then follow the instructions for those plans throughout the rest of this chapter.

___ *Non-qualified Deferred Compensation Plans*. A small percentage of executives and upper level key employees have deferred compensation plans. These special plans do not meet federal tax deductibility requirements of most (qualified) plans. Generally, the plan provides that the employee's current compensation is delayed until the future, theoretically, when the employee will be retired and in a lower tax bracket. At that time, the employee receives bonuses, incentive stock options, cash value insurance plans, loans from the company or any other creative deferred payment.

These agreements are usually made directly between the employer and employee and are not reported to the IRS. That makes them difficult to document—unless you're the employed spouse who will get the deferred compensation. If a spouse wants to hide this type of retirement plan, he or she could simply make arrangements with an employer to delay compensation until after the divorce is final. Unless the other spouse knows about these benefits, they won't be included in the property settlement. Similarly, a court may view

these benefits as income, not property, and therefore not subject to division.

___ *Social Security*. Social Security benefits are not considered marital property and are not divisible at divorce. If you have been married at least 10 years, however, you may be entitled to benefits from your spouse's account. These benefits may be higher than those you earned yourself as a worker. If so, then you will probably want to apply for the share of benefits you would receive as a spouse, rather than getting the benefits you earned on your own. Either way, you will need to check on your own account and ask what you would be entitled to as an ex-spouse. You can find out about Social Security benefits by calling 1-800-772-1213.

---

### Social Security and Retirement Planning

Even though your Social Security benefits are not divided at divorce, this is a good time to check the status of your account anyway to see what kind of benefits you'll be getting when you retire. If you're like most workers, you'll probably find that Social Security will not provide enough income for you to live on after retirement. That means you should begin retirement planning now by investing in a plan at work or into an Individual Retirement Account (IRA).

---

### ⚠ If your spouse has a non-qualified deferred compensation plan

If your spouse has—or you think your spouse has—a non-qualified deferred compensation plan, you will have to contact his or her employer for information—or have an attorney do so on your behalf. Talk to an attorney to find out whether the non-qualified deferred compensation plan is considered income, or property subject to division.

## b.  Where To Go for Information

Before you start making decisions about your retirement plans, you must know precisely what you're dealing with. Yet, you may not know who to ask or what you are seeking. This section introduces you to the people and vocabulary you will probably encounter on your search for information.

### i.  What Information You're Looking For

Familiarize yourself with the terms you are likely to hear when you investigate your retirement plans. You are more likely to get answers to your questions if you know what to ask for.

*Summary Plan Description.* Employers are required to issue a description (annually in most cases) which outlines the status and terms of retirement plans. This summary should tell you the amount of benefits (in dollars) that have accumulated in your name or your spouse's.

*Full Plan.* You may or may not need a copy of the full plan, depending on how well the summary plan description is written. Do not hesitate to ask for the full plan if you have questions or need to check details.

*Trust/Custodial Agreement.* Specific provisions of the retirement plan and the agreements between the legal owner of the plan (the "trustee") and the employee (the beneficial owner) are spelled out in a trust or custodial agreement. Understanding these agreements is particularly important with IRAs because they describe the costs of establishing, maintaining and terminating IRA accounts.

*Accrued Benefit.* Often when you look at a summary or talk to a plan administrator, you hear about the accrued benefit. This term refers to the amount that has been earned (or accrued) while a worker has been participating in a retirement program.

*Account Balance.* For plans such as IRAs and Defined Contribution Plans, you simply want to know how much is in the account. This amount may simply be called the balance.

*Annuity Contracts.* A legal contract between a life insurance company and the investor or owner of the annuity. The contract typically states the amount of interest (both the guaranteed minimum and the current), surrender charges, and penalties and options at retirement, among other provisions.

### ii.  Who Can Help You Find the Information

These are the people and the professionals you should talk with to get details on retirement plans.

*Plan Administrator.* The plan administrator is an independent third party who keeps the books and records on retirement plans. That person should be able to answer your questions. Ask in writing—or have an attorney send a letter for you. The administrator also usually prepares the plan's annual tax return. At a divorce, a potential conflict of interest can arise because the administrator works for the company, not you.

*Trustee/Custodian.* Authorized to administer (and sometimes invest or manage) the assets in a plan, the trustee may be directed by the plan administrator to make distributions (payouts) from the plan.

*Actuary.* Actuaries can help you if you have a defined benefit plan. Actuaries are professional statisticians who calculate the amount of benefits to which an employee will be entitled upon retirement. Actuaries primarily work for insurance companies calculating risks, premiums, dividends and other factors by studying population and mortality patterns as well as trends among insurers. In disputed cases, each spouse may hire an actuary to analyze the retirement plan and, if necessary, to testify in court.

*Others.* The banker, broker, financial planner, personnel officer, insurance agent or contact person who handles your retirement plan or its investments could also help you find the account balance on your plan and details regarding investments in the plan.

### iii. If You Can't Find What You Need

If, for any reason, you do not get the straight answers you need to make decisions in divorce, do not hesitate to make extra efforts to find accurate information. Use these tips for help.

*Contact the Internal Revenue Service.* Ask for a copy of your (or your spouse's) employer's pension-fund tax return, Form 5500. You'll need to know the employer's Employer Identification Number and the plan identification number—both of which the employer should provide. Employers with only one participant in a plan, or with fewer than $100,000 in aggregate plan assets, do not have to file this form.

*Write to the plan administrator or company president* or anyone else who could help you get the information you need. You might even engage the services of an attorney or a consumer advocate if you're having particular problems. However you do it, persist until you get what you need. Retirement plans are too complex not to leave a "paper trail," so do not let your spouse or spouse's attorney intimidate you into thinking that the information you need does not exist.

## 2.   Who Is the Plan Participant?

If you are self-employed, or an employee covered by a retirement plan, you are called the *plan participant*. Usually, your spouse is called the *alternate payee*. In some situations, a child or other person chosen by the plan participant might be the alternate payee.[1]

For each plan at stake in your divorce, mark in the chart below whether you are the plan participant or the alternate payee. You do not have to try to define which portions of your plans are marital property and which are separate property. (See Section 3.) Just note the date on which you or your spouse enrolled in the plan, the date you were married and the date you separated. Also note the vesting date in the last column. (See Section 5.a.ii, below.)

---

[1] If the alternate payee is someone other than the spouse, the plan participant is responsible for taxes on the benefits when they are distributed or paid out.

## 3.   What Is the "Legal Value" of Your Retirement Plans?

As we've often stressed in this book, the value of an asset that is recognized by a court may be vastly different than what the asset is worth outside the courtroom. So it is with retirement plans. Normally, the value of a plan recognized by the court—its "legal value"—is either:

- for *defined contribution plans, personal annuities or IRAs*, the amount that appears on your statement as the account value; or

- for *defined benefit plans*, what the plan administrator or an actuary tells you it's worth.

You need to know the legal value because it is often the only dollar value lawyers and judges will take into consideration. This value represents the amount you and your spouse will argue over if you disagree about the value of the benefits.

But the legal value does not account for important financial realities: taxes, early withdrawal penalties, surrender charges and other assessments. In Section 4 you will determine the financial value of the benefits.

## Retirement Benefits: General Information

| Type of Plan | Plan Participant | Alternate Payee | Date Enrolled | Date Married | Date Separated | Amount Vested |
|---|---|---|---|---|---|---|
| *Qualified Plans* —Defined Contribution Plans | | | | | | |
| Money Purchase Plans | | | | | | |
| Profit Sharing Plans | | | | | | |
| Salary Saving or 401(k) Plans | | | | | | |
| Thrift Plans | | | | | | |
| ESOPs—Employee Stock Ownership Programs | | | | | | |
| *Qualified Plans* Defined Benefit Plans | | | | | | |
| Government Plans or Military Pensions | | | | | | |
| Business or Corporate Defined Benefit Plans | | | | | | |
| *Personal Annuities* | | | | | | |
| Deferred Annuities | | | | | | |
| TSAs—Tax Sheltered Annuities | | | | | | |
| *IRAs* | | | | | | |
| IRAs | | | | | | |
| SEP IRAs | | | | | | |

### a. Defined Contribution Plans, Personal Annuities or IRAs

If you have a defined contribution plan, personal annuity or IRA, your job is somewhat simple. The plan statement gives the value. If you can't find the information you need, consult the plan administrator. (See Section 1.b.iii, above.)

Once you know the legal value of any defined contribution plans, personal annuities or IRAs, fill in the amounts in the chart, below, and then figure the marital portions.

➡ If you have no defined benefit plans, skip ahead to Section 4.

### b. Defined Benefit Plans

If you have any defined benefit plans, you'll need to do some work to find the legal value. Because these plans promise a payment in the future, they are harder to value in the present.

The legal value of a defined benefit plan is the plan's actuarial value—that is the value calculated by an actuary. The plan administrator or the company may be able to give you this value. Otherwise, you will need to hire an actuary to get it.

An actuary's valuation of your retirement plan should be relatively inexpensive—perhaps $100 to $200. The bill could run higher if your spouse hires his or her own actuary to argue that your actuary's assumptions about the future are wrong, and you find yourself having to call the actuary as an expert witness to testify in a court trial. Disputes can arise with these types of plans because their value lies in the future and is therefore speculative.

After you get the actuarial value for each plan, fill in the amounts in the chart, below, and then figure the marital portions.

## Retirement Benefits: Value of Plans

| Type of Plan | Legal Value | Marital Portion |
|---|---|---|
| Qualified Plans—Defined Contribution Plans | | |
| Money Purchase Plans | $ | $ |
| Profit Sharing Plans | $ | $ |
| Salary Saving or 410(k) Plans | $ | $ |
| Thrift Plans | $ | $ |
| ESOPs—Employee Stock Ownership Programs | $ | $ |
| Qualified Plans—Defined Benefit Plans | | |
| Government Plans or Military Pensions | $ | $ |
| Business or Corporate Defined Benefit Plans | $ | $ |
| Personal Annuities | | |
| Deferred Annuities | $ | $ |
| TSAs—Tax Sheltered Annuities | $ | $ |
| IRAs | | |
| IRAs | $ | $ |
| SEP IRAs | $ | $ |

*Determining the marital portion.* Only the portion of a retirement plan that was earned during the marriage will be divided at divorce. One formula for finding the marital portion is to divide the number of days worked by the number of days married. For example, suppose someone worked for a company 10 years and was married for eight of those years. The portion which accumulated in the retirement plan during marriage would therefore be 80%. If the total value of the plan is $100,000, 80%—or $80,000—is at stake in the divorce. Money put into an IRA before marriage and benefits that vested (see Section 5.a.ii, below) prior to marriage, are considered separate property.

If necessary, the plan administrator or your lawyer can help you figure out the marital portion.

## c. How an Actuary Values Retirement Plans (or "Back to the Future")

If you're not interested in learning how actuaries do their jobs, skip ahead to Section 4.

Actuaries are the soothsayers in divorce. Many work for insurance companies, compiling mortality tables (the charts which track when people are most likely to die) and extrapolating population data so that insurers can spread risks and remain profitable. Actuaries also help companies determine how much they need to put into your retirement plan each year so that the money you are promised—and not one penny more—will be available when it's supposed to be.

An actuary's primary role in the divorce is to figure out the total value of a retirement plan from the present day until the day the employee is likely to die. Basically it's a prediction of the amount you will be paid from the time you retire until your death.

Figuring total value is not as straightforward as it might sound. Because a dollar tomorrow is worth less than a dollar today, an actuary must go through a series of complicated calculations, working backwards from the total *future* value to the *present* day value. Actuaries use different assumptions about the future—such as salaries, interest rates, inflation, and the like—to predict the value of your retirement benefits.

Very few people have been trained in actuarial arts and so have little experience in evaluating the job the actuary does. Even worse, because actuarial predictions are based on assumptions about the future, disputes about values can easily arise if different actuaries use different assumptions. If your spouse doesn't like the value your actuary arrived at, he or she can hire another actuary to contradict the claims of your actuary. If you're unable to reach a settlement on the value, hiring two actuaries as "dueling" experts to testify in a court trial will increase the cost of your divorce considerably.

To minimize the disagreement between actuaries, make sure that they use the same assumptions. In other words, actuaries need to be comparing apples to apples, not apples to oranges. If one actuary assumes a 6% inflation rate while the other assumes 4%, the results will obviously be different.

### i. Factors Used in Evaluating Retirement Plans

While formulas and methods may differ, actuaries commonly look at the following universal factors when calculating the value of retirement plans:

*Current salary.* Often, retirement plans assign benefits based on the highest three years of earnings; during divorce, however, current salary is used in the calculations.

*Payout under the plan.* Payments from the plan may be based on the number of years worked or other requirements spelled out in your plan.

*Year of retirement.* Calculations of future worth will be different if a person retires at age 62 rather than age 65.

*Projected year of death.* The difference between the year of retirement and the projected year of death equals the number of years your plan will pay benefits.

*Estimated inflation rate.* Values will differ if inflation is assumed to be 5% rather than some other percentage.

*Cost of living increase.* If a plan includes a COLA—Cost of Living Adjustment—its value goes up. If not, the value of the plan is lower.

*Estimated interest rate generated by retirement plan investments.* Because retirement dollars are investments which should grow in value, the estimated rate of that investment growth must be factored in. Some actuaries assume a consistent rate of growth—such as 5%—and others do not.

**Example:** *Joe has worked for the same company for 20 years and is now 50 years old. The actuary for his company values Joe's plan based on his early retirement at age 62. The value of the plan using that retirement age is $75,000. Joe's wife hires an actuary to value the plan. This actuary assumes Joe will retire at age 65 and estimates the plan to be worth $100,000. By using different assumptions, the actuaries arrived at different conclusions about the value of the plan—and created a point of contention for Joe and his wife (and their attorneys).*

---

### How the Separation Date Can Affect a Retirement Plan's Value

A doctor in California requested that the pension plan administrator of his medical group tell him the value of his plan. The doctor had separated from his wife four years earlier and was finally ready to file for the divorce. The administrator valued the plan at $200,000. Wanting a second opinion on this obviously valuable asset, the doctor went to an actuary for another valuation of the plan. The actuary valued the plan at only $150,000. Why the difference? In California, the marital portion of the doctor's retirement plan stopped on the day of separation four years previous—the doctor's wife was entitled to only a portion of the amount that had accrued from their wedding day to the date they separated. The plan administrator had calculated the entire value of the plan, including the four-year period that the couple had been separated.

For more on the separation date, See Chapter 6.

---

### ii. How Can a Pension Worth Hundreds of Thousands Later Be Worth So Little Now?

That question reflects one of the most typical misunderstandings about retirement benefits—and the value of money.

Let's take the case of John and Andrea. An actuary tells Andrea that the marital portion of John's plan will pay out approximately $100,000 during John's retirement, but is worth only about $38,000 in today's dollars. If she and John divide the plan at divorce, she will get $19,000, one-half of the $38,000. If she waits until John retires to receive a portion of the payments, she could get $50,000. (But she is putting herself in a risky position. See Section 6, below.) Understandably, Andrea wants to know how something that is supposed to be so valuable tomorrow can have such a low value today.

It's simple. John's pension plan shows that he will get $10,000 per year during retirement. He's supposed to retire at age 65, and according to the actuarial tables, he's expected to live 10 years after that. Theoretically, then, he will receive $100,000 for his entire retired life.

John, however, is only 45, which means he won't be retiring for another 20 years. Assuming an inflation rate of 4%, the $10,000 that he will be paid in 20 years (the first year of his retirement) is worth only $4,564 today. As the years progress (for example, the second year of his retirement is 21 years from now), the $10,000 is worth even less. See the table, below, for the full value.

| Retirement Years | Payout in 20 Years | Value Today |
|---|---|---|
| Year 1 | $ 10,000 | $ 4,564 |
| Year 2 | $ 10,000 | $ 4,388 |
| Year 3 | $ 10,000 | $ 4,220 |
| Year 4 | $ 10,000 | $ 4,057 |
| Year 5 | $ 10,000 | $ 3,901 |
| Year 6 | $ 10,000 | $ 3,751 |
| Year 7 | $ 10,000 | $ 3,607 |
| Year 8 | $ 10,000 | $ 3,468 |
| Year 9 | $ 10,000 | $ 3,335 |
| Year 10 | $ 10,000 | $ 3,207 |
| Total | $100,000 | $38,498 |

The actuary arrived at the "value today" amounts using a procedure called "discounting to the present." This process involves estimating the value of John's plan in the future using the factors listed above. Sophisticated computer programs or calculators can help actuaries arrive at the numbers.

The Present Value Factor chart in the Appendix can help you make a rough estimate of the value of benefits. This chart compares time periods with inflation. The column down the left side of the page represents time periods in years, while the percentages across the top of the page are rates of inflation. Follow the 20-year line (the year we assumed John would retire) to the 4% rate of inflation (the rate we used) to find the Present Value Factor of .4564. To find the "value today" for John's pension in

year 1, we multiplied $10,000 by .4564, which equals $4,564. Follow the 21-30 year lines to see how out the value of the rest of his plan was calculated.

## 4. What Is the "Financial Value" of Your Retirement Plans?

The financial value of a retirement plan encompasses a view large enough to include everything from unexpected pleasantries (a cash settlement upon divorce) to nasty surprises (penalties from the IRS). The financial value is almost always lower than the legal value of a retirement plan.

Although retirement benefits are often years away from being paid out and you may not see the financial value for some time, you nevertheless want to compare all assets on an equal basis during your divorce. Just as you may be contemplating a sale of the family home, so, too, must you assume the "sale" (or liquidation) value of a retirement plan. When negotiating the overall settlement, you'll want to be able to compare each asset's legal value and financial value.

The simplified formula for finding the financial value of a retirement plan is:

| | | |
|---|---|---|
| Legal Value | | $ _____ |
| Income Taxes | - | $ _____ |
| After-Tax Value | = | $ _____ |
| Charges and Penalties | - | $ _____ |
| Financial Value | = | $ _____ |

To apply this formula to your situation, you'll have to investigate three factors—taxability, income taxes and charges and penalties. Below is an overview of each. Read them and then use the instructions that follow to apply them to your situation.

*Taxability.* Uncle Sam does not let you simply accrue money for retirement without receiving a share sooner or later. Your job is to find out when taxes on benefits are paid—either *before* the money goes into the retirement plan or *when it comes out* during retirement. The plan will specify which. You will probably want to pay taxes after you retire and start collecting the money, not as it goes into the account. Presumably, you'll be in a lower tax bracket during retirement than you are while working. When dividing plans at divorce, however, look to keep the plan in which the contributions—or at least some of the contributions—were made with after-tax dollars. Because they are funded with after-tax dollars, these plans won't be taxed when the money comes out during retirement. But this intrinsic value is not measured by actuaries, judges or lawyers.

To make decisions at divorce, you need to know *when* the taxes have to be paid in order to know *how much* in taxes you'll have to pay.

*Income taxes.* The income taxes you will have to pay on your retirement plans are based on both your tax bracket and the tax basis of the plan. The tax basis is the base line value from which tax losses and gains are calculated. Essentially, the tax basis is the total amount of contributions made with after-tax dollars less any withdrawals made or loans paid that have not been taxed. Employer contributions, and interest earned on *all* contributions—employer and employee—are not added in because those dollars are not taxed until they are paid out. The plan administrator should be able to help you find the tax basis.

*Charges and penalties.* Banks, insurance companies and other holders of retirement plans often assess charges and penalties when there is an early withdrawal—that is, when money is taken out prior to a certain date. Check your plans carefully so you do not unknowingly incur these charges.

To find the financial value of your retirement plans, first find your type of plans below and calculate your taxability, income taxes, and charges and penalties. Once you have read the sections that apply to your type of plans, move on to Section B.4.c to actually figure out the financial value of your plan(s).

### a. IRAs and Deferred Annuities

Because IRAs and deferred annuities are more likely to be funded by individuals, the taxes and other charges are calculated using special guidelines. Check these points if you have such plans.

#### i. Taxability

*IRAs.* When you deposit money into an IRA, you do not report that money as income—that is, you pay no taxes on it—as long as you have no retirement plan through your work and you don't deposit over $2,000 a year. For people who qualify, taxes aren't paid until the money comes out of the plan. At divorce time, you won't owe taxes on an IRA that is divided as long as your portion remains in the IRA or is rolled over into a new one.

*Deferred annuities.* The money put into a deferred annuity usually comes from your savings—or from income on which you have already been taxed. Because you pay taxes on the money the year you put it into a deferred annuity, you will not pay taxes on it when it comes out of the annuity. You will pay taxes on accrued earnings (interest) only.

*The money in my IRA or deferred annuity is taxable this year:* _____ Yes _____ No

#### ii. Income Taxes

*IRAs.* IRAs do not have a Tax Basis for federal tax purposes. As mentioned earlier, only those retirement plans into which you deposit *after-tax dollars* have a tax basis. The money deposited into an IRA (assuming it meets IRS qualifications) isn't taxed until those dollars are removed.

*Deferred annuities.* Because you purchase a deferred annuity with your own salary or savings—money you've already paid taxes on—the tax basis of your annuity equals the purchase price of that annuity less the amount received as a loan or withdrawal. You will owe taxes only on the profit (gain)—that is, the current account value minus the original purchase price.

$ _____    **Potential income taxes on the plan**

### iii.  Charges and Penalties

*IRAs and deferred annuities.* If you withdraw money from either of these types of plans before the plan participant reaches age 59 1/2, then you must pay a 10% early withdrawal penalty to the IRS. Also, be aware that insurance companies, banks and some investment companies impose surrender charges if you withdraw the money from an IRA prematurely. To understand the financial value of your plan, fill in any charges and penalties, even if you don't, ultimately, remove the money early.

$ _____     **Charges and penalties on my IRA(s)**

$ _____     **Charges and penalties on my Deferred Annuities**

### b.  Defined Contribution Plans, Defined Benefit Plans and Tax Sheltered Annuities

Qualified plans—such as defined contribution and defined benefit plans—must meet certain regulations of the IRS so that employers get tax benefits. These requirements can also affect the financial value of your plans. While not technically considered "qualified" plans, tax sheltered annuities (TSAs) tend to be affected by the same regulations.

### i.  Taxability

The IRS asks two questions to determine the taxability of money contributed to a pension or retirement plan.

1.  Did *your employer* contribute money?

Pension plans are sometimes referred to as contributory or non-contributory. Contributory plans are those to which the employee makes a contribution. Often, though, employers make a matching contribution to the plan. Some employers chip in 50 cents for every dollar the employee contributes. In other plans, the employer matches the employee's contribution dollar for dollar.

When you begin collecting your retirement benefits, you'll have to pay taxes on the amount contributed by your employer and interest earned on that contribution.

2.  Was *your contribution* made with pre- or after-tax dollars?

You don't have to pay taxes twice on your income. If you are currently reporting as income the money you are contributing to your plan, you will not have to pay taxes on those contributions when the money comes out of the plan at retirement.

If you do not know which percentage of your retirement plan contributions was made with pre- or after-tax dollars, you can:

• Contact the plan administrator, personnel manager or benefits coordinator. Ask for an accounting of pre- and after-tax contributions.

• Check the annual benefits statement. This document breaks down pre- and after-tax contributions.

### ii.  Income Taxes

Suppose your once-beloved offers to keep the house but to give you all of the pension plan benefits? Would you take the deal? You cannot answer that question unless you know what income tax you will owe when the benefits begin paying out.

On first glance, your share of the retirement benefits and your share of the house may equal the same dollar amounts. But those amounts probably reflect legal reality only. You may have to pay substantial income taxes when you begin receiving the retirement benefits, while your spouse may get the house while avoiding any tax liability. Your spouse could use the one-time exclusion for taxes on the house (see Chapter 14, Section C.7) and never pay taxes on up to $125,000 of profit. Remember to include financial factors when you analyze assets, because in a divorce, it's not what you *get* that count—it's what you *keep*.

$ _____     **Potential income taxes on the plan**

### iii.  Charges and Penalties

Check your plan documents carefully or ask the plan administrator to see if any of these charges or penalties apply to your retirement plan(s).

*Surrender charges.* Insurance and some investment companies impose surrender charges on annuity products to discourage participants from terminating their plans or withdrawing funds prior to the date specified in the contract. Enter all charges you would have to pay if you withdrew the funds early.

$ _____    **Surrender charges**

_____    **Not applicable**

*Early withdrawal penalties.* If a plan participant takes money out of a plan prior to retirement, he or she may be hit with an early withdrawal penalty (also called an excise tax) as high as 10 percent of the amount withdrawn. If the early withdrawal includes a distribution (payout) to the alternate payee, no penalty is charged to that alternate payee as long as the distribution is subject to a QDRO. (See Section B.5.a, below.)

Enter all penalties you would have to pay if you removed the funds early.

$ _____    **Early withdrawal penalties**

_____    **Not applicable**

Using information you calculated above—the legal value (B.3, above), tax basis, income taxes, and charges and penalties—you can determine the financial value of your retirement plan(s). Do this calculation for each plan.

1.  Find the Gain by subtracting the Tax Basis from the Legal Value.

2.  Find the Taxes Due on Gain by multiplying the Gain by your Tax Bracket. If you have an IRA or Deferred Annuity, find the Early Withdrawal Penalty by multiplying the Legal Value times 10%. Find the Total Taxes Due by adding the Early Withdrawal Penalty to the Taxes Due on Gain. If your retirement plan is neither an IRA or Deferred Annuity, use the Taxes Due on Gain as the Total Taxes Due.

3.  Find the After-Tax Value by subtracting the Total Taxes Due from the Legal Value.

4.  Find the Financial Value by subtracting any Surrender Charges or other Penalties from the After-Tax Value.

---

### Tax Brackets and State Income Taxes

Throughout this book, we assume that you fall into the 28% federal income tax bracket. Because some states tax a percentage of IRA deposits and other retirement plans (Thrift Plans and Employee Stock Option Plans), you'll need to ask a tax advisor if you might owe state taxes on your benefits. You won't owe state income taxes in Alaska, Florida, Nevada, New Hampshire, South Dakota, Texas, Washington and Wyoming, the states that currently impose no state income taxes. If you owe state income taxes, increase your tax bracket in all calculations accordingly.

---

**Example:**

1.  Find the Gain by subtracting the Tax Basis from the Legal Value.

| | |
|---|---|
| *Legal Value* | $ 75,000 |
| *Tax Basis* | -  20,000 |
| *Gain* | = $55,000 |

2.  Find the Taxes Due on Gain by multiplying the Gain by your Tax Bracket.

| | | |
|---|---|---|
| *Gain* | | $55,000 |
| *Tax Bracket* | x | 28% |
| *Taxes Due on Gain* | = | $15,400 |

If you have an IRA or deferred annuity, find the Early Withdrawal Penalty by multiplying the Legal Value times 10%.

| | | |
|---|---|---|
| *Legal Value* | | $75,000 |
| *Penalty Percentage* | x | 10% |
| *Early Withdrawal Penalty* | = | $ 7,500 |

If you have an IRA or deferred annuity, find the Total Taxes Due by adding the Early Withdrawal Penalty to the Taxes Due on Gain. If your retirement plan is neither an IRA or Deferred Annuity, use the Taxes Due on Gain as the Total Taxes Due.

| | |
|---|---|
| Early Withdrawal Penalty | $ 7,500 |
| Taxes Due on Gain | + <u>15,400</u> |
| Total Taxes Due | = $22,900 |

3. Find the After-Tax Value by subtracting the Total Taxes Due from the Legal Value.

| | |
|---|---|
| Legal Value | $75,000 |
| Total Taxes Due | - <u>22,900</u> |
| After-Tax Value | = $52,100 |

4. Find the Financial Value by subtracting any Surrender Charges or other Penalties from the After-Tax Value.

| | |
|---|---|
| After-Tax Value | $52,100 |
| Surrender Charges and Penalties | - <u>0</u> |
| Financial Value | = $52,100 |

Note the difference between the Legal Value and Financial Value of our hypothetical retirement plan. If you had assumed your plan was worth $75,000 and therefore kept it in exchange for another item worth $75,000, you'd have actually given away $22,900.

Now fill in the numbers for your retirement benefits and enter them in the Financial Value chart that follows. Remember to do this calculation for each plan.

1. Find the Gain by subtracting the Tax Basis from the Legal Value.

| | |
|---|---|
| Legal Value | $ _____ |
| Tax Basis | - $ _____ |
| Gain | = $ _____ |

2. Find the Taxes Due on Gain by multiplying the Gain by your Tax Bracket.

| | |
|---|---|
| Gain | $ _____ |
| Tax Bracket | x $ _____ |
| Taxes Due on Gain | = $ _____ |

If you have an IRA or Deferred Annuity, find the Early Withdrawal Penalty by multiplying the Legal Value times 10%.

| | |
|---|---|
| Legal Value | $ _____ |
| Penalty Percentage | x $ _____ |
| Early Withdrawal Penalty | = $ _____ |

Find the Total Taxes Due by adding the Early Withdrawal Penalty to the Taxes Due on Gain. If your retirement plan is neither an IRA or Deferred Annuity, use the Taxes Due on Gain as the Total Taxes Due.

| | |
|---|---|
| Early Withdrawal Penalty | $ _____ |
| Taxes Due on Gain | + $ _____ |
| Total Taxes Due | = $ _____ |

3. Find the After-Tax Value by subtracting the Total Taxes Due from the Legal Value.

| | |
|---|---|
| Legal Value | $ _____ |
| Total Taxes Due | - $ _____ |
| After-Tax Value | = $ _____ |

4. Find the Financial Value by subtracting any Surrender Charges or other Penalties from the After-Tax Value.

| | |
|---|---|
| After-Tax Value | $ _____ |
| Surrender Charges/Penalties | - $ _____ |
| Financial Value | = $ _____ |

**Retirement Benefits: Value of Marital Portion**

| Type of Plan | Financial Value | Marital Portion |
|---|---|---|
| Qualified Plans—Defined Contribution Plans | | |
| Money Purchase Plans | $ | $ |
| Profit Sharing Plans | $ | $ |
| Salary Saving or 401(k) Plans | $ | $ |
| Thrift Plans | $ | $ |
| ESOPs—Employee Stock Ownership Programs | $ | $ |
| Qualified Plans—Defined Benefit Plans | | |
| Government Plans or Military Pensions | $ | $ |
| Business or Corporate Defined Benefit Plans | $ | $ |
| Personal Annuities | | |
| Deferred Annuities | $ | $ |
| TSAs—Tax Sheltered Annuities | $ | $ |
| IRAs | | |
| IRAs | $ | $ |
| SEP IRAs | $ | $ |

*Determining the marital portion.* Follow the instructions for determining the marital portion of the legal value of your plans for figuring the marital portion of the financial value. See Section B.3, above.

## 5. How Will You and Your Spouse Divide Your Retirement Plans?

In most divorces, spouses keep "their" own retirement benefits in exchange for other assets. As a simplified example, if each spouse's share of the house is $75,000 and the non-working spouse's share of the other's retirement plan is $75,000, then the employee would keep the retirement plan while the other spouse would take the house.

### a. Financial Factors Affecting Retirement Plan Divisions

Dividing assets during a divorce, however, is not that simple. To truly exchange assets of equal value, you must look beyond the legal value, and even the financial value, of your retirement plans. Consider the following five factors before you propose how to divide the retirement benefits from your marriage with your spouse.

- Qualified Domestic Relations Orders (QDROs)
- Vesting
- Matured Benefits
- Cost of Living Adjustments
- Access to Cash

### i. Qualified Domestic Relations Orders

If you weren't getting divorced, you'd never hear about fascinating legal concepts such as the QDRO. (It's pronounced quadro.)

QDRO stands for Qualified Domestic Relations Order. It is an order from the court to the retirement plan administrator spelling out how the plan's benefits are to be assigned to each party in a divorce.[2] A QDRO is quite important because if something is omitted from it, you cannot get it—even if the plan says you are entitled to the money or benefits. Amanda is a case in point. Her husband died shortly after the divorce was final. Even though his plan stated that his surviving ex-spouse was entitled to "survivor benefits," the QDRO didn't and she received nothing.

Sometimes, an order concerning the retirement plans is in a document called a Domestic Relations Order, Marital Settlement Agreement or Divorce Settlement Agreement. These don't qualify as QDROs.

---

[2] Don't be frightened by the phrase "court order." In most cases, the divorcing couple agrees on how to divide their property, including their retirement plans. They put their agreement in writing, and then get the judge's signature as a formality. Getting the signature usually means dropping the papers off for the judge and then going back and picking them up after they are signed. Once the judge has signed the papers, you have an order—or a QDRO.

---

**What Constitutes a QDRO**

For an order dividing a retirement plan to qualify as a QDRO, it must specify:

- the name and last known mailing address of the participant;

- and the name and mailing address of each alternate payee;

- the amount or percentage of the participant's benefits that is to be paid to each alternate payee, or the manner in which the amount or percentage is to be determined;

- the number of payments or the period to which the order applies; and

- the name of the plan, such as the Walton Company Pension Plan, to which the order applies.

A QDRO cannot:

- require a plan to pay any benefit or option not otherwise provided by the plan;

- require a plan to provide increased benefits as determined by an actuary; and

- require the payment of benefits to an alternate payee that are required to be paid to another alternate payee (that is, another ex-spouse) under a previous qualified order.

---

Not all plans are subject to QDROs. In other words, you don't always have to get a court order describing how the plan's benefits are to be distributed. That's mostly because some plans have no administrators; they are administered by the plan participant (you or your spouse). Other plans for which you don't need a QDRO are usually government plans, beyond the reach of private plan administrators. Also, if you aren't going to be receiving benefits from your spouse's retirement plan—that is, you trade different assets for the retirement plans or "she keeps hers and he keeps his"—then you don't have to worry about a QDRO. Check off the plans you have that are subject to QRDOs.

Plans subject to QDROs include:

- Qualified Plans—Defined Contribution Plans and Defined Benefit Plans; and

- Tax Sheltered Annuities (TSAs).

Plans exempt from QDROs include:

- Deferred Annuities;

- IRAs (Individual Retirement Accounts);

- SEP IRAs (Simplified Employee Pension IRAs); and

- Non-Qualified Deferred Compensation Plans (also government and church plans).

*List all retirement plans that must be spelled out in a QDRO:*

_____

_____

_____

_____

### ii. Vesting

One retirement plan concept that is especially important at divorce is *vesting*. You've probably heard people say they'll be "fully vested" after a certain number of years or that they'll "be vested in another year." Vesting means that you are entitled to the retirement benefits your employer has contributed to the plan for you. Even if you quit your job or are fired, you're entitled to those benefits. Being *fully* vested means that you are entitled to *all* the benefits your employer has contributed. Being partially vested, for example, 30 percent vested, means that if you were to begin receiving the benefits from your employer's contribution to the plan, you'd receive only that percentage. If the plan paid $100 a month upon retirement, you'd receive $30.

Keep in mind that vesting affects only the amount your *employer* contributes toward your retirement plan. You are always entitled to the full amount that *you* contribute to your retirement plan.

Another consideration if you are not fully vested is whether or not your state considers non-vested retirement benefits marital property. If it doesn't, and a plan participant has not vested, then division of that plan in that state is not affected by vesting. If the state does, however, and you divorce before you fully vest, you could face the awful prospect of paying your spouse a portion of the retirement benefits—even though you might *never* receive them yourself. If you are not fully vested and will potentially encounter this costly dilemma, be sure you know your rights and obligations before negotiating over your retirement plan.

For example, in such a state, the *total* value of your retirement plan is calculated and that amount is divided. If you want to keep the retirement plan, you might have to buy out your spouse's share or exchange it for another asset. If you're fired or change jobs, you might not receive your employer's contributions to your retirement plan, even though you paid your spouse for them.

To reduce these risks, carefully consider whether to divide your plan in the future or in the present. See Section 5, below.

If you are fully vested (and therefore entitled to your employer's contribution and required to divide them at divorce) double check details of your benefits package to be sure you know about any provisions that could be affected by divorce or death. In some cases, when a single (unmarried) employee dies before the age of 55, even though fully vested, that person's estate may not be entitled to the benefits.

*List all retirement plans that have vested (specify percentage):*

_____

_____

_____

_____

### iii.  Maturing

Once pension benefits vest, the employee may still have to wait before actually receiving the benefits. Usually, vested pensions do not pay out ("mature") until the worker reaches a certain age, such as 62 or 65. Some employees choose to continue to work even after the pension matures because the pension payments increase the longer the employee works past the maturity date. If you continue to work to prevent your ex from getting matured benefits, a court may order you to retire (or to pay your former spouse for his or her share from the benefits).

When dividing matured benefits in a divorce, the employee-spouse must be aware of two financial risks: taxes and double payments.

*Taxes.* Many divorce settlements specify that the non-participant spouse gets a share of the other spouse's retirement benefits when the employed spouse retires. Usually, the pension plan administrator sends a check to the retired employee, who in turn sends a check to the ex-spouse. But this means that only the retired employee pays income taxes on the benefits.

To reduce your tax burden, make sure the QDRO orders the pension plan administrator to send two checks—one to you and one to your ex-spouse. Each person pays income taxes on the benefits he or she receives. If your plan is not subject to a QDRO, it may be possible to reduce the retired person's tax liability, by using the domestic relations order, marital settlement agreement or divorce agreement to specify how the benefits are to be paid.

*Specify how you will minimize taxes:*

_____

_____

_____

_____

*Double payments.* You should not have to pay your spouse twice for the retirement benefits you are receiving as income. If your spouse is given a portion of your retirement benefits as part of the property settlement, you do not want your retirement benefits to be considered part of your income when alimony and child support is calculated. To protect yourself against double dipping, remember the following: *You can divide the plan or divide the stream of income, but do not divide both.*

This double dipping of payments is one of the most common ways in which pension benefits are lost at divorce. Don't let it happen to you. One way to protect yourself is to include a provision in your settlement exempting your pension payments from being considered income for the purposes of alimony or support.

*Specify how you will prevent double dipping:*

_____

_____

_____

_____

### iv.  Cost of Living Adjustments

Cost of Living Adjustments (COLAs) are provisions in retirement plans that provide for an increase in benefits based on your life expectancy and the formula by which benefits are paid out. A plan with a cost-of-living provision is usually more valuable than another plan without it. Check with your plan administrator to see if your retirement plan includes a cost-of-living provision.

*List the retirement plans that have Cost of Living Adjustments (COLAs):*

_____

_____

_____

_____

### v.  Access to Cash

In getting cash out of a retirement plan at divorce, the alternate payee holds the advantage.

If you are the *alternate payee* (non-employee spouse), you can request that the QDRO provide for a payout when a marital property settlement becomes final. You'll have to pay taxes on that money unless you deposit it into an IRA or any other qualified pension plan within 60 days of receiving it.

If money is tight (as it often is during divorce), you may want to open a savings account with all or part of the money you receive from a retirement plan distribution. Although you'll have to pay taxes on this money, you will have easy access to these funds should you need them. Most importantly, you won't be hit with the 10% early withdrawal penalty as you would have had you put it into an IRA and then needed to withdraw money to live on.

If you are the *plan participant* (employee spouse), you probably won't get an early payout from your plan even though your spouse may. Your divorce does not change your status with respect to your benefit payments. It's rare that you will be able get to your benefits prior to the date on which the plan specifies you are to receive them—the exceptions are if you become disabled, if quit your job or get fired, or if the plan itself ends.

*Specify your access to cash from a retirement plan during your divorce:*

_____

_____

_____

_____


## b.  The Division Decision

### Decision Time . . .
Now that you understand the financial factors that can affect your retirement benefits, you are ready to move on to the division decision itself.

Generally, you can divide a pension plan or take a payout in one of two ways:

*Present Division.* You divide the value of the plan now, at divorce, instead of later, at retirement.

*Future (Deferred) Division.* You divide the value of the plan at retirement or at that point in the employee's career when benefits would normally be paid out. Most future divisions involve only Defined Benefit plans which promise payment in the future.

Remember—no matter which approach you take, everything must be spelled out in the QDRO.

What follows are the pros and cons of a present versus a future division for each type of retirement plan. Read only those that apply.


### i.  IRAs

Present and future divisions are not really relevant with IRAs. IRAs are not subject to QDROs, but can be divided in half or in any way the court orders. IRAs can also be transferred from one spouse to the other. In most divorces, a spouse keeps any IRAs in his or her name.

Unlike distributions from plans covered by QDROs, distributing the proceeds from an IRA triggers a 10% early withdrawal penalty. The only way to avoid the penalty—and immediately paying taxes on the money withdrawn—is to open another IRA account within 60 days.

*I would like to divide the IRAs as follows:*

_____

_____

_____

_____


### ii.  Defined Contribution Plans or TSAs

In each case the advantages to a present or future division depend on whether you are the Alternate Payee or the Plan Participant.

## Why Do a Present Division of Retirement Benefits?

| *Alternate Payee* | *Plan Participant* |
|---|---|
| 1. Economic ties with your spouse are severed. The division is over and done with and you do not have to worry about it in the future. | 1. Economic ties with your spouse are severed. The division is over and done with and you do not have to worry about it in the future. |
| 2. Deferred divisions are difficult for the court to administer. | 2. Deferred divisions are difficult for the court to administer. |
| 3. You do not need to use the services of an actuary. The value of the plan is clear in the present and they can be divided in the present. | 3. You do not need to use the services of an actuary. The value of the plan is clear in the present and it can be divided in the present. |
| 4. Each spouse gains control over his/her share of the funds. The QDRO can instruct the plan administrator to segregate the alternate payee's interest so that each spouse has an account within the existing retirement plan. The alternate payee can then:<br><br>a. keep the benefits within the existing plan. You would have the services of the plan's managers to invest the money. If you're not confident about your abilities in this area, you might be better off leaving your share of the retirement benefits where they are. The drawback is that you lose control over your money and cannot make your own investment decisions.<br><br>b. take the cash out upon divorce. You get these tax advantages:<br><br>• 10% early withdrawal penalty does not apply and<br><br>• you can roll your taxable portion into an IRA, as long as you receive all of your portions in one taxable year. | 4. Each spouse gains control over his/her share of the funds. |

## Why Do a Deferred Division of Retirement Benefits?

| *Alternate Payee* | *Plan Participant* |
|---|---|
| 1. If you or your spouse has unvested benefits, and there is any doubt about the value of those benefits, a deferred division allows time for vesting to occur. | 1. If you or your spouse has unvested benefits, and there is any doubt about the value of those benefits, a deferred division allows time for vesting to occur. |
| 2. If you have insufficient property or cash to buy out your spouse's share of other marital property, then deferred division may be the only way to even up the property split. | 2. If you have insufficient property or cash to buy out your spouse's share, then deferred division may be the only way to even up the property split. |
| | 3. You will not receive money from the plan until the plan provides for it anyway, so why divide it early? |
| | 4. If you have unvested benefits and you divide the plan in the present, you may end up paying more to your spouse than you yourself receive. |

### Using Retirement Plan Distributions To Pay Child Support

Child support is non-taxable income to the person receiving it. Using a retirement plan distribution to pay child support converts what would be non-taxable inome into taxable income to the person receiving it. The recipient should make sure that other money is used to pay child support, or that the support amount is increased to cover the taxes.

*I would like to divide the defined contribution plans or TSAs as follows:*

_____

_____

_____

_____

### iii.  Defined Benefit Plans

In each case the advantages to a present or future division depend on whether you are the Alternate Payee or the Plan Participant.

## Why Do a Present Division of Retirement Benefits?

| Alternate Payee | Plan Participant |
|---|---|
| 1. You can get money now (access to cash). <br><br> 2. Vesting risk is eliminated. <br><br> 3. No 10% early withdrawal penalty for distribution. <br><br> 4. You can avoid the risk of the plan suffering large investment losses or the company or plan going bankrupt. (If you are a better investor than the plan managers you could get a better return on your money.) | 1. The value of your plan is based on your present earnings rather than future earnings. Therefore your spouse does not receive the benefit of your future work when your earned pay increases. <br><br> 2. If you are older than your spouse and expect to live a long life, it may be to your advantage to do a present division because you may outlive the mortality tables. This means you will ultimately receive more income than the actuary predicted you would. |

## Why Do a Deferred Division of Retirement Benefits?

| Alternate Payee | Plan Participant |
|---|---|
| 1. Often, benefits are based on the plan participant's future higher earning rather than today's salary. <br><br> 2. You enjoy the benefits of your ex-spouse's increased earnings. | 1. Share vesting risk with your ex-spouse. <br><br> 2. Your ex-spouse has no access to cash now. |

*I would like to divide the defined benefit plans as follows:*

_____

_____

_____

_____

## 6. How Do You Feel About Your Decision?

Take a few moments to consider your attitude about the decisions you've just made.

Working through the numbers as you've done can sometimes defuse anger and other feelings. Nevertheless, if you are highly upset about how your retirement will be affected by divorce, do not ignore your instincts.

Use the following questions to examine your emotional state regarding your benefits, or jot down your own thoughts in the space below. (Remember, no one has to see your reactions or comments. This exercise is strictly to help you manage the "money crazies" of divorce.)

*My retirement plan symbolizes…*

*…my future*

*…my only compensation for putting up with a terrible job for so long*

*…the plans we made together for our "golden years"*

*…my security*

*…other*

*During this divorce…*

*I'm not going to give up any part of my pension no matter what.*

*I hate to do it, but I'm going to stick with my decision to split the plan (___ in the present ___ in the future) with my spouse.*

*I don't care about the stupid pension. I just want my house.*

*I'll split my pension—but only if I get a very attractive offer on the house or something else.*

*other...*

## C. Questions To Ask Your Attorney

Retirement plans raise several important legal and financial questions. Below is a list of important questions for you to ask your attorney or research at your local law library.

1. Does your state treat retirement benefits upon divorce as marital property to be divided, or as income that may belong only to the earner? Benefits treated like income could affect the amount you pay or receive in alimony or child support.

2. Is a non-qualified deferred compensation plan considered income, or property subject to division?

3. What is the marital portion of our retirement benefits?

4. Must you be fully vested to receive your employer's contribution to your retirement plan?

5. Does your state consider non-vested retirement plans to be marital property?

# 16

# Financial Investments: How To Divide the Portfolio Pie

*In divorce, when you split up the investments made by you and your partner during marriage, it's doubtful you'll get exactly what you want. But, you should get what you need.*

In other words, objectively analyze your portfolio—that is, the stocks, bonds, mutual funds, real estate investments, gold coins and the like that make up your investment holdings. Then work to get the assets that can put you in the best position to build toward your future after divorce.

How do you know which investments will serve you best?

Ask a dozen financial planners and you'll get the same answer: "That depends."

The investments that will serve you best depends on several factors—your future plans, current age, risk tolerance, income needs and investment experience. You should aim for investments which meet your individual needs, allow you to sleep at night and keep your taxes to a minimum.

As you read this chapter and evaluate your investments, keep in mind the following two questions:

- Is the investment performing well?
- Is the investment appropriate for me?

Whether you are a novice or veteran investor, use the formulas and tips in this chapter to select the investments that will best support you after the divorce. Even if you are completely unfamiliar with the investments you and your spouse share, you need not be intimidated—if you do your homework.

In some instances, because trading restrictions and tax laws can complicate certain investments, you may need to consult with financial experts before making decisions at divorce. Tax advisors, stockbrokers or financial planners may be particularly useful. Nevertheless, you can save time and money by doing the groundwork and information gathering yourself.

## A. Concepts To Consider

To get started, here are a few basic investment concepts to help you select investments when a marriage ends.

### 1. An Investment from Marriage May Make Little Sense in Singlehood

While married, the two of you may have chosen certain investments because they met your shared goals—such as a mutual fund to help save for the down payment on a house or an annuity to increase the retirement kitty. Once you divorce, however, your goals, tax bracket and ability to withstand losses may change. Perhaps as a couple you could afford to hold on to a stock with great potential, even when its value fell. As a single person, however, such a stock may be totally unsuitable if you're looking for a stable income. Similarly, a spouse in a high income tax bracket may not want to keep an investment that generates substantial taxable interest.

### 2. Don't Take an Investment You Can't Live With

Does the mere mention of Wall Street give you the jitters? Can you bear to sit by and watch what happens to the bond market? Do you have the time, energy, and interest to keep up with the performance of your investments? Think about these questions carefully as you look at each asset. You should only keep an investment (like a spouse) if you can stand living with it. Don't take an asset if you don't understand its risks.

### 3. Use Your Divorce To Cut Your Losses

When it comes to investments, no one likes to admit they made a bad call or a poor decision—especially if your spouse warned you not to buy the loser in the first place. But you wouldn't fight to keep the awful picture Aunt Lucille gave you for a wedding present, would you? Why hold on to investments that are not doing well? Because of the emotional distress of divorce—or simple "investment inertia"—some people hang on to certain investments they ought to sell. Divorce is the perfect time to review *all* of your investments and unload those that drain your portfolio value.

## 4. No Investment Is Risk Free

"Risk free" investing is one of the great illusions of the American marketplace. Regardless of what you see, hear or want to believe, every investment contains risk. Even what was once the most trusted places for money—banks and savings and loans—have shown this to be true. Ignoring risk is common among today's investors who have been hit by a virtual avalanche of new financial products, each promising rewards which may or may not materialize. Take time to ask questions about the downside of any investment you plan to keep as part of your settlement. Keep in mind one general rule: *the greater the potential for gain, the greater the risk.*

In addition, never keep an investment which carries a greater risk than you can afford. Doing so increases the risk of loss, because you will probably sell the investment when its value drops rather than ride out its ups and downs.

**Example:** *In the property settlement, Cheryl received 300 shares of WOW Mutual Fund, a fund investing in small capitalization computer companies. The fund had a high return of 22% in the prior year. Her husband Jim convinced her that with the $14,000 worth of WOW shares, she would make more money than with the lower-return Treasury bonds he was taking as part of the settlement. Cheryl quickly learned, however, that the greater the potential for gain, the greater the risk; her $14,000 investment dropped to $8,700 when the stock market fell.*

## 5. Asset Options: Sell Now, Take It Forever or Take It for a Loss

Assume sale. Those two words sum up the best advice you can follow when deciding what to do with assets at divorce. So often, cherished investments you thought you would keep forever end up on the auction block after divorce. Ideally, you should select only those investments that financially fit your future lifestyle—and you should sell together or transfer to your spouse those that do not. If you sell the investment at divorce, you share the selling costs and potential tax bite with your soon-to-be ex-spouse. Waiting until after the divorce means you incur all those expenses yourself.

Too often, divorcing couples overlook the simple fact that an asset they are planning to sell eventually can be sold *prior* to the divorce. They get caught up in making tradeoffs to reach a fair or expedient property settlement and accept assets they don't want or intend to keep. If, however, you assume sale, you're forced to consider taxation and other costs. Then your negotiations can be based on the true cost of keeping the asset and not an illusory value. And if you do keep the asset, you know its true financial value.

An exception to the idea of "sell now or take it forever," is to determine if the asset would provide you with a tax loss when you sell it. If it would, and if you have another asset on which you expect a gain, it may make financial sense to take the loss-producing asset in the settlement. Then you can sell the "loser" after the divorce to offset the tax gain you have from the sale of another asset and reduce your overall tax liability. It pays therefore to know which stocks, bonds or mutual funds carry a tax loss with them.[1]

---

[1]Limited partnerships and rental real estate which produce a loss because of depreciating costs actually *increase* your tax liability. Be sure to consult a tax advisor before taking one of these items that show a loss.

**Example:** *Suppose you bought a stock for $2,000 and sold it for $1,500. Your loss is $500. If you have another stock you bought for $1,500 and sold for $2,500, your gain is $1,000. If you didn't sell the first stock, you'd pay $280 on the $1,000 gain assuming you are in the 28% tax bracket. If you sold both assets, however, the loss would offset the gain and your tax liability would be 28% of $500, or $140.*

---

**Sell Now**

Elliot accepted his wife's offer of their coin collection even though he did not particularly care about the coin market and didn't really want the collection. Nevertheless, he accepted it with the illusion that his concession would speed up the settlement. Not only did the settlement proceedings drag on, but after the divorce, when he sold the collection, Elliot owed substantial taxes on the gain and had to pay a sales commission.

---

## 6. Balance Security, Income and Growth

Your investments should give you more than headaches. In fact, a portfolio should balance three financial needs over your lifetime: security, income and growth.

During your divorce, analyze whether or not your investments meet these needs—and in what proportions. The degree to which you need security, income and growth will change depending on what phase of life you're in. Generally, you will want more growth than income while you are young and more income than growth when you get older.

*Security.* The conventional wisdom among financial advisors holds that you should have an emergency fund in place before you even consider investing. This fund should equal three to six months of your cost-of-living expenses such as mortgage, rent, utilities and food. It should be readily available in a money market fund or some other easy-to-tap source of cash. Disability or life insurance can also provide important sources of income or cash in the event of an emergency. Once your emergency needs are met, you can consider investments for income or growth.

*Income.* Income investments pay monthly, quarterly, semi-annual or annual dividends or pay interest to supplement your salary or provide an income during retirement.

*Growth.* Growth investments should "make your money work for you," offering steady growth beyond what you would earn from conservative vehicles like Certificates of Deposit or money markets. Growth investments include individual stocks, high-tech stocks, real estate and artwork (paintings).

---

**Income vs. Growth Needs**

Susan, a young executive, had just gotten a raise when her husband decided he wanted a divorce. A conservative investor, her husband had a large number of utility stocks which provided a steady but small flow of dividends. Because Susan's salary increase gave her a more than adequate income, she accepted cash for her share of the stock rather than the stock itself. With cash in hand, she invested in aggressive stocks which could provide what she wanted most now: growth.

---

## 7. If You Don't Know the Tax Basis, the Tax Bill May Shock You

"Buy low and sell high." That cliche of the marketplace leaves out an important piece of information: when you sell high you owe Uncle Sam taxes on the profit. Just how much you owe is determined by the amount of profit you realized on the investment.

And that profit is derived from your tax basis in the investment.

If you read Chapter 14, you learned how to find the tax basis of the family home. The tax basis is the original purchase price plus improvements minus any tax benefits. For your investments, your tax basis is the original purchase price plus any reinvestment of dividends minus tax benefits (losses you have declared). Specific formulas for finding the tax basis are given throughout this chapter.

**Example:** *Leslie bought 100 shares of stock at $12 per share in May and another 100 shares of the same stock in December for $30 per share. When the stock soare]d in value to $80 per share, Leslie decided to sell it. Assuming a 28% federal tax bracket, here's what Leslie's gain and tax bill would look like:*

| May Stocks | | December Stocks | |
|---|---|---|---|
| Sell 100 shares @ $80 | $ 8,000 | Sell 100 shares @ $80 | $ 8,000 |
| Bought 100 shares @ $12 | - 1,200 | Bought 100 shares @ $30 | - 3,000 |
| Gain | $ 6,800 | Gain | $ 5,000 |
| (times tax bracket) | x .28 | (times tax bracket) | x .28 |
| Taxes Due | $ 1,904 | Taxes Due | $ 1,400 |

The tax basis for the May stocks is $12 per share price. That leads to a greater gain which in turn creates a bigger tax bill. For the December stocks, with the $30 per share purchase price, the gain is less and so are the taxes. If Leslie had to sell half of the shares, Leslie would be better off selling the December stocks and saving $501 in taxes ($1,904 - $1,400 = $504).

Suppose Leslie's spouse offers to split the 200 shares of stock. Should Leslie take the May stocks or the December stocks? Leslie would be better off taking the December stocks, where the taxes owed are lower. The fairest settlement would be for each spouse to take 50 of the May stocks and 50 of the December stocks. Another possibility would be to sell the stocks and split the tax bill equally. In that case, the calculations would look like this:

| | | |
|---|---|---|
| May stocks Gain | | $ 6,800 |
| Monthly Tax Savings | + | 5,000 |
| Total Gain | = | $11,800 |
| Tax Bracket | x | 28% |
| Total Taxes on Gain | = | $ 3,304 |
| Each Spouse's Share of Taxes Due | = | $ 1,652 |

---

**Tax Basis and the IRS**

When spouses divorce, information concerning the tax basis of an asset must be given to the spouse who receives the asset when title (ownership) changes.[2] Because tax consequences are so fundamental to the selection of an asset, however, you should know the tax basis before you divide your assets, not after.

---

## 8. Beware of Inflation and Inflated Claims

Nothing takes the fun out of investing faster than losing money. Yet investors often overlook the simple factor of inflation which constantly erodes the value of their holdings. To determine the true amount of return you earn from an investment, you must consider inflation.

Take the simple example of a $10,000 Certificate of Deposit paying 7% interest at a time when inflation is running 4.5% annually. At the end

---

[2]Internal Revenue Code § 1041.

of a year, the CD would seem to be worth $10,700 (the $700 earned via the 7% interest payment).

Assuming a federal tax bracket of 28%, the amount due the government would equal $196, reducing the $10,700 to only $10,504. Now factor in inflation. The $10,000 loses $450 (inflation of 4.5%) a year. At the end of a year, instead of $10,700, the CD is really worth only $10,054 ($10,504 - $450). The investment gained only $54, less than 1%.

Be on guard, too, for inflated, or misunderstood claims. Quite commonly, investors consider only one dimension, such as the interest rate, an investment pays. They often forget about the numerous other factors which affect value such as risks, inflation, sales charges, management fees, dividend payments and taxes.

The commonly misunderstood differences between yield and total return illustrate the problem of one-dimensional analysis. *Yield* represents income in the form of dividends, interest or capital gains. *Total return* is the yield plus the percentage of appreciation (growth) or loss in the per share value of an investment.

**Example:** *Ron saw an advertisement for a mutual fund offering a yield of 11%. Later that day, his broker called him and told him about another fund with an 8% yield. Which should he buy?*

*Ron must look beyond yield to total return. The yield represents only the dividends he'll receive on his shares. The total return takes into account both the yield and the percentage increase (appreciation) or decrease (loss) in the value of the shares.*

*Ron's broker explained that the shares in the fund yielding 11% decreased in value by 20% the previous year, meaning the total return was a negative 9% (11% - 20%). The shares in the fund yielding 8%, on the other hand, increased 8.3% for a total return of 16.3%. Note that the higher yield fund actually produced a lower total return.*

## B. Steps to a Settlement

Now that you have an overview of the concepts to consider when making investment choices, here is your basic plan of action for reaching decisions.

1. What investments do you and your spouse hold?

2. Who owns each investment?

3. What is the legal value of each investment?

4. What is the after-tax/after-sale value of each investment?

5. Which assets should you keep?

6. How will you and your spouse divide the investments?

7. How do you feel about your decision?

To answer these questions, you will complete the investment chart, below. Begin by writing in your investments in the far left column, Section 1. As you move on through Sections 2, 3 and 4, you can come back to this chart and fill in the remaining columns.

**Investment Chart**

| Investments (Section 1) | Who Owns It?<br>H —Husband<br>W—Wife<br>J —Jointly  (Section 2) | Legal Value<br>(Section 3) | After-Tax/After-Sale Value<br>(Section 4) |
|---|---|---|---|
| **Cash & Cash Equivalents** | | | |
| Bank Checking Accounts<br>1.<br>2.<br>3.<br>4. | | | |
| Bank Savings Accounts<br>1.<br>2.<br>3.<br>4. | | | |
| Certificates of Deposit<br>1.<br>2.<br>3. | | | |
| Bank Money Market Funds<br>1.<br>2.<br>3. | | | |
| Money Market Mutual Funds<br>1.<br>2.<br>3. | | | |
| Personal Notes<br>1.<br>2.<br>3. | | | |
| Other<br>1.<br>2.<br>3. | | | |
| **Stocks & Bonds** | | | |
| Common Stocks<br>1. ___ Domestic ___ International<br>2. ___ Domestic ___ International<br>3. ___ Domestic ___ International | | | |
| Preferred Stock<br>1.<br>2. | | | |

| | | | |
|---|---|---|---|
| Mutual Funds<br>1.<br>2.<br>3. | | | |
| Treasury Bills<br>1.<br>2.<br>3. | | | |
| Government Bonds (such as Ginnie Maes)<br>1.<br>2. | | | |
| Municipal Bonds<br>1.　__　Mutual Funds<br>　　__　Unit Trusts<br>　　__　Individual Bonds<br>2.　__　Mutual Funds<br>　　__　Unit Trusts<br>　　__　Individual Bonds | | | |
| Corporate Bonds<br>1.<br>2.<br>3. | | | |
| EE U.S. Savings Bonds<br>1.<br>2.<br>3. | | | |
| Zero Coupon Bonds<br>1.<br>2.<br>3. | | | |
| Other<br>1.<br>2. | | | |
| *Real Estate* | | | |
| Income or Rental Properties<br>1.<br>2. | | | |
| Real Estate Investments Trusts (REITs)<br>1.<br>2. | | | |
| Raw Land<br>1.<br>2. | | | |
| Other<br>1.<br>2. | | | |

## Insurance Investments

| Cash Value of Life Insurance Policies<br>1.<br>2.<br>3. | | | |
|---|---|---|---|
| Annuities<br>1.<br>2.<br>3. | | | |
| Other<br>1.<br>2.<br>3. | | | |

## Limited Partnerships

| Real Estate<br>1.<br>2.<br>3. | | | |
|---|---|---|---|
| Oil & Gas<br>1.<br>2.<br>3. | | | |
| Cable Television<br>1.<br>2.<br>3. | | | |
| Equipment Leasing, etc.<br>1.<br>2.<br>3. | | | |
| Other<br>1.<br>2. | | | |

## Commodities & Collectibles

| Gold & Silver<br>1.<br>2.<br>3. | | | |
|---|---|---|---|
| Coins, Jewelry, Art & Collectibles<br>1.<br>2.<br>3. | | | |
| Other<br>1.<br>2.<br>3. | | | |

## 1. What Investments Do You and Your Spouse Hold?

Using the investment chart, list all investments owned by you, your spouse and the two of you together. If you're unsure of certain investments, check old tax returns, or give a call to your banker, stockbroker, accountant or other tax advisor.

## 2. Who Owns Each Investment?

In Column 2, show whether the investment is owned by husband (H), wife (W) or jointly (J). Only those investments owned jointly are divided at divorce. List the investments owned separately by you and your spouse anyway. As you negotiate the settlement, it is possible that your or your spouse's separate investments will be considered in terms of income needs or for alimony.

If you need more information on what constitutes separate and marital property, see Chapter 13, Section A.

## 3. What Is the "Legal Value" of Each Investment?

With investments, the legal value basically equals the fair market value or face value—that is, the amount the investment is worth before any debt is subtracted. The legal value is generally the dollar amount attorneys use when discussing investments in trying to settle your divorce. In Sections 4 and 5, below, you will take a closer look at the financial value of your investments.

To find the legal or fair market value of your investments, you often need to do no more than place a phone call.

You may, however, run into problems determining which date to use in valuing the account. As mentioned in Chapter 6, many states value portfolio assets, like houses, as close to the *date of divorce or settlement* as possible, not the *date of separation*. Be sure to ask your attorney on what date assets are valued in your state.

Even if your state legally values assets at the date of separation, you and your spouse can agree to a later date—and you should. Stocks, bonds, mutual funds and other liquid assets, particularly should be valued as of the date you take control of them. Otherwise, if you value assets as of the date of separation, but then don't transfer them until months or years later, you may incur losses because of market forces.

Ultimately, to get through your divorce, you will probably need to find the account balance at different times. But you can begin by completing Column 3 in the investment chart, above. Use the following information to help you calculate or locate the legal value for each investment. Some of this information may be listed on your Net Worth statement from Chapter 13.

*Cash and Cash Equivalents.* For your bank checking and savings accounts, certificates of deposit and bank money market funds, call the bank or look at your statement. For money market mutual funds, call the fund manager or administrator. The value of personal notes will probably be found amongst your personal papers. Be sure to investigate your spouse's possible business or personal loans.

*Stocks and bonds.* For most stocks and bonds, you can call your broker. If you call another brokerage firm, ask for the discount trading department. You can also look at stock tables in the business section of the newspaper. For stocks, look at the price in the column labeled "Close." That's the price the stock was selling at when the market closed the day before. Multiply this number by the number of shares you have to get a ballpark value. Get an estimate of bonds by calling a broker. Banks can give you the value of permanent savings bonds. For mutual funds, look in the business section of the newspaper in the column labeled "NAV," the Net Asset Value.

*Real estate.* For income or rental property, you can use the services of an appraiser. (See Chapter 14, Section C.2.)[3] For Real Estate Investments Trusts (REITs), ask a broker, brokerage firm or check the published values in a newspaper. To find the value of raw land, check the purchase price, and ask a few real estate agents to find out whether land values have gone up or down in your area.

*Insurance.* Call or write the insurance company or broker and ask for the policy's current value and surrender value. If you're not the policyholder, the insurance company may refuse to give you the information. Call your spouse, or have your attorney call your spouse's attorney to get what you need.

*Limited partnerships.* Limited partnerships are difficult to value. A new industry—called secondary markets—however, has sprung up which buys "used" limited partnerships and re-sells them. These markets may assign widely divergent values to your limited partnerships. Ask a stockbroker or financial planner for the names of several secondary market firms. In your survey, ask for the price at which the partnership would be bought and if additional costs would be incurred. There will probably be a big difference between what secondary markets say the partnership is

worth and the amount you will actually realize from it. Generally, these markets buy partnership shares at a deeply discounted price from the amount you originally paid or might receive if held until maturity. Use the amount the firms give you to fill in this chart, or write in the amount of your original purchase price (knowing that the amount is not the true financial value of that partnership).

*Commodities and collectibles.* Gold and silver values are listed, per ounce, in the daily newspaper. Coins, jewelry, art and collectibles must be appraised. Be sure to find the wholesale or re-sale price, not the retail price.

## 4. What Is the After-Tax/After-Sale Value of Each Investment?

Remember: You will need to know tax bases for your investments for your own calculations. But also, the IRS requires that when you transfer property at divorce, you must provide tax basis information to the party who will keep the asset. If you are in the dark about investments, you may need to press matters with your spouse to get the information to figure the tax basis. You cannot make informed decisions about which investments to accept or sell in the settlement unless you know your potential tax liabilities *before* any property transfer takes place.

Knowing the tax basis will help you find the After-Tax/After-Sale Value of your investments. For most investments, you will probably enlist the services of a professional tax advisor, but the following formulas and tips should help you get a ballpark estimate of your taxes and other costs.

After calculating the After-Tax/After-Sale Value of each investment, talk to a broker, financial planner or other investment professional to find out if your investments carry any other additional or hidden costs. If they do, subtract those amounts from the After-Tax/After-Sale Value before entering the values in Column 4 of the Investment chart. Be on the lookout for:

---

[3] Be careful when you have income property appraised. Two identical pieces of property can have different values if the rents charged in one building are not the same as the rents charged in another building. Rent control laws can also affect (bring down) the value of property. A spouse trying to artificially lower the value of rental property may rent units at below-market rates on a month-to-month basis, and then raise rates (and the property's value) after the divorce. If you suspect this is happening, check previous tax returns to see what rents were charged and ask realtors what comparable units in the area are renting for.

*Account charges.* An amount charged for having an account with a broker, brokerage house or firm.

*Redemption fees.* What you pay to redeem or sell the investment.

*Trading fees.* A commission for buying or selling stocks or bonds.

## a. Cash and Cash Equivalents

Because these assets are not technically "sold," there are no taxes due when you liquidate or cash them in. To the extent that you earn interest on checking accounts, savings accounts, money market accounts or certificates of deposit, you must report that interest as income and pay taxes on the interest the year you earned it. To estimate the interest you will earn this year, call your banker. Then simply use the Market (or Face) Value ascertained in Section 3, above, as the After-Tax/After-Sale Value.

## b. Stocks, Bonds and Mutual Funds

Calculating taxes and other costs associated with stocks and bonds will require you to do some tedious paperwork. Old statements will have to be gathered to reconstruct trading activity that has occurred in the past (perhaps, even, over several years). Only you can decide whether it's worth it to do that work yourself or hire someone else for the job. No matter who does it, you will need this information to complete your tax return when you sell stocks or bonds.

### i.    Bonds

See an accountant or tax advisor to analyze the tax aspects of bonds. The Internal Revenue Code has numerous complicated rules depending on *when* the bonds were purchased and the *type* of bonds they are. For instance, some bonds are tax exempt.

Also keep in mind these general rules:

- EE U.S. Savings Bonds. You can pay taxes on the interest generated on EE bonds each year, like most investments, or when you redeem the bonds. You can defer paying taxes on the interest if you roll it forward into an HH bond.

- HH Bonds. These are government bonds which pay you interest semiannually.

- Zero Coupon (or Corporate) Bonds. You must pay taxes on interest earned each year even though you don't receive that interest until the bond matures.

Once you talk to an accountant or other tax advisor about your bonds, enter in Column 4 the After-Tax/After-Sale Value. This value equals the purchase price, plus interest earned on which you've paid taxes, minus any commissions you've paid.

### ii.    Stocks and Mutual Funds

Use the following formula and instructions to find the After-Tax/After-Sale Value for your stocks and mutual funds. To complete the calculations, you will need to know the following:

$ _____    **Purchase Price**

Check your confirmation statement or call your broker. Be sure to include the initial investment plus any subsequent purchases you made.

$ _____    **Dividends Reinvested**

These should be shown on your monthly statement from the brokerage firm. You can also look on tax form 1099, sent annually to you from the company, showing dividends or interest earned each tax year.

$ _____    **Commissions and Transaction Fees**

These are fees paid when you purchase stocks and mutual funds. The amount is on your confirmation statement; if it's not, call your broker. For "load" mutual funds, the commissions, which are automatically charged, are reflected in the Purchase Price. Ask your broker if the fund has a redemption charge or surrender charge, a fee you pay when the fund is sold.

$ _____    **Fair Market Value**

Enter the Legal Value from Section 3, above.

$ _____     **Tax Bracket**

Check the income tax schedule or ask an accountant to verify your current bracket. Or, simply use .28 to represent the 28% federal tax bracket.

To find the After-Tax/After-Sale Value of stocks and mutual funds, use the following formula:

1. Find the Tax Basis by adding the Purchase Price, Reinvested Dividends and Commissions and Transaction Fees (paid at purchase).

2. Find the Adjusted Sales Price by subtracting Commissions and Transaction Fees (to be paid when you sell) from the Fair Market Value.

3. Find the Gain (or Loss) by subtracting the Tax Basis from the Adjusted Sales Price.

4. Find the Taxes Due (or Tax Refund) by multiplying the Gain (or Loss) by your Tax Bracket.

5. Find the After-Tax/After-Sale Value by subtracting the Taxes Due (or adding the Tax Refund) from (or to) the Adjusted Sales Price.

**Example:**

1. Find the Tax Basis by adding the Purchase Price, Reinvested Dividends and Commissions and Transaction Fees (paid at purchase).

| | | |
|---|---|---|
| Purchase Price | | $1,000 |
| Dividends Reinvested | + | 60 |
| Commissions & Transaction Fees | + | 65 |
| Tax Basis | = | $1,125 |

2. Find the Adjusted Sales Price by subtracting Commissions and Transaction Fees (to be paid when you sell) from the Fair Market Value.

| | | |
|---|---|---|
| Fair Market Value | | $2,200 |
| Commissions & Transaction Fees | - | 68 |
| Adjusted Sales Price | = | $2,132 |

3. Find the Gain (or Loss) by subtracting the Tax Basis from the Adjusted Sales Price.

| | | |
|---|---|---|
| Adjusted Sales Price | | $2,152 |
| Tax Basis | - | 1,125 |
| Gain (or Loss) | = | $1,027 |

4. Find the Taxes Due (or Tax Refund) by multiplying the Gain (or Loss) by your Tax Bracket.

| | | |
|---|---|---|
| Gain (or Loss) | | $1,027 |
| Your Tax Bracket | x | 28% |
| Taxes Due (or Tax Refund) | = | $ 288 |

5. Find the After-Tax/After-Sale Value by subtracting the Taxes Due (or adding the Tax Refund) from (or to) the Adjusted Sales Price.

| | | |
|---|---|---|
| Adjusted Sales Price | | $2,152 |
| Taxes Due (or Tax Refund) | - or + | 288 |
| After Tax/After-Sale Value | = | $1,864 |

To apply this formula to your situation, fill in the blanks below. Copy this page to use as a worksheet if you'd like or to calculate the value of additional investments.

1. Find the Tax Basis by adding the Purchase Price, Reinvested Dividends and Commissions and Transaction Fees (paid at purchase).

| | | |
|---|---|---|
| Purchase Price | $ | _____ |
| Dividends Reinvested | + $ | _____ |
| Commissions & Transaction Fees | + $ | _____ |
| Tax Basis | = $ | _____ |

2. Find the Adjusted Sales Price by subtracting Commissions and Transaction Fees (to be paid when you sell) from the Fair Market Value.

| | | |
|---|---|---|
| Fair Market Value | $ | _____ |
| Commissions & Transaction Fees | - $ | _____ |
| Adjusted Sales Price | = $ | _____ |

3. Find the Gain (or Loss) by subtracting the Tax Basis from the Adjusted Sales Price.

| | | |
|---|---|---|
| Adjusted Sales Price | $ | _____ |
| Tax Basis | - $ | _____ |
| Gain (or Loss) | = $ | _____ |

4. Find the Taxes Due (or Tax Refund) by multiplying the Gain (or Loss) by your Tax Bracket.

| | | |
|---|---|---|
| Gain (or Loss) | $ _____ | |
| Your Tax Bracket | x  $ _____ | |
| Taxes Due (or Tax Refund) | =  $ _____ | |

5. Find the After-Tax/After-Sale Value by subtracting the Taxes Due (or adding the Tax Refund) from (or to) the Adjusted Sales Price.

| | |
|---|---|
| Adjusted Sales Price | $ _____ |
| Taxes Due (or Tax Refund) - or + | $ _____ |
| After Tax/After-Sale Value[4] | =  $ _____ |

### iii.  Dividing Stocks, Bonds and Mutual Funds: Consider the Tax Basis

As noted at the beginning of this section, the IRS requires that you give information about the tax basis of an asset to the person receiving it at the time of transfer. It's very important for you to understand the tax basis of an asset. If you don't, you could decide to keep investments that give you a higher tax burden than those your spouse will carry. At the least, you ought to share the tax burden equally.

Once you know the tax basis, you can calculate the taxes on the assets. Knowing the tax liability enables you to make an equal comparison between investment assets and other assets. This knowledge will also influence your tax strategy after the divorce, if you sell the investments.

The IRS allows three different methods to calculate the taxes.[5]

*First In-First Out.* If you've purchased shares of stock over several years at different prices, this method lets you sell the first batch you bought. For example, Mindy and Ryan bought 300 shares of stock at $13 per share in 1991 and another 300 shares of the same stock at $20 per share in 1992. The stock is now worth $25 per share. They decide to sell 300 shares before they divorce. But which 300?

Using the "First In-First Out" option, they would sell the 300 shares bought in 1991. They would have to pay taxes on the gain of $12 per share ($25 Fair Market Value - $13 Purchase Price = $12 Gain). Had they sold the 1992 shares, they'd owe taxes on a gain of only $5 per share ($25 Fair Market Value - $20 Purchase Price = $5 Gain). But by selling the shares that gave them a larger profit, they can split the taxes owed.

As an alternative to selling shares before the divorce, Mindy and Ryan consider splitting the 600 shares in half. It's fair on the surface. If one spouse keeps the 1991 shares and the other keeps the 1992 shares, however, the division becomes unfair because the tax liabilities differ. They could even things up again if they divide other property to cover the tax difference.

*Specific Identification.* This time, assume that Mindy and Ryan bought their 600 shares at various times paying prices ranging from $13 to $20 per share. If they decide to sell 300 shares before their divorce and use the Specific Identification option, they would pinpoint precisely which 300 shares to sell—perhaps 100 bought at $13, another 100 bought at $18 and the final 100 purchased at $20 per share.

If they split the shares as part of their divorce settlement, they should consider the tax liability for the shares bought at each price. If Mindy wants 300 of the "$20 stocks"—leaving Ryan with all of the stocks purchased at $13 and $18 per share—Ryan will pay more in taxes than Mindy will pay.

*Average Basis.* Mindy and Ryan's third option is the Average Basis. As the name implies, this option lets them take an across-the-board average tax basis on all the shares of stock, no matter when purchased and at what price per share. They would simply take the total amount purchased (and dividends reinvested) and divide it by the total number of shares owned.

---

[4] If you incur a loss, entitling you to a Tax Refund, the After-Tax/After Sale Value will be greater than the Fair Market Value, which means you should try to keep this asset in the settlement and sell it immediately after your divorce is final.

[5] In these examples, a Gain is assumed. If you have experienced a Loss on your investments, the investment offers a Tax Refund which is more valuable than the asset's face value, but only if you sell the asset immediately.

Because of the difficult calculations and the fact that supporting documentation regarding reinvestments and commissions is often missing, many divorcing couples use the Average Basis to divide stocks and mutual funds. Before settling on it, however, compare it to the First In-First Out and Specific Identification options. Incorporate the calculations from this section on Tax Basis option with After-Tax/After-Sale Values when you reach Sections 5 and 6, below.

---

### Document Dividends and Reinvestments

When Evelyn divorced in 1984, she got $5,000 worth of shares in a mutual fund as part of her settlement. A savvy investor, she sold the shares in the last week of September 1987 for $10,000. Initially, it appeared Evelyn would pay taxes on the $5,000 gain—$10,000 (sales price) - $5,000 (original price) = $5,000 (gain).

But Evelyn had kept records showing every time she reinvested her dividends. In adding up each reinvestment, she found that she had reinvested total dividends of $2,000 into the fund. This finding lowered her tax liability. Remember—her tax basis is the original purchase price plus reinvested dividends. Her original $5,000 investment, plus the dividend reinvestments of $2,000 totalled $7,000. Her gain, therefore, was $3,000, not $5,000.

---

### c. Real Estate

In valuing real estate investments, you can consider many of the factors raised in Chapter 14, assuming you own a family house. If you haven't read that material, refer to it for basic formulas and an explanation of real estate terms.

Unlike the family home, however, investment properties can be hard to value. The property is affected by the local economy, rental vacancy rates, rental control or stabilization laws, property management and other market forces. Nevertheless, you can estimate the After-Tax/After-Sale Values of your real estate investments by using these guidelines.

$ _____    **REITs (Real estate investment trusts)**

A real estate investment trust company invests in a variety of holdings which can range from apartments and hotels to office buildings and shopping centers. Because most REITs are publicly traded, their value is easily identified. Refer to the stock tables in the newspaper, or ask your broker for current values. To find the After-Tax/After-Sale Value, subtract any commissions or fees from the market (or face) value.

$ _____    **Raw land**

Real estate agents and appraisers normally base the value of raw land on current comparables, that is, the amount at which comparable parcels of land are currently selling. Other factors to consider in determining the real financial value of raw land are:

- how land will be affected by a city's general plans;
- the kind of building permits that have been issued in the area; and
- how land surrounding your land will be used.

  Real estate agents can help you answer these questions. Also, talk with the county building permit office and the city office regarding permits and future land use. Then, use your best "guesstimate" for the value and use that number as the After-Tax/After-Sale Value.

$ _____    **Income or rental properties**

For most income-producing property, use the formula in Chapter 14, Section C.7 to determine the After-Tax/After-Sale Value. With rental property, you must also consider total depreciation taken.

To find After-Tax/After-Sale Value of rental real estate you must:

- Find the Current Market Value.
- Determine the Debt on the Property.
- Document Total Capital Improvements and Depreciation taken.
- Verify your Tax Bracket.
- Calculate the Cost of Sale.

### i.   Find the Current Market Value

Single-family homes are somewhat easier to value than commercial, industrial or multi-family dwellings. For single family residential real estate, you can ask several real estate agents or appraisers for current comparable values. With other types of rental units, however, you will need to consult an appraiser or a broker who specializes in evaluating the type of property you have. See Chapter 14, Section C.2, for information on finding an appraiser.

An appraiser will use one—or a combination—of these three recognized calculations:

*Cost Approach.* The Fair Market Value equals the amount it would cost to replace a building, plus the land's value. This approach usually applies to single-family dwellings.

*Market Data Approach.* Also used with single-family dwellings, this approach compares properties that all provide similar cash flows to determine the Fair Market Value.

*Income Approach.* The Fair Market Value is based on the cash flow a building currently generates plus an estimate of the amount it will generate in the future. Commercial, industrial or multi-family dwellings are often appraised with this approach.

Ask the appraiser which approach is being used to value your property—and why. Just as a retirement plan can be worth different amounts if appraisers use different assumptions, so too can real estate values vary if different approaches are used. Avoid disputes by making sure you and your spouse or your appraisers are basing the Fair Market Value on the same approaches.

When you've found the Fair Market Value on your properties, use the chart below to keep track of the values. Write the address or the description by which you and your spouse will refer to the property in the first column, and the Fair Market Value in the second column. The remaining columns will be addressed in Sections ii and iii which follow.

### Real Estate Values

| Property Address or Description | Fair Market Value | Current Debt on Property | Total Capital Improvements | Total Depreciation Taken |
|---|---|---|---|---|
| Rental house, 323 Third Street, Rye, NY | $ 100,000 | $ 60,000 | $ 20,000 | $ 40,000 |
| Duplex, Sun Court, Surf City, CA | $ 280,000 | $ 100,000 | $ 0 | $ 32,000 |
| | $ | $ | $ | $ |
| | $ | $ | $ | $ |
| | $ | $ | $ | $ |

### ii.   Determine the Debt on the Property

The debt connected to real estate equals what you owe to any lenders (mortgages) plus any liabilities (liens) on the house. All liabilities must be paid before any cash disbursements can be made from the sale of real estate. The mortgage due is sometimes called the "payoff balance."

To find the current debt on the house, talk to a banker or loan officer and check the property's title for any liens you're unaware of. (See Chapter 14, Section C.4.) List the debt in Column 3 of the chart, above.

### iii.   Document Total Capital Improvements or Depreciation

To find total capital improvements made or depreciation taken on rental properties, check your records or previous tax returns, or talk to your accountant or tax advisor. List the totals in the fourth column of the chart.

### iv.   Verify your Tax Bracket

By now, you have probably established your tax bracket, either by checking income tax schedules or talking with your accountant. You will need this information in the upcoming formula.

_____ %   **Tax Bracket**

### v.   Calculate the Cost of Sale

In calculating how much money it takes to actually sell your rental property, you can do a quick ballpark estimate or you can follow the steps to find as precise a figure as possible. To find a precise figure, you'll have to include not only the costs of sale, but also the amount it will take to fix up the property and prepare it for a sale.

To get a ballpark amount for the sales cost, multiply the fair market value by .08. Eight percent is an accepted estimate of what it costs to sell a house.

Obviously, some sales will yield higher or lower costs of sale, but 8% will do.

To obtain a more accurate cost of sale figure, you need to total the following amounts:

$ _____   **Agent's commission**

The amount a real estate agent charges you for selling property. Generally, it averages 6% of the final selling price. This fee can often be negotiated down.

$ _____   **Closing costs**

Included in these costs are escrow fees, recording costs, appraisal fees and miscellaneous expenses which can add up to several thousands of dollars. A lender or real estate agent can help you figure the exact amount.

$ _____   **Attorney's fees**

In a few states, you will need to hire an attorney to help you "close" the sale of real property. If you used an attorney when you bought the property, base your figure on that amount, taking into account the fact that most lawyers raise their fees over time. Otherwise, ask a real estate agent for an estimate.

$ _____   **Fix up costs**

Estimate here the amount of money you will have to spend to prepare the property for sale.

$ _____   **Cost of sale**

To find the After-Tax/After-Sale Value of rental Real Estate, use this formula:

1. Find the Equity by subtracting the Debt from the Fair Market Value.

2. Find the Tax Basis by adding Total Capital Improvements to the Purchase Price and then subtracting Total Depreciation taken.

3. Find the Adjusted Sales Price by subtracting the Cost of Sale from the Fair Market Value.

4. Find the Gain (or Loss) on the potential sale of the property by subtracting the Tax Basis from the

Adjusted Sales Price. If you experienced a Loss, you will have no tax liability and will receive a Tax Refund.

5. Find the Taxes Due (or Tax Refund) by multiplying the Gain (or Loss) by your Tax Bracket.

6. Find the After-Tax/After-Sale Value by subtracting Cost of Sale from the Equity and then subtracting the Taxes Due (or adding the Tax Refund).

**Example:**

1. Find the Equity by subtracting the Debt from the Fair Market Value.

| | |
|---|---|
| Fair Market Value | $100,000 |
| Debt | - 60,000 |
| Equity | = $ 40,000 |

2. Find the Tax Basis by adding Total Capital Improvements to the Purchase Price and then subtracting Total Depreciation taken.

| | |
|---|---|
| Purchase Price | $ 50,000 |
| Total Improvements | + 5,000 |
| | = 45,000 |
| Total Depreciation | - 12,500 |
| Tax Basis | = $ 32,500 |

3. Find the Adjusted Sales Price by subtracting the Cost of Sale from the Fair Market Value.

| | |
|---|---|
| Fair Market Value | = $100,000 |
| Cost of Sale | - 8,000 |
| Adjusted Sales Price | = $ 92,000 |

4. Find the Gain (or Loss) on the potential sale of the property by subtracting the Tax Basis from the Adjusted Sales Price.

| | |
|---|---|
| Adjusted Sales Price | = $ 92,000 |
| Tax Basis | - 32,500 |
| Gain (or Loss) | = $ 59,500 |

5. Find the Taxes Due (or Tax Refund) by multiplying the Gain (or Loss) by your Tax Bracket.

| | | |
|---|---|---|
| Gain (or Loss) | = | $ 59,500 |
| Tax Bracket | x | 28% |
| Taxes Due (or Tax Refund) | = | $ 16,660 |

6. Find the After-Tax/After-Sale Value by subtracting Cost of Sale from the Equity and then subtracting the Taxes Due (or adding the Tax Refund).

| | | |
|---|---|---|
| Equity | = | $ 40,000 |
| Cost of Sale | - | 8,000 |
| Taxes Due (or Tax Refund) | + or - | 16,660 |
| After-Tax/After Sale Value | = | $ 15,400 |

To apply this formula to your situation, fill in the blanks below:

1. Find the Equity by subtracting the Debt from the Fair Market Value.

| | |
|---|---|
| Fair Market Value | $ _____ |
| Debt | - $ _____ |
| Equity | = $ _____ |

2. Find the Tax Basis by adding Total Capital Improvements to the Purchase Price and then subtracting Total Depreciation taken.

| | |
|---|---|
| Purchase Price | $ _____ |
| Total Improvements | + $ _____ |
| | = $ _____ |
| Total Depreciation | - $ _____ |
| Tax Basis | = $ _____ |

3. Find the Adjusted Sales Price by subtracting the Cost of Sale from the Fair Market Value.

| | |
|---|---|
| Fair Market Value | $ _____ |
| Cost of Sale | - $ _____ |
| Adjusted Sales Price | = $ _____ |

4. Find the Gain (or Loss) on the potential sale of the property by subtracting the Tax Basis from the Adjusted Sales Price.

| | | |
|---|---|---|
| *Adjusted Sales Price* | | $ _____ |
| *Tax Basis* | - $ | _____ |
| *Gain (or Loss)* | = $ | _____ |

5. Find the Taxes Due (or Tax Refund) by multiplying the Gain (or Loss) by your Tax Bracket.

| | | |
|---|---|---|
| *Gain (or Loss)* | | $ _____ |
| *Tax Bracket* | x $ | _____ |
| *Taxes due (or Tax Refund)* | = $ | _____ |

6. Find the After-Tax/After-Sale Value by subtracting Cost of Sale from the Equity and then subtracting the Taxes Due (or adding the Tax Refund).

| | | |
|---|---|---|
| *Equity* | | $ _____ |
| *Cost of Sale* | - $ | _____ |
| *Taxes Due (or Tax Refund) + or -* | $ | _____ |
| *After-Tax/After Sale Value* | = $ | _____ |

---

### Who Pays the Rent

If you or your spouse moves from the family home, you can make temporary arrangements for paying the mortgage and other bills. But what if you own rental property and the renters move? Who will pay the mortgage? Or suppose you and your spouse decide to sell the property. Who will pay for repairs. Who will be reimbursed for capital improvements to the property? You and your spouse must settle these questions. If you pay these costs alone, keep good records of every expense so that you will have a chance to get reimbursed as part of the final settlement.

---

## d. Insurance

Buying more insurance than you need or paying too much in insurance premiums are common mistakes. At divorce, you have the opportunity to take a good look at your policies.

Whole life or universal life insurance not only provides income in the event of someone's death, but also has investment benefits. As you pay your premiums a cash reserve builds up. This reserve increases over and above the premiums you pay because you earn interest on your premiums. The reserve also grows because the expenses, such as commissions paid to brokers, decrease over time. Be aware though, that the cash value will have decreased if you borrowed any money against the policy. In other words, the cash value may be zero.

Term policies, on the other hand, provide death benefits only. They have no cash buildup and serve no investment purpose.

Select only those policies you truly need for insurance and/or for your investment objectives. Never surrender an essential policy or let it lapse without having replacement insurance but do get rid of any unnecessary policies. Life insurance companies select policyholders with care. If you have to apply for insurance in the future, you may be denied coverage because of a yet unknown health problem. Keep in mind, however, if you surrender policies with cash value—that is, you turn them in and collect the cash—you will have to pay taxes on interest earned. You figure the interest by subtracting the total premiums paid and the surrender charges from the cash value. The difference is the interest and that amount is what you'd have to report to the IRS as profit.

### i.  Annuities

Annuities are investments offered by insurance companies that are meant to provide income at retirement. Annuities are discussed in Chapter 15.

### ii.  Cash Value Policies

Any policy with a cash value is sometimes referred to as a "cash value policy." If you decide that your policy is not the most cost-effective for you, you can use the cash value to purchase another insurance policy that is more suitable. The benefit of buying another policy versus taking the cash out of your current policy is that you can defer the taxes you would owe on you will have to pay a commission when you purchase the new policy and these costs can initially decrease the cash value of the new policy.

To quickly estimate the After-Tax/After-Sale Value of your insurance (a detailed analysis is not necessary), you need to obtain the following:

$ _____ **Cash Value**

Take a look at the most current policy statement and see if it shows the cash value. If it doesn't, ask your insurance agent.

$ _____ **Surrender Charges**

Again, this information should be on the current policy or with your agent.

$ _____ **Premiums Paid**

Check the most current policy statement or ask your agent.

Use the following formula to find the After-Tax/After-Sale Value on cash value insurance policies.

### Value of Insurance Policy

|  | Example | Your Policy |
|---|---|---|
| Cash Value | $10,000 | |
| Surrender Charges | - 500 | |
| Cash Surrender Value | $9,500 | |
| Cash Surrender Value | $9,500 | |
| Premiums Paid | - 6,000 | |
| Gain (or Loss) | $3,500 | |
| Gain (or Loss) | $3,500 | |
| Tax Bracket | x .28 | |
| Taxes Due | $980 | |
| Cash Surrender Value | $9,500 | |
| Taxes Due | - 980 | |
| After-Tax/After-Sale Value | $8,520 | |

### e. Limited Partnerships

You may have difficulty finding an accurate value for your interests in a limited partnership. It's often difficult to tell how much was invested and how much has been received in tax benefits (write offs). We do not provide detailed information on figuring the After-Tax/After-Sale Value of limited partnerships. Instead, we urge you to consult your accountant to get an understanding of the value of these assets.

Also, call the general partner (and any other limited partners) to find out everything you can about the partnership, especially its economic health and the competence and ethics of the general partner. Be alert to these problems with limited partnerships:

• You may not be able to divide your interest. General partners may not be willing to divide the investment in the limited partnership between you and your spouse. If you can't divide your interest, and neither of you wants to give up your interest to the other in exchange for other property, be sure you and your ex-spouse have a carefully written agreement about how taxes, bookkeeping and dividend checks will be handled after the divorce.

- A limited partnership can generate taxable income which you never receive, called phantom income. Ask the general partner whether phantom income is expected and how much of this income will be taxable.

- Some limited partnerships make requests for additional investments (called capital calls) from the limited partners. Before keeping a limited partnership, check the original investment document, contact your accountant or ask the general partner if you may be liable for additional investments.

- All limited partnerships are risky investments because the general partner has almost complete control over the assets of the partnership. A general partner's decision to sell an asset or allow a foreclosure can create a tax liability for you. The only way to prepare for this eventuality is to deposit money into an account in anticipation of possible taxes.

- Bookkeeping can be difficult. When the partnership sends out its IRS reporting form (K-1) each tax year, it sends only one form to each investor. The partnership usually sends only one dividend check as well. If you and your spouse are unable to divide the partnership interest, then only one of you will receive the form and the check.

Unless you've been lucky, limited partnerships are more trouble to keep than they are usually worth.

## f.  Commodities and Collectibles

Your biggest problem in determining the After-Tax/After-Sale Value of Commodities and Collectibles (like art, special plates or even baseball cards) will be finding a valuation on which you and

your spouse can agree. You may hear any number of conflicting values depending on who is making the appraisal.

To find the After-Tax/After-Sale Value of Commodities or Collectibles, first list the following:

$ _____   **Purchase Price**

Check original receipts, look at old tax returns or consult with a broker.

$ _____   **Selling Price (commodities)**

Ask a broker for current prices. You may be quoted a Bid Price—the amount you can sell it for, or an Ask Price—what you would have to buy it for. Use the Bid Price as the Selling Price.

$ _____   **Wholesale Price (collectibles)**

Ask a dealer, auctioneer or consignment shop to give you an estimate of the wholesale value of your holdings. Many people mistakenly assume that some items, such as diamonds, are worth a great deal because they consider only the retail value. But jewelers buy loose diamonds at wholesale prices and will not pay you more than that price when they buy from you.

$ _____   **Commissions**

Talk with a broker, wholesaler or anyone familiar with the market for your item. With commodities, the commission is the difference between the Bid Price and the Ask Price. With collectibles, the commission is as high as 30% of the sale price.

_____ %   **Tax Bracket**

Consult accountant or previous tax schedules.

To find the After-Tax/After-Sale Value of Commodities or Collectibles, use this formula:

1. Find Tax Basis by adding Commissions (paid at purchase) and Purchase Price.

2. Find Adjusted Sale Price by subtracting Commissions (due at sale) from the Selling Price or Wholesale Value.

3. Find Gain (or Loss) by subtracting the Tax Basis from the Adjusted Sales Price.

4. Find Taxes Due (or Tax Refund) by multiplying the Gain (or Loss) times your Tax Bracket.

5. Find After-Tax/After-Sale Value by subtracting (or adding) Taxes Due (or Tax Refund) from (or to) the Adjusted Sale Price.

**Example:**

1. Find Tax Basis by adding Commissions (paid at purchase) and Purchase Price.

| | |
|---|---|
| *Purchase Price* | $10,000 |
| *Commissions* | + ___1,000___ |
| *Tax Basis* | = $11,000 |

2. Find Adjusted Sale Price by subtracting Commissions (due at sale) from the Selling Price or Wholesale Value.

| | |
|---|---|
| *Selling Price or Wholesale Value* | $ 5,000 |
| *Commissions* | - ___500___ |
| *Adjusted Sales Price* | = $ 4,500 |

3. Find Gain (or Loss) by subtracting the Tax Basis from the Adjusted Sales Price.

| | |
|---|---|
| *Adjusted Sales Price* | $ 4,500 |
| *Tax Basis* | - ___11,000___ |
| *Gain (or Loss)* | = $(6,500) |

4. Find Taxes Due (or Tax Refund) by multiplying the Gain (or Loss) times your Tax Bracket.

| | |
|---|---|
| *Gain (or Loss)* | $(6,500) |
| *Tax Bracket* | x ___28%___ |
| *Taxes Due (or Tax Refund* | = $(1,820) |

5. Find After-Tax/After-Sale Value by subtracting (or adding) Taxes Due (or Tax Refund) from (or to) the Adjusted Sale Price.

| | |
|---|---|
| *Adjusted Sales Price* | $ 4,500 |
| *Taxes Due (or Tax Refund)* | + or - ($1,820) |
| *After-Tax/After-Sale Value* | = $ 6,320 |

To apply this formula to your situation, fill in the blanks below:

1. Find Tax Basis by adding Commissions (paid at purchase) and Purchase Price.

| | | |
|---|---|---|
| *Purchase Price* | | $ _____ |
| *Commissions* | + | $ _____ |
| *Tax Basis* | = | $ _____ |

2. Find Adjusted Sale Price by subtracting Commissions (due at sale) from the Selling Price or Wholesale Value.

| | | |
|---|---|---|
| *Selling Price or Wholesale Value* | | $ _____ |
| *Commissions* | - | $ _____ |
| *Adjusted Sales Price* | = | $ _____ |

3. Find Gain (or Loss) by subtracting the Tax Basis from the Adjusted Sales Price.

| | | |
|---|---|---|
| *Adjusted Sales Price* | | $ _____ |
| *Tax Basis* | - | $ _____ |
| *Gain (or Loss)* | = | $ _____ |

4. Find Taxes Due (or Tax Refund) by multiplying the Gain (or Loss) times your Tax Bracket.

| | | |
|---|---|---|
| *Gain (or Loss)* | | $ _____ |
| *Tax Bracket* | x | _____ |
| *Taxes Due (or Tax Refund)* | = | $ _____ |

5. Find After-Tax/After-Sale Value by subtracting (or adding) Taxes Due (or Tax Refund) from (or to) the Adjusted Sale Price.

| | | |
|---|---|---|
| *Adjusted Sales Price* | | $ _____ |
| *Taxes Due (or Tax Refund)* | + or - | $ _____ |
| *After-Tax/After-Sale Value* | = | $ _____ |

---

### Negative Arithmetic

Calculating the After-Tax/After-Sale Value on an asset you're holding at a loss can be confusing. You first must multiply the amount of the Loss by your Tax Bracket to find your Tax Refund. This amount is *added* to the Adjusted Sales Price to give the After-Tax/After-Sale Value. We designate Losses and Tax Refunds by putting parentheses ( ) around the numbers. Be sure to read the formula carefully if you're confused.

---

## 5. Which Assets Should You Keep?

Once you know the After-Tax/After-Sale Value of investments you have a starting point for negotiating with your spouse. The values are useful whether you want to sell your assets to the person you're divorcing, buy them for yourself or divide them between you.

The decision to keep an investment depends on many factors including your age, risk tolerance, income needs and investment experience. Here are two different approaches toward making the decision:

*Investment Policy.* A financial planning tool used by professionals when working with investors. It enables you to make investment decisions on an analytical level, and questions your need or desire for certain assets.

*Decision Tree.* provides you with a matrix of questions to follow any time you need to make financial decisions about investments.

### a. Investment Policy

Policies guide us toward the future and help keep us on track when pressing questions demand immediate attention. When employees know a company's vacation policy, they can plan their work around it. Parents of teenagers know the value of having a curfew policy when a child asks to go out with friends and stay out late.

It's important that you, too, develop policies for your financial life, especially when the emotions of divorce can cloud your judgment or sway your decisions. Developing a policy about what you will or won't invest in helps you shape your future by giving guidance in the present.

Your investment policy should suit your personal needs and guide you when market conditions, stockbrokers or others press you to make investment decisions. It also shapes your choices so your money can generate the kind of returns you want. It serves as a map for telling you which way to go, which detours to avoid and the length of time it will take to reach your destination. But to draw that map, you must know where you're going—your goals; the amount of risk you can afford—the detours; and what kind of performance you expect from your investments and the economy—the length of time it will take to reach your destination.

### i. Questions to Help Shape Your Investment Policy

Use these questions to define your investment policy.

*Income, Growth and Security Needs.* From what sources are you receiving income? What risks could cause that income to decrease or cease altogether? How much cash do you need on hand in the event that your income ceases?

Do you have adequate emergency reserves—that is, at least 3-6 months worth of cost-of-living expenses put aside?

What's more important to you—to have your assets grow or to conserve your principal?

What do you expect your tax bracket to be during the current year and next year? Have you updated your investments to bring them in line with your current tax situation?

Do you feel that the economy will experience inflation, deflation or moderate growth over the short and long term? What's your opinion on interest rates—will they increase, decrease or remain the same over the short and long term? Are your investment decisions consistent with your views?

*Risk Tolerance.* Are you a "buy and hold," "sell when the market is down" or "buy more when the market is down" type of investor?

How much are you willing to lose? Can you live with fluctuations in the value of your investments? What types of investments do you want to avoid?

*Management of Investments.* Do you have investment experience? Are you comfortable working with investment advisors and financial planners? Do you have the time to monitor and manage your investments and assets?

### ii.   Identify Your Goals

Take a moment to consider your major goals for the future. (You may have listed these in Chapter 12.) Try, also, to estimate what it could cost you to reach those goals. Think about this question for each of the time spans listed below.

## Your Investment Policy

| One Year |
| --- |
| Example:   Buy new car for $20,000—$8,000 from cash account; $12,000 to be financed. |
| 1. |
| 2. |
| 3. |
| 4. |
| 5. |
| 6. |

| Five Years |
| --- |
| Example:   Sell current home, buy another. Approximate cost—$200,000. Build short-term bond fund to $25,000. |
| 1. |
| 2. |
| 3. |
| 4. |
| 5. |
| 6. |

| Retirement Years |
| --- |
| Example:   Retire in 18 years. Will need $3,000/month income for living expenses in today's dollars. Invest $300 into XYZ mutual fund and $300 into ABC every other month. |
| 1. |
| 2. |
| 3. |
| 4. |
| 5. |

## b. Decision Tree

To simplify your investment choices, you can answer one question at a time on the decision tree. The answer to each question will then determine which direction you will take next. Like a cat climbing a tree, once you choose a certain limb, you will continue in that direction, moving out along certain branches until you can go no more or you have to turn around and start over. (Unlike a wayward cat, however, the fire department can't rescue you.)

Using the information you have gathered up to this point, answer two questions about each investment:

*1. Has this investment performed well?*

If Yes, go to Question 2.

If No, consider these options:

___ Sell the asset before the divorce so you and your soon-to-be ex-spouse share costs of sale, taxes and other expenses.

___ Take the asset for yourself, but only if it provides you with the benefit of a tax loss. That is, it can offset a gain you may have earned on another asset. You should consult a tax expert to determine your need to take any losses.

___ Offer to sell the asset to your spouse in the divorce settlement.

*2. Is this investment appropriate for me—is it providing the income, growth, liquidity or security I need?*

If Yes, how long do you plan to keep it?

___ Long Term—buy out your spouse's interest and keep this investment.

___ Short Term—sell before your divorce becomes final, sharing the proceeds, taxes and other costs with your spouse.

If No, consider these options:

___ Sell before your divorce if final, sharing the proceeds, taxes and other costs with your spouse.

___ Buy out your spouse and sell immediately to take advantage of tax losses.

___ Let your spouse buy out your share or interest in the investment.

## 6. How Will You and Your Spouse Divide the Investments?

You are now ready to prepare your position for negotiating over investment assets. Pull out the Investment Chart you completed in this chapter and use it to list which assets you want to keep, which could be transferred to your spouse, and which should be sold together before finalizing the divorce. If you have cash value life insurance or rental property, be sure to read the appropriate sections, below.

## a. Special Problems With Cash Value Life Insurance

The After-Tax/After-Sale value of the policy isn't the only consideration with cash value life insurance. Be sure to consider the following before selecting this asset in your divorce.

• What is the quality of the insurance company? You may be able to evaluate the quality of an insurance company by checking its Standard and Poors, Moody and A.M. Best ratings, but these ratings are no guarantees. Before it folded in 1990, Executive Life received an A+ rating from Best, considered the top rating company.

- What interest rate are you receiving on the premiums accruing as your cash value? Would alternate—yet safe—investments, such as corporate bonds, municipal bonds or federal government bonds yield you more?

- Are there any loans outstanding on the policy? If so, the amount paid at death will be reduced by the outstanding loan. Before taking this asset at divorce, be sure the loans are paid back so the full amount is paid, or recognize that the death benefits will be reduced.

## b. Special Problems With Rental Property

The After-Tax/After-Sale value of the property isn't the only consideration with rental property. Be sure to ask yourself the following questions before selecting this asset in your divorce.

- Where is the property located? Is it on a busy street? On the beach?

- What is the quality of the neighborhood? Is it improving or deteriorating?

- How will your property be affected by changes in the local economy?

- Are newer and nicer buildings directly competing for your renters?

- Are your rents above or below market?

- What does it cost to maintain and manage the property? Is your cash flow positive or negative? Can you afford the property when renters vacate and the income is down?

- What are the tax incentives or disincentives to keeping the property?

- What would it cost to improve the property?

- How much income can you expect the property to generate?

- When might you sell? Can you determine your rate of return over that time?

- What is the vacancy rate?

- What kind of loan do you have—fixed or adjustable rate? If it's adjustable and interest rates rise, can you still afford it?

Your answers will help you to reach one of three conclusions:

1. The property has strong potential (the location is great, there's little rental competition, operating costs and vacancy rates are low) to appreciate faster than other investments I could make using the same amount of money.

   *It would be a good asset to keep.*

2. The property has some potential, but it's uncertain; and other investments using the same amount of money may outperform this one.

   *We should probably sell now and split the proceeds, or my spouse can take it.*

3. This property has little potential (operating costs are high, the location is bad and vacancy rates are high) and other investments have a higher probability of meeting my needs.

   *We should probably sell now and split the proceeds, or my spouse can take it.*

 **Decision Time . . .**
Now review all your properties—rental real estate, limited partnerships and others—and write your decisions below.

## Review Your Properties

| Name or Description of Investment | I Keep | Spouse Keeps | Sell & Split Proceeds |
|---|---|---|---|
| 1. | | | |
| 2. | | | |
| 3. | | | |
| 4. | | | |
| 5. | | | |
| 6. | | | |
| 7. | | | |
| 8. | | | |
| 9. | | | |
| 10. | | | |
| 11. | | | |
| 12. | | | |
| 13. | | | |
| 14. | | | |
| 15. | | | |

## 7.  How Do You Feel About Your Decision?

Use this space to write out your feelings—pro or con—about your decisions, or use the statements, below, to examine your emotions. Your goal is to outline the needs and logic that went into your decision making so that in the future, you can refer to this section to recall why you acted as you did in your divorce. Having this record can help you avoid unnecessary bitterness, regrets and misunderstanding.

*The real financial value of my portfolio is more important to me than fighting with my spouse. I am satisfied that I have made the best choices.*

*I worked hard to get these investments and put a lot of work into making the most of our money. I resent having to let go of them now.*

*My spouse doesn't know the first thing about investments. He/She is going to blow it all and that makes me angry.*

*I feel. . .*

# 17

# Business Assets: What Are They Worth?

*When business partners go their separate ways, one person usually buys out the other's interest in the enterprise. If neither can afford it—or has any desire to continue the business—they close it down and split the assets. Similarly in divorce, when the marital property includes a business, one spouse typically buys out the other's share or trades that share for assets of equal value.*

Businesses are bought and sold every day with no more fanfare than the purchase of a car—unless the partners start fighting. Divorcing spouses, too, can transfer business interests smoothly—or they can use the business as an excuse for a bitter battle.

Most divorce fights over a business revolve around one issue—the financial value. Is a small printing company worth a small fortune? What's the value of a doctor's practice? Who decides?

## A. Valuing Businesses at Divorce— the Basic Concept

The job of placing a dollar value on a business at divorce is best done by a business appraiser. An appraiser might total the value of equipment, study the cash flow, compare the company to similar ones on the market or use any number of other techniques to determine the worth of the business. The goal is to establish a fair market value for the enterprise—that is, the amount the business would bring in if it was sold on the open market.

Business appraisers' valuations are rarely rejected—reputable business appraisers usually come up with estimates that are relatively close to each other, or at least in the same ballpark. Occasionally, however, appraisers differ substantially. For example, if the appraiser for one spouse says a business is worth $300,000 and the appraiser hired by the other spouse says it's worthless, there's obviously a problem. If neither side will move from his or her appraiser's value—and mediation won't work—the question will have to be resolved in court.

A trial will highlight "dueling experts," as each appraiser testifies as to how he or she arrived at the business' value. Not only will this be expensive, but no one is likely to be satisfied with the outcome, because judges usually know little about how to value a business. When a judge is left to decide what to do with the business—and appraisers present conflicting values—the judge may simply split the difference, perhaps turning a $300,000 business into one worth half that amount with the stroke of a pen. Or, a judge may simply lose patience with extreme claims and order the parties back to the negotiating table.

As with all issues facing divorcing couples, they are usually better off making their own decisions, rather than letting the court decide the fate of their assets.

This chapter outlines how you can protect your business or your marital interest in one. It shows you how to find an appraiser who can value the business, understand common valuation methods and avoid costly mistakes.

## B. Steps to a Settlement

 To find the value of a business and divide it with your spouse, answer these questions:

1. Which businesses are at stake?

2. How does your state value businesses?

3. Who will determine the value of the businesses?

4. How are businesses appraised?

5. How will you and your spouse divide the businesses?

6. How do you feel about this decision?

## 1. Which Businesses Are at Stake?

Are you—or are you married to—a plumber, painter or printer? Does your mate practice law or sell insurance? Do you? These and other professions are pursued by both sole proprietors and ambitious entrepreneurs with a hundred employees.

In the chart that follows, list—in the first column—the name or a description of all businesses in which you or your spouse have any ownership. Include even those businesses owned before you were married. As you will find when you read Section B, in some states a non-owner can develop some ownership interest in a pre-marital business. After reading Section B, enter the owner—and ownership percentages of jointly owned businesses—in the second column. You can fill in column 3 after reading Section E.

| Business Name or Description | Who Owns It? H—Husband W—Wife J—Joint (if joint, list ownership percentages) | Appraised Value |
|---|---|---|
| | | |
| | | |
| | | |
| | | |
| | | |
| | | |

## 2. How Does Your State Value Businesses?

The key to appraising a business during divorce is to understand the laws that apply to valuing this asset in your state. For example, what date does your state use in setting the value? If you and your spouse separated two years ago when your veterinarian practice was worth $100,000—but is now worth $175,000—is your spouse entitled to a share of the increase? You also need to know how your state defines a jointly owned business.

Here are some questions to ask an attorney or research at your local law library.

*Is our business legally considered mine, my spouse's or both of ours?*

Chapter 13 explains how to determine separate and marital property in your state. If you haven't yet read that chapter, do so now.

Usually, the value of a business is divided by the court to reflect the portion that belongs to each spouse. How much of a business will be considered marital property often depends on whose money went into the business and the amount of time spent by each spouse in making the business grow. When the business has been run or managed by one spouse only, that spouse will most likely be awarded the business, and the other spouse will be given a share of other marital property.

*What date is used to calculate the value of a business?*

A business worth a great deal today may have been worth very little yesterday—or may be worthless tomorrow. In some states, businesses are valued at the date of separation. Other places use the value closest to the settlement date. Market forces, the state of the economy and the efforts of the spouse working in the business can cause major fluctuations in the business's value. If your state values the business at a date which diminishes your share, you can try to negotiate for another asset to offset the loss.

*Is "good will" considered part of the value of the business?*

Any established business has a name and reputation which, by themselves, can be expected to generate a certain amount of income in the future. This is called good will. The good will of a business depends on a number of factors including its name recognition, length of existence and revenues. IBM, for example, has significant good will based on name recognition alone.

Most states require that the business good will be included as part of the overall appraisal of the business. Be sure to find out what happens in your state.

*Can I obtain copies of business records in my spouse's control?*

Settlement negotiations will go smoothly if both spouses cooperate and exchange honest information. If you can't get information from your spouse on a business in his or her control, however, you may need to go through legal discovery procedures to get what you need. (See Chapter 13.)

---

### Professional Degrees as Business Assets

Some spouses support their mates financially through professional, graduate or trade school. When they divorce, alimony is not necessarily awarded to the spouse who supported the couple. Yet, those spouses may have made sacrifices (such as delaying their own education) in order to support their mates. Where the spouse who supported the couple earns less than the other at divorce, courts have tried a number of solutions to even out the income imbalance: Michigan views a professional degree as marital property to be valued and divided. New York values and divides the license, but not the degree. Arkansas and Missouri will value and divide degrees when no other way exists to equally divide the property.

Many other states, such as California and Pennsylvania, reimburse the supporting spouse for the costs contributed to the education or support while the student was in school. Some states use the degreed spouse's ability to earn in setting alimony. Others states, when setting alimony, look at the post-graduation living standard, not the standard of living during the student days. A few states combine these methods.

---

## 3.   Who Will Determine the Value of the Businesses?

Most commonly, the valuation of the business is left to appraisers, but you and your spouse will still need to decide how you will work with these professionals. If you can't agree on the business value or your relationship with the appraiser(s), you may wind up fighting in court.

### a.  Valuing a Business

There are four possible ways to value a business at divorce.

- Do it yourself

- Use one appraiser
- Use separate appraisers
- Leave it to a judge.

You might think that the accountant who works for the company can give a fair value for the business. That is not always a wise course. The accountant may not consider the larger market factors that affect business values, and may lean toward one spouse or the other rather than remain neutral.

### i. Do It Yourself

If you and your spouse are on good terms, you might assign a mutually acceptable value to the business. If the business was recently appraised for purposes of getting a loan or paying taxes, you could use that amount. Or you could compare the business to similar ones which have recently sold in your community. Other tips are in Section D, below. The do-it-yourself option will work, however, only if the spouses are in equal positions regarding their personal stake in the business and their sophistication about the transaction.

### ii. Use One Appraiser

If you and your spouse can agree on and work with one good appraiser, by all means use this approach. The two of you should sit down with the appraiser and have him or her review the evaluation step by step, showing you how calculations were made. This option is probably the least costly, but make sure that the appraiser can give you a fair, impartial and realistic evaluation. This method will not work if the appraiser favors one party's interest over the other.

### iii. Use Separate Appraisers

In contested cases, each spouse hires a business appraiser and the two appraisers value the business separately. Especially if you and your spouse are not on good terms, your attorney might recommend that you hire an appraiser to protect your interests or to testify in court should it later become necessary. If

the two appraisals are only a few thousand dollars apart, you and your spouse (or your attorneys) might propose splitting the difference and moving the settlement forward.

### iv. Leave It to the Judge

In the worst case, you each hire a business appraiser, but the values they assign to the business are vastly different. Compromise becomes impossible, and you decide to let the judge set the value of your business. You can spend a great deal of money preparing for the trial where your appraiser gives testimony and also tries to discredit the method used by your spouse's attorney.

### b. Finding and Working With a Business Appraiser

Certain business accountants qualify as CBAs, Certified Business Appraisers. If you have never worked with an appraiser before, you will want to find one who has the CBA designation. To earn this designation, appraisers must pass a rigorous written exam and submit appraisals for review by a committee of experienced peers.

### i. Finding an Appraiser

The best way to find a business appraiser is to get a referral from an owner of a similar business or get a

*Contact business appraisal organizations.* Consider contacting one of the following professional organizations to find the names of appraisers in your area. Before hiring one, ask for references—names of clients—and then call those people to see if they were satisfied.

- American Society of Appraisers, 2777 So. Colorado Blvd., Suite 200, Denver, CO 80222; 303-758-6148
- Institute of Business Appraisers, P.O. Box 1447, Boynton Beach, FL 33425; 407-732-3202

*Check public records.* Your ideal appraiser is someone who is experienced with your type of business and is known and trusted locally. When a business is sold, it is usually a matter of public record, so you can contact your state's Office of the Secretary of State where business sales are registered. Check for the names of appraisers who have worked on sales in your area. Study the records and talk to the buyers or sellers (also listed in the public records) to find out about the performance of appraisers.

### ii.  Working With an Appraiser

Business appraisers must do more than compare one business with another. Most business appraisers, therefore, charge an hourly fee, somewhere between $100 to $200 per hour for their services. A few charge a flat fee. Before hiring any appraiser, be sure you know the fee and what the appraisal will include.

An appraisal for a small business could take 20 to 30 hours and cost from $2,000 to $6,000. Larger businesses might cost $20,000 for a complete appraisal. If you can't agree on a value and must go to court, the appraiser will charge you an hourly—or possibly daily—fee to testify.

With these kinds of charges, it's obvious why accepting the opinion of a reputable appraiser is less costly than fighting over the business's value.

---

**Do You Go High or Low?**

Appraisers often hear that question from attorneys or potential clients. These callers want to know if the appraiser will give a high (or low) value to make it look as though the business is worth more (or less) than it actually is. Honest appraisers will tell you that a business cannot be valued over the phone and that they work to produce an accurate valuation—not one that is skewed high or low. Because outlandish appraisals may only serve to inflate divorce expenses—and may be disregarded in court—go with a competent and impartial appraiser.

---

## 4.  How Are Businesses Appraised?

In valuing a business, the best appraisers make three or four different calculations and then cross check them against each other to insure accuracy.

### a.  Adjusted Book Value

The appraiser's first step is to obtain the business's adjusted book value. The adjusted book value, a term used more by accountants than appraisers, represents the sum of the assets—including their depreciation less the liabilities—including the amortization of their payback.

To get the adjusted book value, the appraiser updates the company's financial records to reflect the current market value of the fixed assets. The appraiser reviews five years of tax returns, income statements and balance sheets. The appraiser then makes other adjustments to the income statements to arrive at the true adjusted earnings for that particular business.

Then, the appraiser will subtract a fair owner's salary from the true adjusted earnings, because that spouse is entitled to keep his or her income separate from the business assets. If the business is paying for other items or perquisites (for instance, a car or pair of season tickets), the cost of those items is added back to the true adjusted earnings of the business.

## b. Comparable Sales

When you look in the classified ads in the Sunday paper, you can usually get a good idea about the price of houses, used cars, furniture or anything else you're interested in buying. If you look under "Businesses For Sale," you can also see the selling price of local outfits. A business appraiser can get a rough idea of the value of your business by comparing it to the prices quoted in these ads. This value in only good for an estimate, however, because the listed price is the asking price—not what the business sells for.

## c. Industry Market Method

This method is sometimes referred to as the Comparable Values approach. An appraiser surveys similar businesses and discusses the industry with other appraisers to establish a basis for buying or selling a particular company. This method relies on industry rules, which are useful for ballpark estimates only. Industry rules suggest the following "Quick Values For Businesses."[1]

*Coffee shop.* Three to six times the monthly average sales. Hours open for business is a key consideration.

*Deli or sandwich shop.* Four to nine times the monthly average sales. Rent and hours open for business are a key consideration.

*Retail businesses.* One to two times yearly true earnings. Inventory is a key consideration.

*Service businesses.* One to two times yearly true earnings. Business specialization is a key.

Professional practices can also be evaluated using industry market methods. For example, a lawyer's

practice might be valued at the amount it would take to buy in as a partner in the firm. The worth of a doctor's practice could be estimated according to the number of patients she has, how long they have been patients and the longevity of staff members. A share of an insurance agency is the amount it would cost for an insurance company to buy back an agency from an individual.

## d. Capitalization of Excess Earnings

By capitalizing the excess earnings, the appraiser arrives at the good will or "blue sky" value of the business. In many cases, this value may exceed the actual net worth of the business. This appraisal method essentially involves an analysis of Internal Revenue Code §§ 59-60 and 68-609.

Once the business appraiser has completed the analysis using any or all of the above four methods, he or she will send you an appraisal report. The report suggests the fair market value of the business and explains the methods used to arrive at the value. Review the report carefully; don't be shy about asking the appraiser questions if there is information you don't understand. Then enter the amount of the appraisal in the chart in Section A.

---

 **Be Aware of Hidden Business Assets**

Having a business may give one spouse the opportunity to hide assets. If you suspect your spouse is hiding assets by siphoning off cash, undercounting accounts receivable or keeping two sets of books, you will probably need a forensic accountant—and your attorney to conduct legal discovery. (See Chapter 13.). This specialized accountant will want to analyze sales, cash flow and inventory. Your lawyer may want to talk to disgruntled former employees.

---

[1] This list is provided courtesy of Gary L. Allen, a Certified Business Appraiser in San Ramon, California.

## 5. How Will You and Your Spouse Divide the Businesses?

A decade or two ago, business appraisers used to joke that the value of the business in a divorce was exactly equal to the amount of equity in the house. That was so the business owner, presumably the husband, would get to keep his business, while the wife would keep the house.

Times have changed, of course. In divorces today, the wife could just as easily be the business owner, and neither spouse may want the house.

As with other major assets in divorce, one spouse's interest in a business can be kept, sold, or exchanged for another property. Or, the entire business could be sold and the proceeds divided between the two spouses according to their marital interests in the property. Because the spouse who works in the business may have no desire to sell it, that person will probably have to offset this asset by allowing the other spouse to have marital property of equal value.

### ⏰ Decision Time . . .

You may write your decision on dividing the business in the space below. Check one of the options listed or devise your own strategy.

\_\_\_   Buy out my spouse's share

\_\_\_   Sell my share to my spouse

\_\_\_   Own and run the business jointly with my spouse

\_\_\_   Sell the business and divide the proceeds

\_\_\_   Other:

_____

_____

_____

_____

_____

 **Does the owner have adequate insurance coverage?**

If you are selling your share to your spouse—who will also be paying alimony or child support—what will happen if the business owner becomes too disabled to work or dies? Your best protection is to be sure that person has disability coverage and life insurance.

---

### Using an Equalization Payment To Buy Out a Spouse

In the economics of divorce, one partner sometimes has to borrow money to buy out the other's share of a business. Sam, the owner of a small print shop, borrowed money to give his wife an equalization payment in their settlement. She also received a high alimony award. When the equipment in his shop broke down, Sam couldn't borrow money to make the repairs because he had exhausted his credit for the equalization payment. Unable to repair his machinery or expand the business, Sam had to close shop and was out of work for almost a year. Because of the change in circumstances, the court agreed to reduce the amount of alimony he had to pay. When he finally went back to work, his salary was much lower than his previous income.

The lesson is simple: When you divorce, analyze the long-term effects of the settlement on the business. A business is not a money machine from which you can draw unlimited cash. Sam lost his business and his ex-wife lost the monthly income she was counting on.

---

## 6. How Do You Feel About This Decision?

A business you have worked hard to build or support can tap into your feelings of pride or need for security. The idea of losing a business in a divorce is no less painful than the thought of letting go of a home. While you could replace a house, a business may be much harder to rebuild. If you are going to lose your share of a business, you can expect a period of grieving. Avoiding it will only lead to displaced anger and other upheavals. For an interim period, you may need to channel your entrepreneurial—or financial investment—energy into other projects.

While you work to secure your financial future in the overall settlement, do not neglect your emotional health. Use this step to come to terms with your decisions on the business assets. The following statements may help trigger your thoughts on this issue.

*We reached a fair decision; it's not going to change my life that much.*

*When I think of losing my interest in the business it makes me feel—*

angry...

relieved...

*I'm actually glad to be out from under all of the responsibility of the business.*

*It will be better to run the business alone instead of having to deal with my ex every time I want to make a decision.*

*It's going to be costly now, but in the long run I'll be happier because of this decision.*

# 18

## How Will We Divide Debts?

*When you divorce, you not only divide property, but debts as well. It's crucial that you and your spouse reach an agreement about how debts will be handled.*

For instance, if you are the one who is willing to assume a debt, you might ask for something in return. You may be able to make tradeoffs—perhaps getting the car or the piano in exchange for paying off credit card debts.

Before negotiating your agreement, you'll want to know who is responsible for paying your various debts in your state. You also need to be aware of the possibility that your spouse will declare bankruptcy, default or fail to live up to your agreement in some other way. Use this chapter to investigate your legal and financial position on debts and divorce.

## A. Your Debts and the Law

You each are responsible for paying your individual debts incurred before you were married and after your divorce is final. In general, you are both responsible for paying any debts that you ran up during the marriage. Debts created during separation, however, aren't as clear. Usually, debts incurred after the separation date but before the divorce is final are the responsibility of the spouse who incurred them and must be paid by that person.[1]

---

[1] One exception is for "family necessities." For example, if, during the period of separation, one spouse incurs a debt for food, clothing, shelter, medical care or for the children, the other spouse is probably obligated to pay that bill if the spouse incurring the debt cannot.

This general rule, however, does not affect your relationship with your creditors. If your partner defaults or simply refuses to pay, the creditors no doubt will come after you for payment. And because you were still married when the debts were incurred, the creditor will assert a right to collect from you. Your only remedy may be to try to get your ex-spouse to reimburse you.

---

**Back Taxes**

Back taxes may be a part of your marital debts. But the IRS has special rules that apply to back taxes. Before allocating your tax bill as part of dividing the debts, read Chapter 11, Section B.

---

A summary of spousal debt laws is listed below. Before relying on this information, you may want to check statutes at a local law library for any amendments. (See Appendix, *Resources Beyond this Book*, for help on doing legal research.) (Note: Torts, or "civil wrongs," include negligence (such as car accidents), assault, battery, libel, slander and infliction of emotional distress.)

| State | Code Section | Spousal Obligations |
|---|---|---|
| Alabama | Const. Art. X § 209 | Wife's separate property—owned before marriage or received during marriage as gift or inheritance—cannot be taken to pay for husband's debts. |
| Alaska | 25.15.010 | Separate property of one spouse cannot be taken to pay for the other's debts. |
|  | 25.15.050 | Neither spouse is responsible for paying the other spouse's separate debts incurred before or during marriage. |
| Arizona | 25-215 | Separate property of one spouse cannot be taken to pay for the other's separate debts. |
|  |  | The portion of a spouse's community property that would have been separate property if that spouse were unmarried can be taken to pay for that spouse's debts incurred before marriage. |
|  |  | Community property can be taken to pay for debts incurred outside the state during marriage if those debts would have been community debts had they been incurred in the state. |
|  |  | Community debts are to be paid first by community property, then by the separate property of the spouse incurring the debt. |
| Arkansas | 9-11-506 | Neither spouse is responsible for paying the other's debts incurred before marriage. |
|  | 9-11-507 | Separate property of one spouse cannot be taken to pay for the other's premarital debts. |
|  | 9-11-508 | Separate contracts entered into by a spouse where the creditor looks for payment only from that spouse's separate property does not bind the other spouse or the other spouse's property. |
| California | CC 5120.110 | Community property can be taken to pay for all debts incurred before or during marriage by either spouse. |
|  |  | Earnings of one spouse earned during marriage cannot be taken to pay for the other spouse's debts incurred before marriage if those earnings are kept in a separate bank account to which the debtor spouse has no access, and those earnings are not mixed with other community property. |
|  | CC 5120.130 | A spouse's separate property can be taken to pay for that spouse's separate debts incurred before or during marriage. |
|  |  | A spouse's separate property cannot be taken to pay for the other's debts incurred before or during marriage. |
|  | CC 5120.140 | A spouse is responsible for paying the other spouse's debts incurred during marriage for necessaries while they are living either together or apart. |
|  | CC 5120.160 | After divorce, a spouse's separate property can be taken to pay for all of that spouse's separate debts incurred before or during marriage, even if the other spouse agreed to pay that debt as part of the divorce settlement. |
|  |  | After divorce, a spouse's separate property cannot be taken to pay for any of the other spouse's separate debts incurred before or during marriage, unless that spouse agreed to pay that debt as part of the divorce settlement. |
| Colorado | 16-6-110 | Both spouses are responsible for paying family expenses and children's education. |

| State | Code Section | Spousal Obligations |
|-------|--------------|---------------------|
| Connecticut | 46b-36 | Husband's property cannot be taken to pay for wife's debts incurred before or during marriage. |
| | 46b-37 | If a spouse makes a purchase in own name, it's assumed to be a separate debt. |
| | | Each spouse is responsible for supporting the family—specifically to pay a doctor, dentist or hospital; to pay rent; to pay for an item used for support or that benefits both spouses; and to pay for the wife's clothes in the event her husband abandons her. |
| | | Spouse is not responsible for paying other's separate debts incurred during separation if paying reasonable support. |
| Delaware | 13 § 314 | Wife is responsible for paying her debts incurred before or during marriage out of her separate property. |
| District of Columbia | 30-201 | Spouse's property cannot be taken to pay for the other's debts, except that both spouses are responsible for paying debts for necessaries for them or their dependant children. |
| Florida | 708.05 | Husband is not responsible for paying wife's debts incurred before marriage. |
| Georgia | 19-6-13 | Both spouses are responsible for paying shelter, food and necessaries for their children. |
| Hawaii | 510-8 | Separate property of spouse can be taken to pay for that spouse's debts. |
| | | Marital property can be taken to pay for wife's separate debts, husband's separate debts or marital debts. Marital property should be used before separate property to pay marital debts. |
| | | Husband and wife's earnings and separate property can be taken to pay for their own debts incurred before marriage. Separate property should be used to pay those debts before marital property is used. |
| | | Husband and wife are obligated to support each other and the family, and to pay for all debts for necessaries during marriage. Marital property should be used to pay those debts before separate property is used. |
| Idaho | 32-910 | Husband's separate property cannot be taken to pay for wife's debts incurred before marriage. |
| | 32-911 | Wife's separate property cannot be taken to pay for any of husband's debts, but can be taken to pay for her debts incurred before or during marriage. |
| Illinois | Ch. 40 ¶ 1005 | Neither spouse is responsible for paying the other's separate debts incurred before or during marriage. |
| | | Wages, property, and rents and profits of a spouse's property, cannot be taken to pay for other's separate debts. |
| | Ch. 121 1/2 ¶ 262H | Creditor cannot try to collect a debt or loan from a spouse unless that spouse cosigned for the debt or loan. |
| Indiana | 31-7-10-3 | Wife is responsible for paying all torts committed by her. |
| | 31-7-10-4 | Husband is not responsible for paying acts committed by wife. |
| Iowa | 597.19 | Spouse is not responsible for paying torts committed by the other. |

| State | Code Section | Spousal Obligations |
|-------|-------------|---------------------|
| Kansas | 23-201 | Spouse's separate property cannot be taken to pay for other spouse's debts. |
| Kentucky | 404.010 | During marriage, wife owns all her property separately; that property cannot be taken to pay for husband's debts. |
| | | Wife's property can be taken to pay her debts incurred before or during marriage. |
| | 404.040 | If wife gives property to husband, or husband receives property from wife by virtue of the marriage, husband is responsible for paying wife's debts incurred before or during marriage to the value of property received. |
| | | Husband is responsible for paying wife's necessaries bought during marriage. |
| Louisiana | 2345 | Separate or community debt incurred during marriage may be paid out of community property or separate property of the spouse who incurred the debt. If community property is used to pay separate debt, non-debtor spouse may ask a court to be reimbursed. |
| | 2360 | Debt incurred by either spouse during marriage for the interest of both or the other is a community debt. |
| | 2363 | Debt incurred before marriage or after divorce, or during marriage but for only one spouse's benefit, is that spouse's separate debt. |
| Maine | 19-164 | Husband is not responsible for paying wife's debts incurred before marriage, incurred in only her name or her torts in which he took no part. |
| Maryland | FL 4-301 | Neither spouse is responsible for paying the other's debts incurred before marriage. |
| | | Spouse is responsible for paying all his or her debts incurred before marriage. |
| | | Husband is not responsible for paying wife's debts incurred before marriage, nor for a court judgment against wife only. |
| | | Wife's property owned before or acquired during marriage cannot be taken to pay for husband's debts. |
| | | Spouses cannot sell or give property to the other if it prejudices rights of creditors. |
| Massachusetts | 209:7 | Wife is not responsible for paying husband's debts, except his debts for necessaries to $100 if those necessaries were sold with her knowledge or consent and she has property of at least $2000. |
| | 209:8 | Husband is not responsible for paying wife's debts incurred before marriage or for court judgments against her. |
| | 209:9 | Wife's contracts made regarding her separate property or her own business are not binding on her husband and do not subject his property to liability for payment. |
| Michigan | 26.165 (1) | Wife's separate property—owned before or acquired during marriage—cannot be taken to pay for husband's debts. |
| | 26.165 (4) | Husband is not responsible for paying wife's debts for breach of contract relating to her separate property. |

| State | Code Section | Spousal Obligations |
|---|---|---|
| Minnesota | 519.02 | Wife's separate property cannot be taken to pay for husband's debts. |
| | 519.05 | Husband is not responsible for paying wife's debts except for necessaries furnished during marriage. If husband and wife live together, they are jointly responsible for paying for all necessaries used by the family. |
| Mississippi | 93-3-13 | If husband receives and uses wife's property or income, he becomes her debtor, but is accountable to her for only one year. |
| Missouri | 451.250, 451.260 | Wife's separate property—owned before or acquired during marriage—cannot be taken to pay for husband's debts, except his debts to provide necessaries for her and the family, or to improve her real property. |
| | 451.270 | Husband's property cannot be taken to pay for wife's debts incurred before marriage. |
| Montana | 40-2-106 | Neither spouse is responsible for paying the other's debts; however, both spouses are responsible for paying for necessaries of family and children's education. |
| | 40-2-209 | Spouse's separate property cannot be taken to pay for other's debts except for necessaries, or if the property is in the exclusive possession and control of the other and a creditor relied on that property for repayment, not knowing it didn't belong to that spouse. |
| Nebraska | 42-201 | Wife's separate property—owned before or acquired during marriage—cannot be taken to pay for husband's debts except that 90% of her wages are responsible for paying family's necessaries, although the creditors must seek payment from husband first. |
| | 42-206 | Husband is not responsible for paying wife's debts incurred before marriage. |
| Nevada | 123.050 | Neither spouse is responsible for paying the other's debts incurred before marriage. |
| New Hampshire | 460:1 | Wife's separate property—owned before or acquired during marriage—cannot be taken to pay for husband's debts. |
| | 460:3 | Husband is not responsible for paying wife's debts incurred before marriage. |
| New Jersey | 37:2-8 | Wife is responsible for paying for her own torts. |
| | 37:2-10 | Husband is responsible for paying wife's debts incurred before or during marriage. |
| | 37:2-15 | Husband cannot dispose of wife's separate property nor can it be taken to pay for his debts. |

| State | Code Section | Spousal Obligations |
|-------|-------------|---------------------|
| New Mexico | 40-3-10 | Separate debts are to be paid with: (1) debtor spouse's separate property, except for separate property that is a portion of joint tenancy or tenancy in common property with the other spouse; (2) debtor spouse's share of joint tenancy, tenancy in common or community property, except the residence; (3) debtor spouse's interest in residence.<br><br>Neither spouse's community property or separate property can be taken to pay for the other spouse's separate debts. |
| | 4-3-10.1 | Court may declare a community debt incurred by one spouse while the spouses live apart to be a separate debt if it does not benefit both spouses or the spouses' dependents. |
| | 4-3-11 | Community debts are to be paid with: (1) community property; (2) tenancy in common or joint tenancy property except the residence; (3) a tenancy in common or joint tenancy residence; (4) the separate property of spouse who incurred debt. If the spouses together incurred the debt, both spouse's separate property can be taken to pay the debt. |
| New York | DRL 50 | Wife's separate property—owned before or acquired during marriage—cannot be taken to pay for husband's debts. |
| | GOL 3-305 | Husband is not responsible for paying wife's contracts. |
| | GOL 3-307 | Husband who acquires some of wife's property owned before marriage by way of a contract with her is responsible for paying her debts incurred before marriage to the value of the property received. |
| North Carolina | 39-18 | Contracts between a man and woman to transfer property in consideration of marriage are invalid against their creditors. |
| | 52-11 | Neither spouse is responsible for paying the other spouse's debts incurred before marriage. |
| North Dakota | 14-07-03 | Spouses must support each other out of their separate property and labor. |
| | 14-07-08 | Neither spouse is answerable for the other's acts.<br><br>Earnings and separate property of spouse cannot be taken to pay for the other's debts.<br><br>Spouses are jointly liable for debts for necessaries contracted by either while they live together. |
| | 14-07-10 | Husband and wife are jointly responsible for paying anyone who in good faith supplied articles necessary for their support. |
| Ohio | 3103.03 | Husband must support himself, wife and their minor children with his property or labor. If he can't, wife must assist in so far as she is able to. |
| | 3103.08 | Neither spouse is responsible for the other's acts. |

| State | Code Section | Spousal Obligations |
|-------|--------------|---------------------|
| Oklahoma | 43-202 | Husband must support himself and wife out of his property or labor. Wife must support husband, if he has not deserted her, out of her property if he has no property and can't support himself. |
| | 43-208 | Neither spouse is responsible for the other's acts. Separate property of wife cannot be taken to pay for husband's debts, but can be taken to pay for her debts incurred before or during marriage. |
| Oregon | 108.020 | Neither spouse is responsible for paying the other's separate debts incurred before or during marriage. The rent or income of property of one spouse cannot be taken to pay for the other's debts. |
| | 108.040 | Both spouses are responsible for paying the debts of the family and education of children. If creditor sues only the wife, creditor must sue within two years of when the debt becomes due. After divorce, wife is not responsible for paying family expenses incurred by husband while they lived together. |
| | 108.050 | Wife's property owed before marriage or acquired during marriage by her own labor cannot be taken to pay for her husband's debts. |
| | 108.060 | Spouse's separate property cannot be taken to pay for debts of the other, except as provided in §108.040. |
| Pennsylvania | 48-64 | Wife's separate property—owned before or acquired during marriage by will, descent, deed of conveyance or otherwise—cannot be taken to pay for husband's debts. Husband is not responsible for paying wife's debts incurred before marriage. |
| | 48-116 | To obtain payment for debts for necessaries, creditors may look to all of husband's property and then separate property of wife if the creditor sued both spouses. Creditor cannot get a judgment against wife unless she contracted for the debt, or if the articles are for the support of husband and wife. |
| Rhode Island | 15-4-9 | If wife carries on her own business or trade, husband is not responsible for paying her business debts. |
| | 15-4-12 | Husband is not responsible for paying wife's debts incurred before marriage. Husband is not responsible for paying wife's debts incurred during marriage unless he participated with her or coerced her to act. Wife is not responsible for paying husband's debts. |
| South Carolina | 20-5-30 | Wife's property cannot be taken to pay for husband's debts. |
| | 20-5-60 | Husband is not responsible for paying wife's debts except for those necessary for her support and the support of their minor children residing with her. |
| South Dakota | 25-2-6 | Separate property of a spouse cannot be taken to pay for the other's debts incurred before marriage. |
| | 25-2-11 | Spouses are jointly liable for all necessaries of life—food, clothing and fuel—purchased by either for their family while they live together as husband and wife. |
| | 25-2-14 | Neither spouse is responsible for the other's acts. |

| State | Code Section | Spousal Obligations |
|-------|--------------|---------------------|
| Tennessee | 36-3-502 | No marital settlement agreement is valid against creditors if under the agreement wife receives more in debts than in property. |
| | 36-3-503 | Husband is not responsible for paying wife's debts incurred before marriage. |
| | 47-18-805 | Spouse of credit applicant is not responsible, except for debts for necessities, if that spouse did not sign the application. |
| Texas | Fam. 4.031 | Spouse is responsible for the other's acts only if acting as agent or if spouse incurs debt for necessaries. In general, community property cannot be taken to pay for debts arising from act of spouse. |
| | Fam. 5.61 | Separate property of a spouse cannot be taken to pay for the other's debts. |
| | | Unless both spouses are liable under § 4.031, community property under one spouse's management and control cannot be taken to pay for other's debts incurred before marriage or non-tort debts incurred during marriage. Community property subject to one spouse's management and control can be taken to pay for that spouse's debts incurred before marriage. All community property can be taken to pay for tort debts of either spouse incurred during marriage. |
| Utah | 30-2-1 | Wife's separate property—owned before or acquired during marriage—cannot be taken to pay for her husband's debts. |
| | 30-2-5 | Neither spouse is responsible for paying other's debts incurred before or during marriage. |
| | | Earnings of one spouse cannot be taken to pay for other's separate debts. |
| | 30-2-7 | Husband is not responsible for wife's torts. |
| | 30-2-9 | Both spouses are responsible for paying family expenses and children's education. |
| Vermont | 15-68 | Wife's real property owned before marriage or acquired by gift or inheritance during marriage, cannot be taken to pay for husband's debts. Rents and profits of wife's real property can be taken to pay husband's debts for necessaries for wife and their family and for debts for improving her real property. |
| | 15-69 | Husband is not responsible for paying wife's debts incurred before or during marriage unless debts incurred with husband's authority or at his direction. |
| Virginia | 55-35 | Wife's property cannot be taken to pay for husband's debts. |
| | 55-38 | Neither spouse is responsible for paying the other's debts incurred before or during marriage. |

| State | Code Section | Spousal Obligations |
|---|---|---|
| Washington | 26.16.010 | Husband's separate property cannot be taken to pay for wife's debts. |
| | 26.16.020 | Wife's separate property cannot be taken to pay for husband's debts. |
| | 26.16.190 | If one spouse causes injuries to a third person, the injured person cannot recover against the other spouse's separate property. |
| | | Neither spouse is responsible for paying the other's separate debts. |
| | | Spouse's earnings and accumulations can be taken to pay for own debts. |
| | 26.16.200 | No separate debt may be basis for claim against a husband or wife unless reduced to court judgment within three years of marriage. |
| West Virginia | 48-3-14 | Husband is not responsible for paying wife's debts incurred before marriage. |
| | 48-3-15 | If spouse gives or sells property to the other in a prenuptial or marital agreement, creditors of original spouse owner may go after spouse who received the property to the value of the property received. |
| | 48-3-17 | If wife runs her own business or carries on a trade or profession, the business is not responsible for paying husband's debts nor subject to his control. |
| | 48-3-20 | Husband is not responsible for wife's torts. |
| | 48-3-22 | A spouse is responsible for paying all debts incurred in his or her name except both spouses are responsible for paying services of physician, rent, support of family, and clothing if husband abandons wife. |
| Wisconsin | 766.55 | Debt incurred by a spouse during marriage is presumed to be in the interest of marriage or family and therefore both spouses are responsible for paying it. |
| | | A spouse's duty to support the other or their child must be paid from community property or the obligated spouse's separate property; a debt incurred by a spouse for the interest of family is to be paid from community property or the incurring spouse's separate property. |
| | | A separate debt incurred before or during marriage may be paid only from that spouse's separate property or from community property that would have been that spouse's separate property but for the marriage. |
| | | Any debt incurred by a spouse during marriage may be paid from that spouse's separate property or that spouse's interest in community property; for non-tort debts, separate property must be used before spouse's interest in community property. |
| Wyoming | 20-1-201 | Separate property cannot be taken to pay for other's debts. |
| | | Separate property can be taken to pay for necessary expenses of family and children's education. |
| | 20-1-202 | Spouse is not responsible for paying the other's debts incurred before marriage. |

## B. Listing Your Debts

Below is a chart that you can use to list all your debts—yours, your spouse's and your joint (marital) debts.

In Column 1, list all current debts you and your spouse are responsible for paying. In Column 2, write the balance owed on each debt. In Column 3, note whether the debt is your separate debt, your spouse's separate debt or a marital (joint) debt. Refer to the Spousal Obligation table in Section A, above, for help in determining what constitutes a marital debt in your state. In Column 4, write in the name of the person who will assume responsibility for paying the debt. Only in unusual circumstances will one of you be responsible for the other's separate debt. You will need to divide the marital debts, however. You may want to make several copies of this chart in the event you negotiate back and forth about who will be responsible for paying which debts. Use the italicized examples as a guide.

### List Your Debts

| Debts—Example | Balance | Husband, Wife or Joint | Who Will Pay |
|---|---|---|---|
| Car Loan | $8,000 | Joint | Wife |
| Franklin Bank Visa | $1,800 | Husband | Husband |
| Marshall Bank Visa | $2,300 | Joint | Husband |
| Personal Loan | $5,000 | Joint | Husband |
| Student Loan | $10,000 | Wife | Wife |
| USA Mastercard | $4,000 | Joint | Husband |

| Debts | Balance | Husband, Wife or Joint | Who Will Pay |
|---|---|---|---|
| | | | |
| | | | |
| | | | |
| | | | |
| | | | |
| | | | |
| | | | |
| | | | |
| | | | |
| | | | |
| | | | |
| | | | |
| | | | |
| | | | |
| | | | |

## C. Marital Debts and Bankruptcy

For many couples, debts and divorce go together the way love and marriage did on their wedding day. Unmanageable debts may serve as a catalyst for the ending of the marriage in some cases. Other couples feel the pinch as their expenses double when one spouse moves out—they maintain two households, yet their incomes stay the same.

For couples or recently divorced individuals overwhelmed by their debt burden, declaring bankruptcy may be the best way out. In most cases, bankruptcy lets you erase your debts in exchange for giving up "non-exempt" property. (Every state declares certain items of property, such as household goods and furniture, clothing, certain equity in a home, certain equity in a car and several other items exempt. You get to keep exempt property when you file for bankruptcy.)

Married couples can file for bankruptcy jointly. Married persons can also file individually, and single people can file on their own. Before filing as an individual or a couple, you must understand what the different outcome will be.

If a married couple files for bankruptcy together, they can eliminate all separate debts of the husband, separate debts of the wife and all jointly in- curred marital debts.[2] If only one spouse files, that spouse can eliminate his or her separate debts, as well as his or her obligation to pay the marital debts. The non-filing spouse, however, remains responsible for paying the marital debts, and of course, his or her own separate debts. In community property states (Arizona, California, Idaho, Louisiana, Nevada, New Mexico, Texas, Washington and Wisconsin), the non-filing spouse can pay the marital debts out of community property (joint fund), including the share of the spouse who files. In community property states therefore, it's almost never worth it for a married person to file individually for bankruptcy.

A spouse wanting to file for bankruptcy might decide to wait until after the divorce, especially if he or she agreed to pay a large share of the marital debts, perhaps in exchange for taking a greater share of the marital property. The non-filing spouse must watch carefully in the event an ex-spouse files for bankruptcy. Remember what we said at the beginning of the chapter—dividing debts at divorce does not affect your original relationship with your creditors. Just because Mark agreed to pay back the marital debt to Sears doesn't mean that Sears cannot go after his ex-wife Sylvia for the payments.

This rule holds true in bankruptcy as well. If Mark agrees to pay the marital debts and then files for bankruptcy, the bankruptcy will wipe out Mark's obligation to pay those bills. But Sylvia, who figured she didn't have to pay them because the divorce agreement gave them to Mark, now is liable for paying. The creditors will seek her out, and if necessary, may send the bill to a collection agency or even sue her to get paid.

In some situations, the bankruptcy court can refuse to let Mark discharge the marital debts. If Mark agreed to pay the debts in lieu of paying alimony—or in exchange for paying lower alimony— the bankruptcy court may declare that the marital

---

[2] Some debts cannot be erased (discharged) in bankruptcy. The most common ones are recent taxes, student loans first payable with the past seven years, child support, alimony and debts obtained by a fraudulent act on your part.

debts are really alimony. Alimony is not erasable in bankruptcy and Mark would still have to pay them.

Here's a situation that is perhaps even more frightening than having your ex-spouse declare bankruptcy and wipe out an obligation to pay the marital debts. Assume that Jackie and Art divorce. Jackie received a larger share of the property, so she gave Art a promissory note, say for $35,000, as an even up payment. Jackie files for bankruptcy and asks the court to erase her obligation to make good on the note—Art falls $35,000 short in getting his share of the marital property.[3]

Bankruptcy isn't for everyone. It stays on your credit record for 10 years, although you can take steps to rebuild your credit and probably obtain credit in two or three years after filing. Nonetheless, be sure you understand that bankruptcy is always a possibility (unless you filed within the previous six years) for you or your spouse. If you're overwhelmed by your debt burden, don't immediately count it out. If your spouse assumes a large share of the marital debts or owes you a large sum to even up the property division, be on the lookout for any bankruptcy filing, especially if your ex starts to complain loudly about being broke.

*Make sure your divorce agreement doesn't leave you vulnerable.* Promissory notes, especially unsecured notes (notes that don't give you a lien on property), are almost always wiped out in bankruptcy. You may have a little more protection with secured notes, but don't count on it.[4] You may be able to protect your-

self by specifying in the settlement agreement that the promissory note or other payments are made in lieu of alimony. If you want to file for bankruptcy, be sure you know what's involved, and whether or not you can wipe out your debts. What's most important is that you get sound legal advice from a bankruptcy attorney or a Nolo Press publication.[5]

## D. Dividing Debts at Divorce

While it is critical that you fully understand your legal position and recourse regarding your debts, do not overlook the financial realities of your situation.

In Chapter 13, you had the chance to complete Net Worth and Cash Flow statements. If you skipped that material, you may want to go back and fill them out now. If you completed the Net Worth and Cash Flow statements in Chapter 13, use this opportunity to update them. You might leave many items blank on these statements, but at least you'll get an idea of what you actually own and owe, and how much it costs you to live. This information is crucial when you divide your debts at divorce.

You have four basic options in allocating your marital debts:

- Sell joint property to raise the cash to pay off your marital debts.

- You agree to pay the bulk of the debts; in exchange, you get a greater share of the marital property or a corresponding increase in alimony.

---

[3] Art could protect himself by taking cash or property worth $300,000, or a promissory note secured by the house—assuming Jackie keeps the house. This kind of note would allow him to force the sale of the house if she doesn't pay. Also, a secured promissory note can't be erased by bankruptcy if the security interest (the note securing the house) is created at the same time the house transfers from the two spouses to the one keeping it after the marriage. (See *Farrey v. Sanderfoot*, 111 S.Ct. 1825 (1991).) This is a very tricky area of law and if it applies to you, see a bankruptcy lawyer as soon as possible.

[4] A secured promissory note can't be erased by bankruptcy if the security interest (the note securing the property) is created at the same time the house transfers from the two spouses to the one keeping it after the marriage. If your spouse has a separate property house and gives you a promissory note securing that house—or you transfer title in the house from the two of you to your spouse a month, week or even day before your get the promissory note

securing the house—your ex-spouse will probably be able to wipe out the note in bankruptcy.

[5] See *How to File for Bankruptcy*, by Elias, Renauer and Leonard or *Money Troubles: Legal Strategies to Cope with Your Debts*, by Robin Leonard. The first book gives all the information necessary to decide whether or not to file, and the forms for filing. A chapter on non-dischargeable debts has information on when marital debts can and cannot be wiped out. The second book includes a chapter on bankruptcy, but it is mostly devoted to alternative strategies for dealing with your debts.

- Your spouse agrees to pay the bulk of the debts; in exchange, your spouse gets a greater share of the marital property or a corresponding increase in alimony.

- Divide your property equally and divide the debts equally—that is, each of you gets half of the property and each of you agrees to pay half of the debts.

From your perspective, the first two options are much less risky than the second two possibilities. Remember the caution we have given throughout this book: *When you're connected to someone financially, you're at risk.* What happens if your spouse agrees to pay all or even half of the debts and then loses his or her job, refuses to pay or files for bankruptcy? You'll damage your credit rating, or be stuck paying—with the likelihood of getting reimbursed or getting a share of the marital property originally given to your spouse being somewhere between slim and nil. So if possible, sell your joint property and pay your joint debts, or agree to pay the debts yourself.

## E. Dividing Debts When There's "Nothing To Fight Over"

As your financial picture gets clearer, you may come to the unhappy conclusion that your bills and liabilities far outweigh your assets and income. Don't feel alone. Not only do most consumers live above their means, but many people going through divorce find they simply do not have enough money to make ends meet. Unlike the bitter battles for property that have stereotyped divorce cases on television, you and your partner may admit in despair that there's "nothing to fight over."

If you're in such a position, it's critical for you to take an honest look at your needs and protect your own interests. Even if you have to borrow money to get through your divorce, it could well be worth it to prevent problems later. Hiring a lawyer and/or financial professional now to review your situation, could cost less than a huge tax bill or other debts in the future.

Extensive information on debts and creditors is in *Money Troubles: Legal Strategies To Cope with Your Debts*, by Robin Leonard (Nolo Press).

# 19

# Alimony and Child Support

➡️ If you have no interest in receiving alimony (and neither does your spouse), skip ahead to Section C, assuming you have children. Keep in mind that if you knowingly give up (waive) alimony, you cannot go back to court later on and try to get some. Once it's waived, it's gone forever.

Unemployment checks and insurance claims can help a couple survive the loss of a job or a house fire. But who pays the bill when the financial disaster of divorce strikes?

Somehow, household expenses must be paid. Someone must come up with the "alimonia"—a word that means "food" or "support" in Latin. Today the word is alimony, although it is increasingly called spousal support, maintenance or even rehabilitative support. The names differ depending on which state you live in, but the impact seems to be the same everywhere: the payor feels the amount is far too much; the recipient knows it's not enough.

Both parties may be right.

Breaking one household into two simply costs more than anyone thinks it will. Besides doubling the basics—mortgage or rent, utilities and phone bills—divorcing couples must admit that the choices they made as a couple may no longer be relevant. A wife who left her job to care for the children cannot retrace her steps and cover the ground she lost when she dropped out of the workforce. A husband who refused a job transfer so his wife could pursue her entrepreneurial ambitions may be stuck in a dead-end job that he can't leave without jeopardizing his pension. When you are "fired" from the job of husband or wife, no one offers you a worker's compensation check. Is it any wonder, then, that alimony often becomes a major battleground in divorce.

If you have children, the struggle to make ends meet can become even more draining. Whether you will pay or receive child support, you must know what it costs. But how can parents put a price tag on their children?

That's hard to answer. It's therefore not surprising that the custodial parent (recipient) never feels he or she is receiving enough and the non-custodial parent (payor) feels hounded for support payment increases.

⚠️ **Do not jeopardize your custody of your children**
Before making any legal moves that affect your children, make sure you are informed about your rights as a parent. Ask attorneys, social workers and anyone else who might help you to get precise information about what can and will happen when custody is disputed. Make sure you know when and where all hearings will take place. Better to ask too many questions than to lose your children because you misunderstood the consequences of your actions. Further, because the court will examine your custody arrangements, be prepared for any stunt your spouse may try to pull in the courtroom. Don't be lulled into a false sense of security because of anything your spouse may have agreed to informally.

This chapter first takes you through the legal, financial and emotional realties of alimony, and then outlines your steps to a settlement. Once you've taken care of alimony, you will follow the same steps with respect to child support.

## A. Alimony—Legal, Financial and Emotional Realities

It helps to think of alimony as a separate issue, distinct from your property settlement. Especially in community property states (Arizona, California, Idaho, Louisiana, Nevada, New Mexico, Washington and Wisconsin), the need to receive or pay alimony is separate from dividing property and assets.[1] Before reviewing the steps toward a settlement, take a few minutes to read about the legal, financial and emotional realties surrounding alimony.

---

[1] Although Texas is a community property state, Texas has been omitted from this list because alimony is unavailable in Texas.

## 1.  Legal Realities

Until the 1970s, alimony was a natural extension of the financial arrangement in traditional marriages, where the husband was the breadwinner and the wife stayed home, caring for the house and children. The amount of alimony was determined by a number of factors—the needs of the parties, their status in life, their wealth and their relative "fault" in ending the marriage. For example, if a husband was committing adultery, or treating his wife with cruelty, he would pay a relatively large amount. If, however, the wife was having an affair or treating her husband cruelly, she would receive little or no alimony.

Today, alimony is increasingly determined based on the following guidelines:

- the recipient's needs
- the payor's ability to pay
- age, health and standard of living of the parties
- length of the marriage
- each party's ability to earn
- the recipient's non-monetary contributions to the marriage
- the recipient's ability to be self-supporting and
- tax advantages and disadvantages.

Except in marriages of long duration (usually 10 years or more) or in the case of an ill or ailing spouse, alimony today usually lasts for a set period of time, with the expectation that the recipient spouse will become self-supporting.

In an effort to make alimony awards more uniform, some individual counties within states have adopted financial schedules to help judges determine the appropriate level of support. Of course, spouses can make arrangements outside of court that differ from the schedules.

Also, in some states, especially non-community property states, the division of property can affect how much alimony is awarded. For example, if one spouse gets a house with no mortgage, plus rental properties that produce a good income, a court is not likely to award a high amount of alimony. You will have an opportunity to examine the interplay between alimony and your property division in Chapter 20, Negotiating the Settlement.

## 2.  Financial Realities

Although legal guidelines and financial schedules have helped eliminate wide-ranging differences for alimony payments in a given locale, these guidelines do not necessarily provide adequate money to live on. Often, there's a big gap between the amount you will receive and what you really need, or between the amount you must pay and what you can actually afford.

To understand the financial reality of alimony, you must know what it really costs for you to live. Then you need to develop strategies for making up the difference between true living expenses and the amount you will receive or pay in alimony. As you work through Section B, you will look at the tax consequences of alimony as well as practical matters such as when, where and how payments should be made.

## 3.  Emotional Realities

Since the advent of no-fault divorce, many couples no longer vent their anger in knock-down, drag-out fights in court. That doesn't mean the anger isn't there. It just manifests itself differently and often leads to fights over alimony, an item directly tied to a person's survival. You may be moving along nicely in the negotiations only to find that when you get to the alimony, your spouse suddenly makes unreasonable demands or starts playing tricks. Focusing on the legal and financial questions, in Section B, below, will help you guard against emotional sabotage. Record your feelings in Section B.5, and get whatever personal and emotional care you need.

## B. Steps to a Settlement

As you move through your divorce, you may find that your choices about alimony are dictated by local financial schedules. For instance, if a schedule shows that a person in your situation should get $500 a month in alimony, your spouse will probably use that number, at least as a starting point.

While you need to be aware of any schedule used in your area, don't rely on those figures in determining the amount you will pay or receive. By answering the following questions, you can analyze the financial consequences of paying or receiving alimony.

1. How much do you need to live on?

2. What, if any, are the financial schedules for alimony in your area?

3. How much alimony do you need—or can you afford to pay?

4. Are there alternatives to paying or receiving monthly alimony?

5. What is your bottom line decision on paying or receiving alimony?

5. How do you feel about this decision?

## 1.  How Much Do You Need To Live On?

If you've completed the Cash Flow statement in Chapter 13, you have already tracked your living expenses. If not, go back now and use the statements to outline these costs. Whether you will pay or receive alimony, your goal is to get a realistic picture of your household costs. If your spouse demands more than you feel you can afford to pay—or offers less than you feel you need to live on—you will have to document your lifestyle. Yes, that lifestyle will probably change after divorce, but for now you need to establish a baseline for expenses.

While you're documenting your own cost of living, estimate your spouse's expenses as well. You will

need this information in your negotiating, and if you can't settle prior to a trial, the court will require that you each submit documentation of your income and expenses.

---

**If You Have Children**

In calculating your expenses, don't overlook the special costs generated by children, such as piano lessons, child care, braces, Little League uniforms and the like. You will need to make a list of ordinary and extra expenses. Some of those expenses may be listed on your Cash Flow statement from Chapter 13. Other expenses are listed in Section D.3, below.

---

Check your Cash Flow statement and other documentation containing your marital costs to estimate the following:

$ _____      **My personal monthly expenses**

$ _____      **My spouse's monthly expenses**

## 2.  What, if Any, Are the Financial Schedules for Alimony in Your Area?

As mentioned previously, a few counties have adopted informal financial schedules to help judges—and spouses—set alimony. Be sure to ask your lawyer if your county follows a financial schedule in setting alimony.

More likely, alimony is determined based on the factors listed in Section A.1, above. In addition, there's a trend for courts to follow principles such as these:

• If a marriage was under five years and the couple has no children, many courts will deny alimony altogether.

• If there are children below school age, most courts will require some alimony.

- If a marriage lasted at least five years, most courts make an alimony award to try to assure a continuity in the standard of living for both parties.

- In marriages that lasted at least 10 years, most courts will award alimony indefinitely, or at least until the recipient remarries or no longer needs alimony.

Based on those factors, judges—and attorneys who regularly appear before those judges—estimate the amount of alimony to be paid or received. There's no universal formula or rule that applies. The amount of an alimony award, perhaps more than any other decision a judge can make, is seldom subject to challenge but often leaves ex-spouses the angriest.

To get an estimate of the amount of alimony you may have to pay or are likely to receive if the issue is presented to a judge for decision, you will need to speak to an attorney or mediator to determine local practice and custom.

## 3. How Much Alimony Do You Need— Or Can You Afford To Pay?

Figuring out how much alimony you need or can afford to pay centers on three concerns—income needs, taxes and payment practicalities.

### a. Income Needs

Only a hard look at the income-alimony gap can reveal potential problems. If you come to terms with this gap, you have a better chance of closing it. Here are a few suggestions if you, like many divorcing people, find that you run out of money before you run out of month.

- Cut expenses to reduce your debt load as much as possible

- Do not use credit cards to finance your lifestyle

- Take on a second job

- Rent out part of your home to offset mortgage costs

- Sell an asset and use the money to pay off debts

Calculate how you would fare today if you had no option other than to pay or receive the alimony amount mandated by local custom or financial schedule. Then brainstorm about possible plans for resolving any budget problems you may face. Write your answers below.

### Alimony Recipients

| Monthly expenses: | $ |
|---|---|
| Estimated alimony I will receive: | $ |
| Difference: | $ |
| How I will make up the shortfall: | |

### Alimony Payors

| Monthly income: | $ |
|---|---|
| Estimated alimony I will pay: | $ |
| Difference: | $ |
| How I will make up the shortfall: | |

*Don't despair.* In negotiating the overall settlement, you may get enough property or other assets to replace the loss of income caused by the divorce. As noted previously, you can explore this possibility in Chapter 20.

## b. Taxes

To understand taxes and alimony, remember this basic rule: Alimony is tax deductible to the payor and taxable as income to the recipient—when the alimony is based on an agreement in writing (such as your divorce settlement papers) or is ordered by a court.

If your taxes are particularly complicated, you will need to consult with your accountant to fully understand alimony's tax consequences. Ideally, you and your spouse (or your attorneys or accountants) should figure the tax consequences for each of you and fashion an agreement  in which each person can receive the greatest number of after-tax dollars. Many attorneys and financial planners have computer programs that can make these calculations. In addition, consider the following points:

*Recipients*. All too often, the person receiving alimony treats it as "free" money, as in "tax free." On April 15, however, you may find yourself scrambling to pay income taxes on it. Be sure you manage your money in such a way that you put aside enough to cover the taxes.

*Payors*. Keep careful records of the payments so you can deduct them properly. And obviously, you want to be sure the alimony award is in writing or ordered by the court. Also, be sure to get an itemized bill from your attorney. Any fees you pay for work your attorney did to try and reduce the amount of alimony you pay are deductible, like the alimony itself.

To be deductible, alimony payments must meet the following conditions:

- They must be in cash. Cash paid to the cover the rent, mortgage, taxes, tuition, health insurance or medical expenses of the recipient also qualify.
- No payment can be made after the death of the recipient.

- Payments cannot be made to people in the same household.
- The payments cannot be disguised as child support.

---

### The IRS Is Watching

Alimony is deductible by the payor in the year it's paid, as long as it hasn't been "frontloaded."

This is not a type of clothes dryer. It's a method some divorcing couples use to load up on tax deductible alimony. Sometimes one spouse will pay a great deal of alimony the first year and then reduce it dramatically in later years. Or, a spouse will give the other some property, but call it alimony. In both cases, the IRS will want its share of money in taxes.

EXAMPLE 1: Biff will be paying Kit $66,000 in total alimony. He decides to pay her $44,000 the first year and $11,000 the second and third years. Because Biff has not spread out the alimony evenly, he will owe a lot of taxes to the IRS. Biff is clearly frontloading his payments—paying most of the alimony in the first year to get a bigger tax break. In cases of frontloading, the IRS would re-compute Biff's taxes at the end of the third year and slap him with a bill to re-capture the tax break he got the first year.

EXAMPLE 2: This time, Biff pays Kit $12,000 in cash and $30,000 for her new BMW in the first year. Even though only $12,000 was for the alimony itself, Biff deducts all $42,000 and calls all of it alimony. Biff plans to pay Kit $12,000 a year for the next two years to come up with the total $66,000. Again, Biff is clearly frontloading and the IRS will hand him a bill at the end of the third year.

Biff could have avoided the frontloading charge by simply paying Kit $22,000 per year for each of the three years—without dramatically decreasing the amount or trying to pass off the transfer of the BMW as alimony. Biff would be safe as long as the total payments in the first year did not exceed the payments in years two and three by more than $15,000.

### c. Payment Practicalities

If you will receive or pay alimony, you must be careful not to overlook the details involved in continuing a financial connection with your ex-spouse. Below are the questions we ask and suggestions we offer to cover the practical issues. Whether you deal with these items as your negotiations progress or wait until the final settlement, use the spaces provided to jot down your ideas which you can refer to later when needed. Put a checkmark in front of the question once it is resolved.

\_\_\_    *How will alimony payments be made?*

_____

_____

_____

_____

If you're the recipient, you basically have three choices:

- you can wait for the proverbial "check in the mail"

- you can set up a voluntary wage deduction through your ex's employer—you can then have that money automatically deposited into your bank account

- you can set up a voluntary account deduction through your ex's bank—that money is then automatically deposited into your bank account.

Most recipients wait for the check, although wage deductions are becoming more common, especially when the payor is also paying child support. (See Section D.4.c, below.) Whatever you arrange, be sure the details are clearly outlined in writing.

Also, keep accurate records of all payments. If you'll be receiving a check in the mail, be sure to make a copy of the check before depositing it. If money will be automatically deposited into your account, be sure to keep copies of your monthly bank statements. Payors should also keep copies of checks and bank statements. If you ever pay in cash, have your ex sign a receipt.

\_\_\_    *On what day of the month will alimony payments be made?*

_____

_____

_____

_____

Payors usually find it most convenient to pay alimony shortly after receiving their salary checks or other income. If you are a recipient, and payments won't arrive until the 15th, while your mortgage, rent or some other large monthly bill is due on the 1st, you'll need to rearrange your budget. Try to manage your cash flow so there's some left over from the previous month. If that won't work, contact the lender and ask that your payment date be pushed ahead to correspond with your cash flow—you don't need to tell the lender you're waiting for your alimony check unless the lender pushes the issue. Most lenders will make arrangements to accommodate payments.

\_\_\_    *How long will alimony payments be made?*

_____

_____

_____

_____

It's rare—except in long-term marriages where the alimony recipient (wife) will not be reentering the workforce—for alimony payments to be made indefinitely. And even in "indefinite" arrangements, alimony almost always ends if the recipient remarries or the payor dies. In most arrangements, alimony lasts for a set number of years—often for the length of time it takes for the recipient to get training to reenter the workforce or to allow the recipient to stay home with young children.

Whatever your arrangement, pay close attention to the termination date. Suppose you are to receive alimony until September 30, 1994 based on the assumption that you will return to school, graduate in June of 1994 and use the summer to find a job. What will you do if your education and career path don't work out as planned? You can usually go back to court and ask for an extension of the alimony, *but only if you make your request before the scheduled termination date.* If you wait until after September 30, 1994, you're probably out of luck because the court will have "reserved jurisdiction"—kept the power to make decisions—only until September 30, 1994.

For the ex-spouse paying alimony, by knowing when payments are supposed to end, you can plan your financial life accordingly. If you intend to build a new deck on your house and need to refinance your mortgage, you could give an accurate picture of your finances to a lender. The lender might give you a loan in 1993, knowing that in just another year your monthly disposable income will rise by the amount of the alimony payment. (If you believe your ex-spouse may get an extension of payments, you'll need to adjust your financial outlook accordingly.)

___ *How will you handle future economic changes, such as inflation or salary increases?*

_____

_____

_____

_____

If your alimony payment does not change, the amount it can actually buy year to year is sure to decrease. That's inflation. It's possible to take inflation into account in your alimony agreement with a COLA—Cost of Living Adjustment—clause. Some couples tie COLA increases to the rise in the Consumer Price Index (CPI); others simply choose a specific dollar amount.

Similarly, couples can avoid extended bitterness over alimony arrangements if they face the question of salary increases in advance. Will the recipient get a share of the payor's raise? Will the recipient's raise mean the alimony payment decreases? Be sure you know ahead of time how these questions will be handled.

___ *What life or disability insurance policies will cover your ex-spouse?*

_____

_____

_____

_____

If you are dependent on someone else for your income, what will you do if that person becomes disabled or dies? If you will be the alimony recipient, you'll want to make sure you have appropriate insurance coverage on your ex-spouse. You could purchase a life insurance policy on your ex. Or, your ex could buy life and disability insurance—naming you as the beneficiary—to protect your income stream. To get a tax deduction on the insurance premiums, the payor can pay the premium money to the recipient by increasing the alimony, and having the recipient make the insurance payments. The alimony recipient must be both owner and beneficiary under the policy. (Remember, however, an increase in alimony may increase the recipient's income taxes.)

___ *What will happen if the payor tries to modify the alimony payments or stops paying altogether?*

_____

_____

_____

_____

If you are the payor and you cannot afford to pay the amount of alimony you've been ordered to pay, you must file a motion for modification with the court. At your hearing, you must show a material change in circumstances since the last court order. Your ex-spouse's cohabitation with someone of the opposite sex may qualify, especially in Alabama, California, Connecticut, Georgia, Illinois, Louisiana, New York, Oklahoma, Pennsylvania, Tennessee and Utah, where such cohabitation raises a presumption of a decreased need for alimony.

Other common reasons for changes include your decreased income or your ex-spouse's substantially increased income. Where you have voluntarily decreased your income, however—for example, you quit your job as a doctor to work in a pastry shop—the judge may instead consider your ability to earn, not just your actual earnings.

If you are a recipient and your ex stops paying, you will need to go to court. Most likely, you will have to schedule a hearing where your ex-spouse is ordered to come to court and explain why he or she isn't paying. You can also ask the court to grant you a judgment for the amount owed or "in arrears." You can then use judgment collection methods, such as wage attachments and property liens, to try and collect the arrears.

---

### Alimony and Bankruptcy

Alimony cannot be erased in bankruptcy. If your ex owes a substantial amount and tries to have it wiped out in bankruptcy, you will be protected. For more on bankruptcy and divorce, see Chapter 18, Section C.

---

## 4. Are There Alternatives to Paying or Receiving Monthly Alimony?

While financial schedules and legal guidelines help establish the amount of alimony, they don't require any certain payment arrangement. Although alimony is traditionally paid monthly, it is possible to pay it in a lump sum, periodically or combined with child support.

### a. Lump Sum Alimony

A lump sum settlement of alimony upon divorce is sometimes called an alimony buyout. Before agreeing to a buyout, consider its pros and cons.

### i. Recipient

There are three major advantages to accepting a lump sum settlement:

1. You reduce the risk of depending on someone else—who could default, become disabled or die—for income. Reducing the risk of depending on someone who could default is important—alimony default rates exceed 50% in many places.

2. You can use the lump sum for a down payment on a house or other purposes, such as paying bills.

3. If you have no children, you can terminate any further contact with your ex-spouse.

There are also disadvantages to a buyout:

1. You lose a steady flow of income.

2. Once you accept a lump sum payment, you cannot go back to court to re-instate or increase alimony.

3. You may receive less than you would have in monthly payments. You and your soon-to-be ex-spouse may agree on a lower amount just to get rid of each other. Also, had you written a COLA (Cost of Living Adjustment) clause into your settlement, your payments would have risen, a consideration usually not factored into a lump sum payment.

4. You run the risk of losing some or all of the amount through bad investments or other unforeseen circumstances such as a debilitating illness.

### ii. Payor

There are three major advantages to making a lump sum settlement:

1. Because writing a monthly alimony check to a former spouse can be a grating experience which creates resentment and ill will after the divorce, a lump sum may be easier emotionally.

2. If you have no children, you can end the marriage with a strong sense of finality.

3. Because a buyout compresses all future payments into one present payment, the total is often less than what would have been paid over a set number of years. For example, Mitch agrees to pay Sara $1,000 per month for the next five years, for a total of $60,000. Mitch figures inflation is around 6%, and in today's dollars, $60,000 is worth only $44,835. Mitch offers that amount in a present-day lump sum settlement.

There are also disadvantages to a buyout:

1. You have to come up with a large sum of money.

2. Under standard alimony plans, payments cease if the recipient dies, remarries, or in some cases, cohabits with someone of the opposite sex. You could pay a lump sum at divorce only to watch your ex remarry in a year.

3. Because a buyout cannot be renegotiated, you could end up paying more in the lump sum than might have been required. For instance, if your ex obtains a high paying job or your income drops a great deal, you might have been able to reduce the monthly alimony payments.

4. Your payment might look like frontloading. (See Section 3.b, above.) If you are not going to pay the entire buyout in one year, the IRS could interpret the arrangement as frontloading and assess taxes at the end of the second year.

### b. Family Support

Sometimes, alimony and child support are combined into one monthly payment called family support. For a payor, the main advantage of family support is that, like alimony, family support is tax deductible.

Recipients enjoy one advantage if a payor defaults. In that situation, the recipient has numerous child support collection techniques available. (See Section D.4.c, below.) If the payor defaults on alimony payments, the only collection method in most states involves taking the payor to court. Be warned, however, that a growing number of courts are disallowing family support, not wanting to burden the child support collection bureaus with collecting what is really alimony.

## 5. What Is Your Bottom Line Decision on Paying or Receiving Alimony?

**Decision Time . . .**
You may have little choice about alimony payments, but you must nevertheless make decisions about them. Will you negotiate for a lump sum buyout? Will you use alimony as a leverage in negotiating for other assets? Use this space to describe your bottom line decision on alimony payments so you can easily refer to this information in Chapter 20, when you bring all your decisions to the negotiating table.

_____

_____

_____

_____

## 6. How Do You Feel About This Decision?

As with everything else you do in divorce, take a few moments to reflect on your emotional state—whether you will pay or receive alimony in a lump sum or monthly payments. Just because you have to accept the reality of paying (or receiving) alimony does not mean you have to like it.

Examine any hidden agendas you may have because buried emotions can hamper negotiations and lead to non-compliance. By expressing your feelings, you can reduce the anger that could cloud your judgment as you move toward your final settlement. Acknowledging feelings is the first step toward accepting them—and is the key to complying with the alimony order.

So think about it.

*How will you feel writing out a check once a month? Receiving one?*

*Do you feel resentful? Guilty? Angry?*

*Or have you accepted it as a fact of life?*

Don't move on until you've answered these questions.

## C. Child Support—Legal, Financial and Emotional Realities

Children, unfortunately, are frequently the emotional pawns of divorce. Parents express their resentments about their mates by fighting over the children through custody and child support. Fighting scares the children and makes them feel guilty. It also wastes time, money and resources that could have been spent more positively on the kids.

As difficult as it sounds, try to keep your emotions in check. This doesn't mean you should hide your angers, fears and resentments about your divorce from your children. It does mean that you should not take them out on your kids.

### 1. Legal Realities

Every parent has an obligation to support his or her children, regardless of divorce. When one parent has physical custody and the other visitation rights (see Section D.1, below), the parent with visitation rights (the non-custodial parent) is usually ordered to pay some child support to the custodial parent. It is assumed that the custodial parent is meeting his or her child support obligation through the custody itself. For parents with joint physical custody, the support obligation of each is often based on the ratio of each parent's income to their combined incomes, and the percentage of time the child spends with each parent.

While divorcing spouses are permitted to decide virtually all terms of their divorce without court intervention, the court often insists on examining the child support arrangement. If the judge approves of the arrangement, the court will include it in the divorce agreement. Some of the factors evaluated by courts in setting child support include:

- the non-custodial parent's ability to earn and ability to pay
- the custodial parent's income

• and the needs of the child.

Unfortunately, a large percentage of parents ordered to pay child support do not. Society has become less tolerant of these parents, and the federal government requires all state governments to enact laws to facilitate enforcement of child support orders. These tools for collecting are discussed in Section D.4.c, below.

## 2.  Financial Realities

Any legal award of child support is probably going to be less than the actual amount needed to meet the needs of growing children. As with the gap between alimony and living expenses, you will have to devise strategies for finding the additional money not provided by child support.

Even if you receive an adequate child support award, financial reality demands that you recognize the problems caused by lack of compliance. If you are the recipient, what will you do when the check does not arrive or comes late? If you are the payor, what happens when your paycheck is suddenly garnished—or worse, you are threatened with jail for non-compliance? Don't dwell on these negative questions, but at least confront them for your children's sake.

Also keep in mind two new, but sad, trends emerging from the financial realities of divorce. Some parents have reached the painful conclusion that they cannot retain custody of their children because they do not have the resources to support them. At the same time, other parents are fighting for joint custody so they can pay less child support . To avoid these situations, you must squarely face the true costs generated by children and prepare your strongest position for negotiating your settlement and protecting the interests of your children.

The true costs of rearing children are highlighted in Section D.3, below.

## 3.  Emotional Realities

Your children's reaction to your divorce can have a major effect on your emotional state. On all issues concerning your children—child support, custody and visitation—you and your mate may inwardly and outwardly struggle over what's best for your children.

A spouse caught up in a power struggle may try to use the children to get back at the other, causing turmoil for all. The "Disneyland Dad" (or Mom) showers the children with gifts, using financial leverage as a way of upstaging the other parent. Be aware of your own behavior and remember that it can do more damage to the kids than to anyone else.

## D.  Steps to a Settlement

As you move through your divorce, you will probably find that your choices about child support are dictated by local financial guidelines. Nevertheless, by answering the following questions, you can analyze the financial consequences of paying or receiving child support.

1.  Who will have custody of the children?

2.  What are the guidelines for child support in your state?

3.  What does it cost to rear your children?

4.  How much child support do you need—or can you afford to pay?

5.  What is your bottom line decision regarding custody and child support?

6.  How do you feel about your decision?

## 1.  Who Will Have Custody of the Children?

Custody is the legal authority to make decisions about the medical, educational, health and welfare needs of a child (legal custody) and physical control over a child (physical custody). Traditionally, legal and physical custody were granted to the mother and visitation rights to the father. In most states, however, courts now have the authority to award joint custody, which lets divorced parents share physical custody, legal custody or both. The most common arrangement is for legal custody to be shared, with one parent (usually the mother) given physical custody and the other parent given visitation rights.

You can work out whatever arrangement you want regarding custody. If you can't agree, you may be able to use mediation. Mediation is a non-adversarial process in which a neutral person (a mediator) meets with parents to help them resolve problems—the mediator cannot impose a solution on the parties. Eight states require mediation in custody disputes, while 13 states encourage it. If you still can't agree (or don't use mediation) and you leave the custody decision to the court, the legal standard the court will use is "the best interests of the child." The factors that make up the best interests usually include:

- the age and sex of the child;
- child's preference (if the child is above a certain age, usually about 12);
- relationship of the child with the parents, siblings and any stepparent ;
- established living pattern for the child concerning school, home, community and the like;
- mental and physical health of the child and parents (including any history of abuse); and
- lifestyle and other social factors of the parents.

## 2.  What Are the Guidelines for Child Support in Your State?

Prior to 1984, family court judges set child support amounts by looking at the parents' income and expenses, assessing the child's needs and then selecting a dollar figure that seemed appropriate. The amounts selected were random and inconsistent —the likelihood that two non-custodial parents with similar incomes and expenses supporting children with similar

needs would pay similar amounts was slim, even if those parents appeared before the same judge.

To minimize inconsistencies within each state, Congress passed the Child Support Enforcement Amendments of 1984. That law required each state, by 1987, to establish non-mandatory guidelines (a formula) for setting child support. Because the state courts were not required to follow their guidelines, however, inconsistencies within each state remained.

Four years later Congress enacted the Family Support Act of 1988, which required states to have mandatory guidelines in place by October of 1989. This has proven a slow process, however, and many states have not yet enacted their guidelines. Nevertheless, the states are working toward conformity with the federal law, and when the guidelines are in place, disparities within states should be at a minimum, although child support will differ among states.

Parents may be able to agree on a child support amount different from that required by the state formula. Clearly, a judge will approve an order providing more than the required amount. Some judges will approve an amount below the guidelines, as long as the judge is convinced that the children are adequately supported by the custodial parent. A judge won't approve zero support—even if it's what the custodial parent wants. Remember: *all* parents are obligated to support their children and a custodial parent cannot give up *the child's* right to receive support.

To find out how much you are likely to pay or receive, you will have to get your state's child support formula. Ask your lawyer, local district attorney (the office obligated to enforce child support orders), parents' support group or court clerk.

## 3.  What Does It Cost To Rear Your Children?

The list below will alert you to items you should consider in figuring the cost of rearing children. As you review the list, calculate the average amount you spend each month. You can make this calculation by totaling the three most recent months and then dividing by three. Check your Cash Flow statement (see Chapter 13), look back through your checkbook or make an educated guess to find your monthly outlays.

After filling in each number, total the expenses at the end.

$ _____    **Birthdays and holidays**

Do you splurge on special occasions and birthdays? Do your children have high expectations about gifts? Depending on how many children you have, these costs can add up. You may need to re-adjust your budget and let your children know about the change. Under the best circumstances, you and your soon-to-be ex-spouse might agree to a spending limit so that one partner does not use "goodies" to turn the children against the less affluent parent.

$ _____    **Child care**

If both parents work, child care costs must be considered. If you relied on informal babysitting arrangements with friends or relatives while married, those arrangements cannot and should not be considered permanent. If you don't know the going rate for child care in your area, investigate. You must factor in the cost of competent care in your children's future.

$ _____    **Education or college funds**

Even after divorce, it's possible to realize the joint goal of providing for a child's private schooling or college education. It takes planning and cooperation, but it can be done. Besides college, your children may want to receive special training for a profession or the arts. These costs can sometimes be staggering. It's necessary to recognize them now, before your settlement is negotiated.

---

**Rising College Costs**

If your children will attend college, don't forget inflation. Throughout your divorce you have to keep an eye on the future—and that includes the real-dollar costs of that future. Tallying the impact of inflation on college expenses can be an eye-opener. Suppose tuition currently averages $10,000 annually. If inflation remains 4% a year and your seven-year-old enrolls as a freshman in 10 years, you will need $16,010 of today's dollars to pay that $10,000 tuition.

You must also consider the fact that college tuition itself will increase. In this example, if tuition increases at 7% per year, you will need $19,672 for that freshman year (not counting any increase for inflation)—almost twice the current tuition. You will need to put your college funds in an investment vehicle that grows at a rate faster than inflation.

---

$ _____    **Emergency savings**

Financial planners make a standard recommendation that you have an emergency cash reserve equal to three to six months of income. Be sure that reserve includes your children's normal expenses. You can also make your life after divorce easier if you include a cash cushion for the unexpected emergencies which only children can create.

$ _____    **Health and dental care**

Divorce affects the health care coverage of children. You and your spouse must reach an agreement as to who will carry the children on his or her health plan or buy coverage. If you cannot agree, a court may make the order for you. Some states mandate that if neither parent has insurance covering the children, one parent must pay for reasonable medical insurance. Also be aware of what benefits are covered and how long they last.

$ _____ **Hobbies**

Are your children involved in sports, music or ballet? Do they act in community theater? Do they expect to be as they grow older? Check how much has been spent on special lessons and hobbies, or talk to parents whose children are involved in similar pursuits to get an idea of future costs.

$ _____ **Total**

## 4. How Much Child Support Do You Need—Or Can You Afford To Pay?

In figuring out how much child support you need or can afford to pay, you will consider the same three items you considered with alimony—income needs, taxes and payment practicalities.

### a. Income Needs

The difference between legal reality and financial reality defines your income needs for child support. Fill in the amount from the legal guidelines (Section 2) on the second line and the total from the cost of rearing children (Section 3) on the first line.

Costs of rearing (Section 3)   $_____

Estimated child support I will
   receive or pay (Section 2)   $_____

Difference   $_____

*Recipients.* If your rearing costs are higher than the amount in the guideline—and you have no way to make up the gap—you'll have to negotiate for a higher amount. Obviously, if your spouse is aware that the guidelines are lower than the amount you are asking for, you may have little leverage. Nevertheless, you can still attempt to push up the amount of support.

If your spouse refuses to agree to a higher amount of support, try negotiating for some other asset to help make up the difference between what you need and what you will be getting.

*Payors.* Recognize that the gap between what your children cost and how much you have to pay has to be closed somehow. If the custodial parent has no other source of revenue, keep in mind that he or she may ask for more money from you now, and into the future. You and your spouse may be able to save yourselves time and trouble by negotiating child support from a realistic financial base right from the start.

### b. Taxes

Child support payments have no tax consequences. They are neither deductible to the payor, nor taxed as income to the recipient.

Children, however, have plenty of tax consequences—first and foremost, they are considered exemptions. The issue parents must decide is who will claim the children as exemptions. Often, the non-custodial parent claims the children in exchange for paying higher support.[2] When the parents have joint

---

[2] The custodial parent must relinquish claim to the exemption by signing IRS Form 8332 (Release of Claim to Exemption for Child of Divorced or Separated Parents).

physical custody, they may each claim a child (if they have more than one) or alternate the claim year to year. No matter who claims the children as exemptions, both parents must list the children's Social Security numbers on their tax returns to ensure that only one parent is claiming the children as exemptions.

### c. Payment Practicalities

The practical matter of getting child support payments from one person to the other can create highly charged problems. Below are questions we ask and suggestions we offer to help prevent these problems. Whether you deal with these items during your negotiations or in the final settlement, use the spaces provided to jot down your ideas. You can refer to these points when needed. Put a checkmark in front of the question once it is resolved.

___    *How will child support be paid?*

_____

_____

_____

_____

You can agree to send or receive a monthly check. The court, however, may want more.

The Family Support Act of 1988 requires that by 1994, all child support orders contain an automatic wage withholding provision. An automatic wage withholding order works quite simply. When the court orders you to pay child support, the court— or your child's other parent—sends a copy of the court order to your employer. The custodial parent's name and address is included with this order. At each pay period, your employer withholds a portion of your pay and sends it on to the custodial parent. Only if you and your child's other parent agree—and the court allows it—can you avoid the wage withholding and make payments directly to the custodial parent.

If you don't receive regular wages, but do have a regular source of income, such as payments from a retirement fund, annuity or Social Security, the court can order the child support withheld.[3] Instead of forwarding a copy of the order and the custodial parent's name and address to an employer, the court sends the information to the retirement plan administrator or public agency from whom you receive your benefits.

Many states have already implemented mandatory wage withholding and most states will do so before 1994. In Texas and Vermont, for example, all current orders include automatic wage withholding, regardless of the parent's payment history. The rationale is that by not distinguishing between parents with poor payment histories and parents who have paid regularly, no parent is stigmatized.

In California, wage withholding orders are automatic as well. But parents who show a reliable history of paying child support may be exempt. And in all states, employers must withhold wages if the payor is one month delinquent in support.

A few states have set up other mechanisms to collect child support as it becomes due. For example, a judge may order a non-custodial parent to pay child support to the state's child support enforcement agency, which in turn pays the custodial parent. This program is often used where automatic wage withholding has not yet taken effect. It may also be used for non-custodial parents without regular income (the self-employed) or when parents agree to waive the automatic wage withholding.

Some other states let judges order non-custodial parents to make payments to court clerks or court trustees who in turn pay the custodial parents. This program is mandatory in Arizona, Idaho and Kansas.

---

[3]If your income is from a private pension governed by either ERISA (Employee Retirement Income Security Act) or REA (Retirement Equity Act)—federal laws that limit access to pension plans—the pension plan administrator might not honor the court order. That is because many private pensions have "anti-alienation" clauses which prohibit the administrator from turning over the funds to anyone other than the plan beneficiary (you).

___ *On what day of the month will payments be made?*

_____

_____

_____

_____

Most custodial parents find it convenient to pay child support shortly after being paid themselves. If you are a recipient, and payments won't arrive until the 15th, while your child's monthly child care bill or health insurance premium is due on the 1st, you'll need to make different arrangements. Try saving money from the previous month. Or, contact the lender and negotiate a new payment schedule. Try to get your payments in sync with your cash flow. You don't need to tell the lender you're waiting for your child support check unless the lender pushes the issue. Lenders may be surprisingly cooperative when you contact them in advance and honestly negotiate so they are assured of getting their payments.

___ *How long will child support payments be made?*

_____

_____

_____

_____

You must pay child support for as long as your child support court order says you must pay. If the order does not contain an ending date, in most states you must support your children until they reach age 18. A few states, however, extend the time and require you to:

- support your children until they are 19 or finished with high school, whichever occurs first

- support your children until they complete college

- or support your adult disabled children as long as they are dependent.

Your child support obligation will end, however, if your child joins the military, gets married or moves out of the house to live independently, or a court declares your child emancipated.

If you owe back support, it doesn't go away when your child turns 18 (or whatever age you are no longer liable for support). Many states give a custodial parent 10 or 20 years to collect back child support—with interest.

___ *How will you handle child support modifications?*

_____

_____

_____

_____

A court retains the power over child support until every last dollar owed is paid. If a non-custodial parent can't afford the payments, he or she must take the offensive to change the child support order. Or, if a custodial parent can't live on the current payment, he or she needs to ask for more. As a first step, the parent wanting the change should call the other parent and try to work out an agreement. If you reach an agreement, be sure to get it in writing. You'll then need to get a judge's signature.

If you can't make satisfactory arrangements with your ex-spouse, the parent wanting the change will have to file papers with the court, schedule a hearing and then show the judge that he or she cannot afford to pay—or to live on—the ordered support. A non-custodial parent needs to understand that a court won't retroactively decrease child support, even if the non-custodial parent was too sick to get out of bed during the affected period. Once child support is owed and unpaid, it remains a debt until it is paid.

To get a judge to change a child support order, you must show a "significant change of circumstance" since the last order. What constitutes a "significant change of circumstance" depends on your situation. Generally, the condition must not have been considered when the original order was made and must affect your—or your child or the other parent's—current standard of living.

Changes that qualify for a *non-custodial* parent include:

- a substantial decrease in income;

- increased expenses, such as a new child;

- a raise you expected—which was the basis of the last order—didn't materialize;

- the custodial parent received a large inheritance; or

- your child's needs have decreased—for example, she is no longer attending private school.

Changes that qualify for a *custodial* parent include:

- a substantial decrease in income;

- increased expenses, such as a new child;

- the non-custodial parent received a raise or large inheritance; or

- your child's needs have increased—for example, he now needs braces.

___ *How will you handle non-payment of child support?*

_____

_____

_____

_____

Unpaid child support can take two forms. The first, arrears, is the money that accumulates when the payor doesn't pay what is owed. If the recipient is owed a great deal in arrears, he or she can go to court and ask a judge to issue a judgment for the amount due.

States' child support enforcement agencies, custodial parents, judges and district attorneys use several different methods to collect child support.

*Interception of income tax refunds.* One of the most powerful collection methods available is an interception of the payor's federal income tax refund. The custodial parent can ask the district attorney to call the Treasury Department for help. States (with income taxes) also intercept tax refunds to satisfy child support debts. In Nebraska, for example, court clerks report all child support arrears to the state for

an interception of the tax refund. Also, many states with lotteries let custodial parents apply to the state for an interception of the other parent's winnings.

*Property liens.* In some states, a custodial parent can place a lien on the payor's real or personal property. The lien stays in effect until the payor pays up, or until the custodial parent agrees to remove the liens. The custodial parent can force the sale of the non-custodial parent's property to be paid, or can wait until the property is sold.

*Posting bonds or assets to guarantee payment.* Some states allow judges to require parents with child support arrears to post bonds or assets, such as stock certificates, to guarantee payment. In California, for example, if a self-employed parent misses a child support payment and the custodial parent requests a court hearing, the court *must* order the non-custodial parent to post assets (such as putting money into an escrow account) equal to one year's support or $6,000, whichever is less.

*Reports to credit bureaus.* If the custodial parent owes more than $1,000 in child support, that information may find its way into a credit file maintained by a credit bureau. Federal law requires child support enforcement agencies to report known child support arrears of $1,000 or more. Many child support enforcement agencies automatically send information about owed child support to credit bureaus, regardless of the amount owed.

*Reporting to "most wanted" lists.* States are encouraged to come up with creative ways to embarrass parents into paying the child support they owe. One method used in a few states is to publish "most wanted" lists of parents who owe child support. In Delaware County, Pennsylvania, the family court lists the names of parents not paying child support on cable television 300 times a week and in a full-page newspaper advertisement once a month.

*Court hearings.* Failing to follow a court order is called "contempt of court." A parent owed child support can schedule a "show cause" hearing before a judge. The other parent must be served with a document ordering him or her to attend the hearing, and then must attend and explain why the support hasn't been paid. If the non-custodial parent is a no-show, the court can issue a warrant for his or her arrest, which could lead to a night or two at the county jail.

If the non-custodial parent attends the hearing, the judge can still throw him or her in jail for violating the support order. To stay out of jail, the parent must first show why the money wasn't paid and then explain why he or she didn't request a modification hearing.

Court hearings (and jail) used to be the major child support enforcement technique used. That is not so anymore. Other methods work better, and throwing a parent in jail for not paying child support has not proven terribly effective.

*Wage and property garnishments.* Child support arrears can often be collected by a wage garnishment. A wage garnishment is similar to a wage withholding— a portion of the non-custodial parent's wages is removed from the paycheck and delivered to the custodial parent. They differ, however, in one way: The amount of a wage withholding is *the amount of child support ordered each month.* The amount of a wage garnishment is *a percentage of the payor's paycheck.* The amount originally ordered to pay is irrelevant.

If the wage garnishment does not cover what's owed, the custodial parent may try to get other property to cover that debt. Common property targets includes bank accounts, cars, motorcycles, boats and airplanes, houses and other real property, stock in corporations and accounts receivable.

*District attorney assistance.* In most states, a local D.A. will help—and in some states is required to help—a custodial parent who hasn't received child support.

## 5. What Is Your Bottom Line Decision Regarding Custody and Child Support?

**Decision Time . . .**
By this point, you've worked through questions on custody and child support. Use the space below to formalize your decision by writing out what you want to accomplish regarding custody and support in the settlement negotiations.

_____

_____

_____

_____

_____

_____

_____

_____

_____

_____

_____

## 6. How Do You Feel About Your Decision?

As you probably recognize by now, no financial decisions are made in a vacuum. Emotions inevitably arise—especially when your children are involved. Examine your feelings about custody and support here so you can sort through the conflicts you may be experiencing.

# 20

# Negotiating the Settlement

*Until this stage of the divorce, you have focused on your personal, individual decisions—that is, the things you "want" in your divorce.*

But how will you get what you want? Through negotiation.

Negotiating the settlement is a process of offers and counteroffers from both sides in the divorce. You and your spouse may be able to compromise and reach a settlement easily; or, your demands and those of your spouse may run headlong into each other. Some couples can state their terms and reach a settlement in hours, others can go through years of bitter fighting.

Your settlement negotiations will probably bear an uncomfortable resemblance to the dynamics of your marriage. If your spouse has been rigid and demanding throughout your relationship, do not expect him or her to suddenly become flexible and reasonable in a settlement conference. Similarly, an uncommunicative mate will probably give you the "silent treatment" as you attempt to complete the settlement. Anticipating your spouse's most likely behavior can make it easier for you to accept and move through the negotiations.

Your decisions—and actions—become crucial in this phase because you are playing for keeps. Once the settlement is final, it is costly, time-consuming and almost impossible to modify it. Better to make changes to the settlement before you complete it, rather than trying to alter it later.

In this chapter, you will address four basic questions regarding negotiating the settlement:

- Have you done your financial homework?
- What kinds of settlement offers will you make, accept and reject?
- How are the offers and counteroffers made?
- How do you finalize the settlement?

## A. Have You Done Your Financial Homework?

Imagine walking into a room and sitting across a table from your spouse who is seated next to an attorney. The attorney smiles while going through a long list of items that your spouse is prepared to "give" you if you will simply forfeit any claim to the items that are on your spouse's much shorter list.

The attorney points out that the dollar amount on the bottom line of both lists is equal. Surely you should agree to such a fair and equitable offer.

But should you?

You can't know whether or not the offer is fair unless you've done your homework. If you've worked through the previous chapters in this book, you should be able to accept or reject your spouse's offer relatively quickly. If you haven't read the prior chapters—analyzing your assets and debts, and evaluating alimony and child support—you're apt to accept an offer that is a bad financial deal for you, regardless of how "equal" the dollar amounts on the bottom line appear to be.

You must know where you stand financially before you negotiate the settlement. We cannot stress this point enough. If you have not already done so, go back and read the material relevant to your divorce from Chapters 14 (house), 15 (retirement plans), 16 (investments), 17 (business assets), 18 (debts) and 19 (alimony and child support). Even if your spouse has made an offer—or is preparing to counter an offer you've made—take no further steps until you have analyzed the financial consequences of any proposed settlement.

## B. What Kinds of Settlement Offers Will You Make, Accept and Reject?

By now you should know which assets you want to keep, which ones you want to get out of your life completely and which ones you can take or leave, depending on how the negotiations progress.

### You Keep the House, I'll Keep the Pension

The family house and the pension plan are often the largest assets a couple has. Commonly, an employed spouse will offer to keep his or her pension while the other spouse gets the house. On the surface, these two assets may be worth similar amounts. But when taxes, penalties and other costs are factored in, they may not be equal. Remember, compare "apples to apples" when you are thinking of exchanging assets—in other words, compare your financial value column with the same column on your spouse's side of the ledger.

If you or your spouse are 55, or near that age, you may have other considerations as well. At age 55, you can take the "one time exclusion" to avoid paying taxes on $125,000 worth of profit realized in a house sale. Suppose one spouse agrees to take the house and the other keeps the pension plan. By taking the one time exclusion, the spouse with the house could be getting the better deal because he or she would save a bundle in taxes. The other spouse, however, could be getting an asset with a high liability to the IRS because taxes are normally owed when a pension plan begins to pay out.

Instructions for completing the chart follow it. Make several copies of the chart and enter all information in pencil. This will allow you to make changes as your negotiations progress.

*Column 1, Assets, Debts, Miscellaneous Property and Other.* List your assets—the family house (jot down the address), your retirement plans, investments, businesses and other assets—your debts, and any miscellaneous property to be included in your property settlement. You don't need to list anything under Other, but note the categories—alimony, child support, tax exemption and custody.

*Column 2, Legal Value.* List the legal value of your assets as you have defined them in previous chapters, and the actual dollar amount of your debts. For your miscellaneous property, use the amount you actually could get for an item if sold it at a garage sale. Don't use the price you paid or the replacement value.

*Column 3, Financial Value.* List the financial value of your assets—remember, this is the amount that takes into consideration taxes, costs of sale or commissions and other liabilities associated with each item. Usually it is the After-Tax/After-Sale Value calculated previously. For your debts and miscellaneous property, enter the same value you entered in Column 2.

The chart, below, helps you bring together the decisions you've made throughout this book.

| | Legal Value | Financial Value | Ideal Offer | | Worst Offer | | Compromise Offer | | Settlement | |
|---|---|---|---|---|---|---|---|---|---|---|
| | | | I Keep | Spouse Keeps | I Keep | Spouse Keeps | I Keep | Spouse Keeps | I Keep | Spouse Keeps |
| Family house | | | | | | | | | | |
| Retirement plans | | | | | | | | | | |
| 1. | | | | | | | | | | |
| 2. | | | | | | | | | | |
| 3. | | | | | | | | | | |
| Investments | | | | | | | | | | |
| 1. | | | | | | | | | | |
| 2. | | | | | | | | | | |
| 3. | | | | | | | | | | |
| 4. | | | | | | | | | | |
| 5. | | | | | | | | | | |
| 6. | | | | | | | | | | |
| 7. | | | | | | | | | | |
| 8. | | | | | | | | | | |
| 9. | | | | | | | | | | |
| Businesses | | | | | | | | | | |
| 1. | | | | | | | | | | |
| 2. | | | | | | | | | | |
| Other Assets | | | | | | | | | | |
| 1. | | | | | | | | | | |
| 2. | | | | | | | | | | |
| 3. | | | | | | | | | | |
| 4. | | | | | | | | | | |
| 5 | | | | | | | | | | |
| **Subtotal—Assets** | | | | | | | | | | |

| | Legal Value | Financial Value | Ideal Offer | | Worst Offer | | Compromise Offer | | Settlement | |
|---|---|---|---|---|---|---|---|---|---|---|
| | | | I Keep | Spouse Keeps | I Keep | Spouse Keeps | I Keep | Spouse Keeps | I Keep | Spouse Keeps |
| **Debts** | | | | | | | | | | |
| 1. | | | | | | | | | | |
| 2. | | | | | | | | | | |
| 3. | | | | | | | | | | |
| 4. | | | | | | | | | | |
| 5. | | | | | | | | | | |
| 6. | | | | | | | | | | |
| 7. | | | | | | | | | | |
| 8. | | | | | | | | | | |
| 9. | | | | | | | | | | |
| **Subtotal—Debts** | | | | | | | | | | |
| *Miscellaneous Property* | | | | | | | | | | |
| 1. | | | | | | | | | | |
| 2. | | | | | | | | | | |
| 3. | | | | | | | | | | |
| 4. | | | | | | | | | | |
| 5. | | | | | | | | | | |
| **Subtotal-Miscellaneous Property** | | | | | | | | | | |
| **TOTAL—ASSETS, DEBTS AND MISCELLANEOUS PROPERTY** | | | | | | | | | | |
| *Equalization Payment, if necessary* | | | | | | | | | | |
| *Other* | | | | | | | | | | |
| Alimony | | | | | | | | | | |
| Child support | | | | | | | | | | |
| Tax exemption | | | | | | | | | | |
| Custody | | | | | | | | | | |

### Dividing Miscellaneous Property

The bulk of your divorce may focus on splitting the miscellaneous items, such as furniture, books, electronic equipment, appliances, kitchenware, tools and the like. The easiest way to divide these items is to make a list of *everything you jointly own*—this includes wedding gifts and joint inheritances—and write your name or your spouse's name next to each item, depending on who wants what. Give the list to your spouse. Ask your spouse to note those items on which he or she disagrees with your assignment of ownership. Then sit down together and review the items in dispute. If you can't resolve your differences, here are three suggestions:

- Flip a coin. The winner gets first choice of the disputed items. Alternate selecting until the list is exhausted.

- Put the disputed items on your settlement chart and divide them as you negotiate the settlement.

- Find a mediator to help you divide what's still on the list.

This property may not be worth the time you spend fighting over it. Do not let the issue of dividing the miscellaneous property interfere with your negotiations over more financially significant assets such as the house or retirement plan.

---

*Columns 4-5, Ideal Offer.* Here you get to fantasize. What is your ideal offer, in light of the fact that your spouse is entitled to half of the items jointly owned? What do you want to keep and what do you want to give away? If your proposal is to sell an asset and divide the proceeds, use its financial value and enter an amount in each column. To keep track of who is getting what, subtotal the assets, debts and miscellaneous property and then total the full list. (Remember to subtract, not add, your debts.) If one of you will have to give the other an equalization payment—the amount of cash one spouse must pay the other so that the division of property comes out even—to equal things up, enter that amount. Finally, write down how you'd like to see alimony, child support—including who gets to claim the children as tax exemptions—and custody resolved.

*Columns 6-7, Worst Offer.* Here, write in settlement terms that are totally unacceptable to you.

### Would You Take This Deal?

Shortly before they divorced, Jeff convinced Terry that they should refinance their home to pay off their debts. They took out a $48,000 loan at 10% interest. In their settlement negotiations, they discussed what will happen to the $48,000 debt. Jeff offered to pay half, or $24,000. Should Terry take the deal?

Absolutely not. Jeff is not offering to pay a penny of the interest due on the money. If Terry accepted Jeff's offer, she would pay $516 a month for 15 years (the length of the loan), for a total repayment of $92,846.

No deal, Jeff.

---

*Columns 8-9, Compromise Offer and Columns 10-11, Settlement.* Use these columns to keep track of changes as your negotiations progress. Again, use a pencil or some of the blank charts if need be. Enter changes in Columns 8 and 9. As you settle issues, enter the terms in the last two columns.

### When Not To Keep the House

After Janet divorced she found herself paralyzed. Not physically—but because of decisions she made during her divorce, she could not afford to move from her home.

Janet owed $60,000 to her uncle—he loaned her the money so that she could buy out her husband. If Janet sold the house, she'd first have to pay her uncle. Then she'd have to pay taxes on the profit from the sale, or buy a new house of equal or greater value. But Janet wants a small condo worth less than her house, which means she will have to pay taxes on some of her profit. Between payments to her uncle and the taxes she'd owe on the profit, however, she does not have enough money for a down payment on a small house.

Janet and her husband had bought a house by rolling over considerable profit from their previous home. When they divorced, their house had gone up nearly $100,000 in value. But the after-tax/after-sale value of the house was far less. Nevertheless, Janet kept the house, and paid her ex-husband $60,000 to do so.

Now, Janet's goal is to keep her monthly house payment low. In her current home, she pays only $650 per month. After Janet repays her uncle and puts money aside for the taxes, she will have money left over from the sale of the house that she can use as a down payment on the condo. She'll still have to finance the deal. If she took a 30-year loan at 10.5% interest, her monthly payment would be $1,000—$350 more per month for housing than she pays now. And she simply cannot afford it on her current salary.

"It's ironic," Janet now muses. "I fought so hard to keep this house and now I have to keep it whether I want to or not. I'm so busy at work that I hardly have time to mow the lawn and I've had to rent out two rooms just to keep everything going. If I had it to do over again, I'd have sold the house during the divorce and started fresh."

## C. How Are the Offers and Counteroffers Made?

Once you identify your ideal offer and worst offer, you can begin the negotiations. In many settlements, the spouses will agree to each other's terms on several issues. To resolve the remaining issues, the couple—perhaps with the help of a mediator or with their attorneys—meet or correspond until all issues are settled. Once the issues are settled, they are reduced to a settlement agreement. The settlement agreement is then taken to the court for a judge's approval. Unless an agreement contains a clause leaving the children unsupported, a judge will approve the agreement as a formality.

### Don't Be Discouraged

In spite of doing your financial homework and the hard work of preparing for settlement negotiations, you may still go through numerous settlement conferences in attempting to hammer out an agreement. Some cooling off time may be needed between offers and counteroffers because of the charged emotional content. Take the time you need and don't give in just because you never want to see "that person" again.

Your settlement may not follow that scenario exactly. Here are other possibilities:

*You and your spouse agree to terms → file your own papers with the court → final decree of divorce is issued → marriage ends*

This kind of easy, simple divorce usually takes place when couples have been married a short time and have no children or major assets to divide. If you fall into this situation, check to see if there's a good "do it yourself" divorce book written for your state.[1]

---

[1] Californians and Texans, of course, can use Nolo's *How To Do Your Own Divorce.*

You can also use the services of an independent paralegal to help you type up your papers.[2]

*You and your spouse agree to terms on some issues →
meet with a mediator to resolve remaining issues → file
papers with the court on your own or using an attorney,
attorney-mediator or typing service → final decree of
divorce is issued → marriage ends*

Mediators are discussed in Chapter 9. Remember that a mediator is not an advocate—it's a person who helps you and your spouse arrive at a settlement you can live with. Once you settle the issues, a mediator will probably not help you file your court papers unless that person is also an attorney. You (or your spouse) can use an attorney for this, but the attorney will probably want to get more involved—find out all the issues of your case, figure out why you settled it as you did and counsel you to resolve it differently. This can mean you might have to start all over.

*You and your spouse—with your attorneys—agree on
certain issues → through your attorneys meeting or corresponding, you resolve remaining issues → attorneys file
papers with the court → final decree of divorce is issued
→ marriage ends*

If you and your spouse cannot settle your case, you'll probably turn to the services of an attorney. The cost will rise and the issues may seem more complicated, but your interests may be better protected. Nevertheless, it is imperative that you retain absolute control over your case. Having come this far in this book, you understand the financial realities of keeping certain assets, assuming (or having your spouse assume) debts and paying or receiving alimony or child support. Be clear with your attorney as to what is an acceptable and unacceptable settlement. Give your lawyer a copy of the chart you completed, above.

---

[2] Call 1-800-542-0034, the National Association of Independent Paralegals, for the name and phone number of a typing service near you.

---

### Understand What You're Getting

Judy and her husband went through an arduous negotiation process. When they couldn't agree on how to divide their property, they scheduled a trial. A few minutes before they were to go before the judge, they settled the issues in the court house cafeteria. Their attorneys initialed papers stipulating the terms they had agreed to.

When Judy received her copy of the stipulations, she noticed that her husband's attorney had added language describing her husband's equalization payment—money owed for receiving a greater share of marital property—as a distribution of retirement benefits subject to a Qualified Domestic Relations Order—QDRO. Instead of receiving tax-free payments, Judy would be getting the payment in the form of a fully taxable distribution from the retirement plan. Judy could roll the money into an IRA to defer taxes, but she did not want a taxable asset when she and her husband had already agreed that she would receive the nontaxable equalization payment.

Fortunately, Judy reviewed the settlement agreement carefully and asked her attorney about it. Judy then demanded—and got—a correction. The equalization payment was separated from the retirement benefits, as was originally intended. Her alertness saved almost $40,000 in taxes.

---

*You and your spouse—with your attorneys—agree on
certain issues → through your attorneys meeting or corresponding, you resolve some, but not all, remaining issues
→ attorneys prepare for trial → trial takes place, judge
makes rulings → final decree of divorce is issued → marriage ends*

Throughout this book, we have warned you against letting your fate be decided by a judge, and letting your marital assets be eaten up in lawyers' fees. If, however, all else fails and you must go to trial, then be prepared. Don't be afraid to ask your lawyer what will happen—and how much the lawyer's bill will be. And don't forget that you'll probably have to pay experts—actuaries, appraisers, financial planners and the like—if you're disputing asset values. If you can't agree on custody, you'll probably need to bring counselors, psychologists and others into court to testify. Be prepared for these bills.

## D. How Do You Finalize the Settlement?

As mentioned above, once the issues are resolved and reduced to a settlement agreement, the agreement is then taken to the court for a judge's approval. Unless it leaves the children unsupported, a judge will sign the agreement.

Usually, when the agreement is taken to court, so are the papers requesting an end of the marriage. Before that, only the complaint or petition request-

ing that the marriage end—and an answer or response from the other spouse—have been filed. Once the couple resolves the property, debt, custody, alimony and child support issues, they also usually end their marriage. In some cases, however, you may actually be divorced before you conclude your settlement. In these cases, the part of the divorce ending the marriage is "bifurcated"—meaning cut off from—the issues of property division, debt allocation, custody, alimony and child support, and resolved first.

Do not expect a grand parade, or even a telegram announcing the end of your marriage. All you're apt to receive is a notice from the court. After all the drama of divorce, the end can be nothing more than an anti-climactic notice in the mail. You might even need to call your attorney's office or the court house to make sure the marriage is really over.

You can, of course, throw yourself a party to mark the occasion.

# 21

# After the Divorce

*Congratulations…you've made it. Your divorce is over and it's probably a tremendous relief. As far as your financial life is concerned, however, the watchword after divorce is caution—not celebration.*

Just as it was important to avoid spending sprees during the divorce, it's wise to keep your expenses down once the divorce is final. You need time to adjust to your new life. The last thing you want to do is run up big bills that you can't pay.

Similarly, don't let your guard down while you wrap up the details and get ready for life as a single person—or single parent. First, you must be sure to follow through—or see that your spouse follows through—on the settlement you've worked so hard to secure. Be on the lookout, too, for people who try to pressure you into investing your money one way or another. Sit tight. You'll have plenty of time to decide what to do once you've made sure there are no loose ends from your divorce which could trip you up in the future.

## A. How Do I Finish the Business of Divorce?

Forgetting to follow through on details after divorce is one of the easiest things in the world to do. It's also one of the costliest.

During the divorce, you were under tremendous stress. Now, you may be more exhausted than you realize, and that can lead you to overlook important tasks. Even if you're feeling exhilarated, not exhausted, that state of excitement can lead to overconfidence and a lack of focus on the business at hand.

You could literally lose the property you fought to keep because of simple errors in divorce paperwork. One man lost his vacation home to his ex-wife when she sold it before the deed transferring ownership to him was recorded. Another woman had to pay off debts her ex-husband incurred because she forgot to close a joint account and he refused to pay the bills he ran up.

You've been through too much to drop the ball now. Don't put off legal and financial chores in this post-settlement phase which is as crucial as any other part of the divorce process. Use the list below to guide you.

_____ **Title documents**

Make sure that new title documents are prepared to indicate new ownership. Deeds—which transfer ownership of real estate—must be recorded at the county recorders office. New registration forms changing title in a motor vehicle (car, boat and the like) must be sent to the state department of motor vehicles. Check investment papers to see that ownership of stocks, bonds and mutual funds is properly listed.

_____ **Will and other estate planning documents**

While you were married, you may have drafted a will, created a trust or taken other steps to determine who will receive your property after you die. These documents must reflect your new status.

_____ **Insurance**

Review your health, dental and disability insurance policies. Be certain you (and your children) have adequate coverage. Also check to see if the beneficiaries of your life insurance policies are who you want them to be.

_____ **Debts**

Verify that all joint accounts are closed and that you pay all debts you agreed to incur. At the same time, contact the creditors your ex-spouse agreed to pay to make sure he or she does so. If your ex isn't paying, you can minimize damage to your own credit by paying the bills. You'll then have to take steps to get reimbursed from your ex-spouse. (See Section B, below.)

**Deposit accounts**

Check your deposit accounts—checking, savings, money markets, certificates of deposit and treasury bills. The names on the accounts should be consistent with the decisions reached in your settlement.

---

### Changing Joint Deposit Accounts

To change joint deposit accounts, write to the financial institution where you have your account. Here's some sample language to use:

Please be advised that as of _____ [date], account number _____, in the names of _____, is to be closed. All assets from that account are to be transferred into a new account in the name of _____.

You and your ex-spouse must sign this form. Some banks and brokerage firms may ask for a copy of your divorce decree, but do not send it unless you're specifically requested to do so.

---

**Children**

Make sure you understand your custody and child support agreements. If you share legal custody of your children, you should have access to their school reports, medical records and other information.

### Tips for Completing the Business of Divorce

Here are a few tips for wrapping up the loose ends:

1. Review settlement details with your lawyer, financial advisors or friends. A few days after your divorce is final—after you've recovered from the euphoria or the exhaustion—meet with your lawyer or financial advisors to go over the details of your settlement. Or, get together with the friends who supported you during your divorce. Make lists of the items that you, your attorney, your ex-spouse or others are responsible for completing. Don't leave these items to memory.

2. Keep records of all payments—for alimony, child support or property exchange—you make or receive. Make copies of all checks you send or receive. Also, use a calendar or log book to show payment amounts and the date payments are made or received. You need to record these details in case you ever go to court to raise or lower support payments or to collect unpaid support.

3. Make a copy of your final judgment and the settlement agreement. Put the original in a safe place, such as a safe deposit box.

4. Start a post-divorce file for essential papers. Keep your payment records and the duplicate of your final judgment and the settlement agreement in the file. If you experience problems, or need to refer to divorce papers for investment or tax purposes, everything will be located in an easy-to-find spot. On an emotional level, hunting for divorce documents can be frustrating. Avoid triggering old angers and reduce stress by keeping these documents within easy reach.

## B. Can I—Or My Ex-Spouse—Change the Settlement?

Your settlement agreement contains several clauses. The main ones probably deal with property division, debt allocation, alimony, child support and custody. You may be wondering if you can change any of those provisions, or if your spouse might try the same. You can *voluntarily* change the terms of your agreement. If your ex-spouse won't cooperate, you will have to go to court. Ask your attorney for the specific rulings in your state and in your case, but below are some general guides.

*Property division.* It's highly unusual that a court will approve a request by one ex-spouse to change the terms of the property division after the divorce. About the only time that such a request will be approved is if the ex-spouse who is asking to change the settlement agreement can show that the other ex-spouse hid assets—such as accounts receivable that should have been used to value a business. The ex-spouse will have to file a motion, schedule a court hearing and then provide convincing evidence at the hearing of the other party's wrongdoing.

*Debt allocation.* If your ex-spouse doesn't pay the debts he or she agreed to pay, you will no doubt need the court's assistance. You can file a motion and ask the court to order your ex to pay—and to insure it, ask the court to have your ex turn money over to the court to assure payment. To avoid damaging your own credit, however, you should go ahead and pay the bills and ask the court for an order requiring reimbursement from your ex. The court can order the reimbursement by changing any equalization payment or property distribution that hasn't yet taken place. The court might also order a wage garnishment from your ex's paycheck, or that other funds belonging to your ex be turned over to you.

*Alimony.* If you knowingly gave up alimony, you usually cannot go back to court and try to get some. Once it's waived, it's gone forever. If you are receiving or paying alimony, pay careful attention to the termination date. If you are the recipient and need money beyond the date, you can usually go back to court and ask for an extension of the alimony, *but you usually must make your request before the scheduled termination date.*

If you are the payor and you can't afford to pay the amount you've been ordered to pay in the settlement agreement, you must file a motion for modification with the court. See Chapter 19, Section B.3.c.

*Child support.* Child support is always subject to modification by a court because a court retains power over child support until the children reach 18 (or to whatever age the agreement specifies support must be paid). If you are the payor and can't afford the payments, or if you are the recipient and you can't live on the current payment, you must file papers with the court, schedule a hearing and show the judge that you cannot afford to pay—or to live on—the current support. See Chapter 19, Section D.4.c.

*Custody or visitation.* Like child support, custody and visitation are always subject to the court's modification. The parent wanting to change custody or visitation must file papers with the court, schedule a hearing and show the judge a "significant change of circumstance" since the original order. Changing custody is usually a difficult and emotionally draining process. The court uses the standard of the "best interests of the child" and does not like to change the status quo. Unless you can show that the current custody arrangement is detrimental to your children—for example, their grades are suffering or they are depressed—you are not likely to win your court hearing.

---

### Get It In Writing

When you want to change an existing court order affecting alimony, child support, custody or visitation, you can ask your ex-spouse to agree to the changes informally before filing papers and scheduling a court hearing. If your ex-spouse agrees on a modification, put it in writing and take it to the court for approval. The court will routinely approve it, as long as child support appears adequate. You may think that if you agree informally, getting court approval is not necessary. If relations later sour, however, not having court approval may cause great difficulty in enforcing the modified agreement.

## C. What Do I Want To Do With My Life?

When your divorce is over, it's more crucial than ever to re-assess where you're going financially. Rarely does anyone's post-divorce life resemble what he or she thought it would look like before the divorce. You need to adapt to changes you didn't expect.

If you have used the goal-setting tools throughout your divorce, you may simply need to make minor adjustments to your basic plans. If, however, your financial position after divorce is drastically different from what you had anticipated, you may need to re-evaluate your objectives, scale down your spending or take a crash course on investing wisely. Whatever your situation, don't jump into risky ventures to try to recoup your losses with your settlement payment.

### 1. If You Have Money To Invest

Unless you're already a successful investor, it's best to put your money into a safe parking place until you get established—personally and professionally—in your new life. First, make sure you have three to six months worth of cost-of-living expenses in savings.

Then, put your cash into a money market fund or a Certificate of Deposit (CD). When you feel you have your post-divorce life under control and your future plans are relatively clear, you can move your assets into investments where your money can work harder for you—that is, earn more return than from a money market or CD. You may start slowly with "dollar cost averaging." With this method, you put the same amount of money into your investment over a long period of time. For example, you might put $200 a month into a mutual fund. Your money will do better in some months than in others. But in the long term, you should come out ahead.

### 2. If Money Is Tight

No matter how well you've planned, you may find yourself with limited resources following your divorce. Cutting costs, then, will be your major priority. Some recently divorced people find it easier to make ends meet by pooling resources. You may be able to connect with others in similar circumstances by contacting singles clubs, Parents Without Partners or groups sponsored by religious or community organizations. Setting up a baby sitting exchange or bartering for other services with members of the group can help everyone lower expenses.

Also consider buying groceries in bulk or purchasing necessities from consumer cooperatives or warehouse distributors. To lower your housing costs, you might rent out a room or part of your home. Alternatively, you could rent part of your house for day use by artists or writers.

Avoid taking cash advances or running up the balance on credit cards, however, if you can help it. Most credit cards carry high interest charges— and that interest is not tax deductible.

You can also try to raise cash. Below are several different suggestions.

#### a. Borrow From Family or Friends

Do not feel discouraged if you have to borrow money from family or friends. Many people find they need short-term loans to get them through this transition period. In times of financial crises, some people are lucky enough to have friends or relatives who can and will help out.

#### b. Sell a Major Asset or Many Minor Items

One of the best ways you can raise cash and keep associated costs to a minimum is to sell a major asset— or hold a garage or yard sale. Few people realize how much money may be lying around their house. Selling a hardly used car you were saving until your oldest child turns 16, or a computer system you no longer use could help you through a rough period.

### c. Cash in a Tax-Deferred Account

If you have an IRA or other tax-deferred account into which you've deposited money, consider cashing it in. You'll have to pay the IRS a penalty—10% of the money you withdraw—and you'll owe income taxes on the money you take out. But paying these penalties to the IRS is probably better than struggling to get by.

### d. Obtain a Home Equity Loan

Many banks, savings and loans, credit unions and other lenders offer home equity loans, also called second mortgages. Lenders usually loan between 50% and 80% of the market value of a house, less what is still owed on it. Home equity loans have advantages and disadvantages. Be sure you understand all the terms before you sign up for one.

#### *Advantages*

- You can obtain a closed-end loan—you borrow a fixed amount of money and repay it in equal monthly installments for a set period. Or you can obtain a line of credit—you borrow as you need the money, drawing against the amount granted when you opened the account.

- The interest you pay is fully deductible on your income tax return.

- Federal law requires that interest rates on adjustable rate home equity loans be capped.

#### *Disadvantages*

- You are obligating yourself to make another monthly or periodic payment. If you are unable to pay, you may have to sell your house, or even worse, face the possibility of the lender foreclos-

ing. *Before you take out a home equity loan, be sure you can make the monthly payment.*

- While interest is deductible and capped for adjustable rate loans, it can be high.

- You may have to pay an assortment of up-front fees for such costs as an appraisal, credit report, title insurance and points that can run close to $1,000. In addition, many lenders charge a yearly fee of $25 to $50.

---

**Cancelling a Home Equity Loan**

If you have second thoughts after taking out a home equity loan, keep in mind that under the Federal Trade Commission's three-day cooling-off rule, you have the right to cancel a home equity loan or second mortgage until midnight of the third business day after you sign the contract. You must be given notice of your right to cancel and a cancellation form when you sign the contract.

---

### e. Get Your Tax Refund Fast

Sometimes, getting a tax refund quickly will help you through a cash-flow crisis, especially if the IRS owes you a lot. Each IRS district office has a Problem Resolution Office (PRO); the offices can help callers get their refunds early. Local offices are listed in the government listing of the phone book; or call the Washington, D.C. office at (202) 566-6475.

## 3. Post-Divorce Financial Planning Tips

Financial planning strategies are often based on the idyllic picture of a couple who moves from struggling to make ends meet in their twenties to a happy retirement in their sixties. This picture hardly resembles the norm for divorced people who must redesign their plans. Below are a few tips to help you do that.

### a. Update Your Net Worth and Cash Flow Statements

Your net worth and cash flow have probably changed because of the property you received or exchanged during the divorce and payments you now make or receive that you didn't before. You can't realize your financial goals in the future unless you know where you're starting from. Update the Net Worth and Cash Flow statements you completed in Chapter 13.

### b. Set Up a Debt Payment Plan

Pay off all debts you agreed to incur as part of your divorce settlement as quickly as possible. Create a payment schedule to match your pay periods. If you're paid on the first and fifteenth of the month, pay your bills then. Keep all bills in a folder. On the first of the month, take out only those bills which you will pay; write your checks, mail the bills and put the folder away until the fifteenth. Then do the same on the fifteenth. By using this system, you won't constantly think about your debts.

### c. Make Sure You Have an "Emergency Fund" and Emergency Plan

As we've recommended previously, you should have an "emergency fund" representing three to six months worth of cost-of-living expenses. Make sure you can get to this money when you need it.

You may also want to make a contingency plan that takes into account your non-financial resources. Could you move in with friends or relatives—includ-ing your adult children—if you had to? Knowing you have some kind of cushion of support makes it easier to face life. Once you've been divorced, you may find yourself dwelling on the "worst cases" you can imagine. Having a contingency plan can dispel fears and let you move on.

### d. Re-evaluate Your Insurance

Most people fall into one of two extremes—either they have too little insurance or too much of the wrong kind. Now that your divorce is over, honestly re-evaluate your insurance coverage. Do research in consumer publications and check with several agents to try to get a good overall update on your insurance position. Buy the proper coverage for your new lifestyle, or let go of old policies you no longer need.

### e. Keep Up With Changes in Your Tax Status

When your marital status changes so does your tax status. Not only might you be in a different tax bracket, but tax laws themselves may change. If you're in a higher tax bracket, you need investments that provide tax-deferred or tax-free income. More likely, however, you are in a lower tax bracket and will want to take advantage of two of the best tax planning opportunities most people have: owning a house (the interest on the mortgage is tax deductible) and contributing to an IRA or a 401k through your work (you don't pay taxes on the money you deposit until you withdraw it).

### f. Re-evaluate Your Retirement Program

How much will it cost you to maintain your current lifestyle once you retire? If you and your ex-spouse divided retirement plans during divorce, be sure to do the follow-up work on securing any payments you are supposed to receive. If you have no retirement plan, go to a brokerage house and ask for a retirement projection. Do not let yourself be pushed into any investment you are not ready to make. Once you have an accurate calculation of post-retirement living costs, investigate several types of plans before choosing one that is right for you.

### g. Take Care of Your Estate

Many people mistakenly assume that they do not have enough property to "plan their estate." If you do not plan, however, the state will do it for you after you die. You may only need a simple will or you might want to investigate a living trust. Nolo Press publishes *Plan Your Estate with a Living Trust*, by Denis Clifford, *The Simple Will Book*, also by Denis Clifford, and two software programs—*WillMaker* (with Legisoft) and *Nolo's Living Trust* (Macintosh), by Mary Randolph. Any of these publications can help you take care of your estate.

## 4.  Setting Goals After Divorce

Right now is the perfect time to look at your financial goals for the time periods listed below. Use this chart to open up ideas about where you'd like to go in the future.

## D.  How Can I Move Beyond the Divorce?

By the time your divorce ends, you may not be sure who won or who lost. You need to give yourself time to re-assess what has happened in your life. You may be so tired of the divorce process that you don't want to hear another word about money. Worse, you may feel bitter or gun shy about moving forward. As it's been said throughout your divorce, you must manage your money and your emotions if you are to end the relationship with your spouse successfully.

Once you've followed up on the legal and financial details of your settlement, check on your emotional state to make sure you won't carry unresolved feelings with you as you move into singlehood. If things are not what you anticipated, don't spend time and money in a continuing connection with your ex-spouse. Recognize your gains and cut your losses so you can get on with your new life.

These questions are designed to help you sort through the emotional-economic fallout of ending a marriage. Your answers can help you move on.

*What changes in my financial life did I not anticipate before the final settlement?*

*What will be different in my children's lives now that the divorce is over?*

*What regrets do I still have about the divorce?*

*What financial steps do I feel good about and what could I have done differently?*

*How can I continue to expand the positive steps I've taken?*

*What can I do to avoid repeating the financial mistakes I made?*

**Setting Goals**

My professional goals are:

| next six months: | next one year: | next five years: |
|---|---|---|
| | | |

My educational goals are:

| next six months: | next one year: | next five years: |
|---|---|---|
| | | |

My recreation-travel-entertainment goals are:

| next six months: | next one year. | next five years: |
|---|---|---|
| | | |

My plans for my children are:

| next six months: | next one year: | next five years: |
|---|---|---|
| | | |

My retirement goals are:

| next six months: | next one year: | next five years: |
|---|---|---|
| | | |

My other goals are:

| next six months: | next one year: | next five years: |
|---|---|---|
| | | |

# Resources Beyond the Book

*This book helps you through the divorce process by giving you strategies for evaluating your assets and debts, your likelihood of paying or receiving alimony or child support, and your children's custody. But you may need help beyond this book. The three best sources of help are a law library, lawyer or typing service.*

Before discussing each of these in detail, here's a general piece of advice: Make all decisions yourself. By reading this book, you've taken on the responsibility of getting information necessary to make informed decisions about your legal and financial affairs. If you decide to get help from others, apply this same self-empowerment principal—shop around until you find an advisor who values your competence and intelligence, and recognizes your right to make your own decisions.

## A. Law Libraries

Often, you can handle a legal problem yourself if you're willing to do some research in a law library. Here, briefly, are the basic steps to researching a legal question. For more detailed, but user-friendly, instructions on legal research, see *Legal Research: How to Find and Understand the Law*, by Steve Elias (Nolo Press).

### 1. Finding a Law Library

To do legal research, you need to find a law library that's open to the public. Public law libraries are often housed in county courthouses, public law schools and state capitals. If you can't find one, ask a public library reference librarian, court clerk or lawyer.

### 2. Finding a State Law that Affects Your Divorce

Laws passed by state legislatures are occasionally referred to in this book. To find a state law, or statute, you need to look in a multi-volume set of books called the state code. State codes are divided into titles—most states divide their titles by number; a few states divide them by subject, such as the civil code, family law code or finance code.

To read a law, find the state codes in your law library, locate the title you need, turn to the section number and read. If you already have a proper reference to the law—called the citation—finding the law is straightforward. If you don't have a citation, you can find the law by referring to the index in the code you're using.

After you read the law in the hardcover book, turn to the back of the book. There should be an insert pamphlet (called a pocket part) for the current or previous year. Look for the statute in the pocket part to see if it has been amended since the hardcover volume was published.

### 3. Going Beyond State Laws

If you want to find the answer to a legal question, rather than simply look up a law, or you want to find cases that interpret the law or otherwise shed light on your problem, you will need some guidance in basic legal research techniques. Good resources—in addition to Nolo's *Legal Research* book—that may be available in your law library are:

*Legal Research Made Easy: A Roadmap Through the Law Library Maze*, by Nolo Press and Robert Berring (Legal Star Video).

*The Legal Research Manual: A Game Plan for Legal Research and Analysis*, by Christopher and Jill Wren (A-R Editions).

*Introduction to Legal Research: A Layperson's Guide to Finding the Law*, by Al Coco (Want Publishing Co.).

*How to Find the Law,* by Morris Cohen, Robert Berring and Kent Olson (West Publishing Co.).

## 4. Using Background Resources

If you want to research a legal question related to family law but don't know where to begin, one of the best resources is the *Family Law Reporter,* published by the Bureau of National Affairs (BNA). This very thorough, four-volume publication covers all 50 states and the District of Columbia, and is updated weekly. It highlights and summarizes cases, new statutes and family law news. It also includes a guide to tax laws affecting family law, a summary of each state's divorce laws and a sample marital settlement agreement.

Most law libraries will have the *Family Law Reporter.* If you can't find it, however, you will need to look at materials written specifically for your state. Ask a law librarian for help.

## B. Lawyers and Typing Services

A lawyer can provide you with information, guidance or legal representation. A typing service can act as a "legal secretary" if you need to have documents prepared and filed in court. Typing services *cannot* give legal advice, but they charge far less than lawyers for their services. Typing services are covered in detail in Chapter 9, Section B.11.

## 1. Finding a Lawyer

Before explaining how to find a lawyer, let's first eliminate the types of lawyers you are not looking for:

- the expensive, flamboyant lawyer who gets his or her name in the newspaper all the time. That lawyer would probably charge you a bundle (several hundred dollars an hour) and pass your case on to a recent law school graduate who works in the office.

- the associate or partner at a giant law firm that represents big businesses. These lawyers charge $200-$400 an hour and few know much about divorce cases or keeping costs down.

- the lawyer who won't tell you how he or she plans to handle your case and wants to make all decisions without consulting you. These lawyers are annoyed—and intimidated—by clients who know anything about the law. What they want is a passive client who doesn't ask a lot of questions and pays the bill on time each month.

What you do want is a dedicated, smart and skilled lawyer who regularly handles family law and divorce cases. The lawyer should understand that your input must be sought for every decision. This being said, here are several ways to find a lawyer:

*Typing services.* The best referrals will probably come from an independent paralegal listed in the yellow pages under "paralegals" or "typing services." You also may be able to find help by calling the National Association of Independent Paralegals at 800-542-0034. Almost daily, independent paralegals refer their clients to lawyers and get feedback on the lawyer's work.

*Personal referrals.* This is the most common approach. If you know someone who was pleased with the services of a lawyer, call that lawyer first. If that lawyer doesn't handle divorces or can't take your case, he or she may recommend someone else. Be careful, however, when selecting a lawyer from a personal referral. A lawyer's satisfactory performance in one situation does not guarantee that the person will perform the same way in your case.

*Group legal plans.* Some unions, employers and consumer action organizations offer group plans to their members or employees, who can obtain comprehensive legal assistance for free or for low rates. If you're a member of such a plan, check it first for a lawyer.

*Prepaid legal insurance.* Prepaid legal insurance plans offer some services for a low monthly fee and charge more for additional work. Participating lawyers may use the plan as a way to get clients who are attracted by the low cost basic services, and then sell them more expensive services. If the lawyer recommends an expensive course of action, get a second opinion before you agree.

But if a plan offers extensive free advice, your initial membership fee may be worth the consultation you receive. You can always join a plan for a specific service and then not renew.

There's no guarantee that the lawyers available through these plans are of the best caliber; sometimes they aren't. Check out the plan carefully before signing up. Ask about the plan's complaint system, whether you get to choose your lawyer and whether or not the lawyer will represent you in court.

*Lawyer referral panels.* Most county bar associations will give out the names of attorneys who practice in your area. But bar associations often fail to provide meaningful screening for the attorneys listed, which means those who participate may not be the most experienced or competent.

## 2.  What to Look for in a Lawyer

No matter what approach you take to finding a lawyer, here are three suggestions on how to make sure you have the best possible working relationship.

First, fight the urge you may have to surrender your will and be intimidated by a lawyer. You should be the one who decides what you feel comfortable doing about your legal and financial affairs. You're hiring the lawyer to perform a service for you; shop around if the price or personality isn't right.

Second, you must be as comfortable as possible with any lawyer you hire. When making an appointment, ask to talk directly to the lawyer. If you can't, this may give you a hint as to how accessible he or she is.

If you do talk directly to the lawyer, ask some specific questions. Do you get clear, concise answers? If not, try someone else. If the lawyer says little ex-

cept to suggest that he or she handle the problem—with a substantial fee—watch out. You're talking with someone who doesn't know the answer and won't admit it, or someone who pulls rank on the basis of professional standing. Don't be a passive client or hire a lawyer who wants you to be one. If the lawyer admits to not knowing an answer, that isn't necessarily bad. In most cases, the lawyer must do some research.

Also, pay attention to how the lawyer responds to the fact that you have considerable information. If you read this book, you know more about divorce and money than the average person. Does the lawyer seem comfortable with that? Does the lawyer give you clear, concise answers to your questions—or does the lawyer want to maintain an aura of mystery about the legal system? Pay attention to your own intuition. Many lawyers are threatened when the client knows too much—or, in some cases, anything.

Once you find a lawyer you like, make an hour-long appointment to discuss your situation fully. Your goal at the initial conference is to find out what the lawyer recommends and how much it will cost. Go home and think about the lawyer's suggestions. If they don't make complete sense or if you have other reservations, call someone else.

Finally, keep in mind that the lawyer works for you. Once you hire a lawyer, you have the absolute right to switch to another—or to fire the lawyer and handle the matter yourself—at any time, for any reason.

## C.  Additional Resources

Below are names, addresses and phone numbers of organizations that may be able to offer additional assistance.

## 1.  Attorneys, Mediators and Therapists

American Academy of Matrimonial Lawyers
150 No. Michigan Avenue, Suite 2040
Chicago, IL 60601
312-263-6477

Center for Dispute Settlement
1666 Connecticut Avenue, N.W., Suite 501
Washington, DC 20009
202-265-9572

Center for the Family in Transition
5725 Paradise Drive, Bldg. B, Suite 300
Corte Madera, CA 94925
415-924-5750

American Association for Marriage and
Family Therapy
1100 17th Street, N.W., 10th Floor
Washington, DC 20036
202-452-0109

## 2.  Child Support

National Child Support Enforcement Association
Hall of the States
444 No. Capitol Street, N.W., Suite 613
Washington, DC 20001
202-624-8180

National Institute of Child Support Enforcement
370 L'Enfant Promenade, S.W.
Washington, DC 20447
202-401-5439
202-401-9381

U.S. Department of Health and Human Services
Office of Child Support Enforcement
6110 Executive Blvd.
Rockville, MD 20852
(Request the "Handbook on Child Support
Enforcement")

## 3.  Custody

Lesbian Mothers Resource Network
P.O. Box 21567
Seattle, WA 98111
206 325-2643

Mothers Without Custody
P.O. Box 56762
Houston, TX 77256-6762
713-840-1622

National Congress for Men and Children
2020 Pennsylvania Ave., N.W., Suite 277
Washington, DC 20006
202-328-4377 (FATHERS)

## 4.  Domestic Violence

National Coalition Against Domestic Violence
1500 Massachusetts Avenue, N.W., Suite 35
Washington, DC 20005
800-333-7233 (SAFE)

## 5.  Employment

National Displaced Homemakers Network
1411 "K" Street, N.W., Suite 930
Washington, DC 20005
202-628-6767

HOME Communications Channel
614-791-0914

## 6.  Financial Assistance

American Society of Appraisers—for a referral to a
business appraiser
2777 So. Colorado Blvd., Suite 200
Denver, CO 80222
303-758-6148

Appraisal Institute
for a referral to a real estate appraiser
875 N. Michigan Avenue, Suite 2400
Chicago, IL 60611
312-335-4100

Bankcard Holders of America
a non-profit organization helping bankcard holders
become informed consumers
560 Herndon Parkway, Suite 120
Herndon, VA 22070
703-481-1110

Institute of Business Appraisers
for a referral to a business appraiser
P.O. Box 1447
Boynton Beach, FL 33425
407-732-3202

Internal Revenue Service (IRS)
to obtain tax forms
800-829-1040

International Association of Financial Planning
for a referral to a financial planner
2 Concourse Parkway, Suite 800
Atlanta, GA 30328
404-395-1605

National Association of Enrolled Agents
for a referral to an enrolled agent
6000 Executive Blvd., Suite 205
Rockville, MD 20852
800-424-4339
301-984-6232

National Association of Independent Paralegals
for a referral to a typing service
635 Fifth Street West
Sonoma, CA 95476
800-542-0034

National Association of Professional Organizers
for a referral to someone who can help you organize
your financial papers
1163 Sherman Road
Northbrook, IL 60062

National Foundation for Consumer Credit
to find a Consumer Credit Counseling office
8611 2nd Avenue, Suite 100
Silver Springs, MD 20910
800-388-2227

Social Security Administration
to confirm work and benefits history
800-234-5772

## PRESENT VALUE FACTORS

| Periods | 1% | 2% | 3% | 4% | 5% | 6% | 7% |
|---|---|---|---|---|---|---|---|
| 1 | .9901 | .9804 | .9709 | .9615 | .9524 | .9434 | .9346 |
| 2 | .9803 | .9612 | .9426 | .9246 | .9070 | .8900 | .8734 |
| 3 | .9707 | .9423 | .9151 | .8890 | .8638 | .8396 | .8163 |
| 4 | .9610 | .9238 | .8885 | .8548 | .8227 | .7921 | .7629 |
| 5 | .9515 | .9057 | .8626 | .8219 | .7835 | .7473 | .7130 |
| 6 | .9420 | .8880 | .8375 | .7903 | .7462 | .7050 | .6663 |
| 7 | .9327 | .8706 | .8131 | .7599 | .7107 | .6651 | .6228 |
| 8 | .9235 | .8535 | .7894 | .7307 | .6768 | .6274 | .5820 |
| 9 | .9143 | .8368 | .7664 | .7026 | .6446 | .5919 | .5439 |
| 10 | .9053 | .8203 | .7441 | .6756 | .6139 | .5584 | .5083 |
| 11 | .8963 | .8043 | .7224 | .6496 | .5847 | .5268 | .4751 |
| 12 | .8874 | .7885 | .7014 | .6246 | .5568 | .4970 | .4440 |
| 13 | .8787 | .7730 | .6810 | .6006 | .5303 | .4688 | .4150 |
| 14 | .8700 | .7579 | .6611 | .5775 | .5051 | .4423 | .3878 |
| 15 | .8613 | .7430 | .6419 | .5553 | .4810 | .4173 | .3624 |
| 16 | .8528 | .7284 | .6232 | .5339 | .4581 | .3936 | .3387 |
| 17 | .8444 | .7142 | .6050 | .5134 | .4363 | .3714 | .3166 |
| 18 | .8360 | .7002 | .5874 | .4936 | .4155 | .3503 | .2959 |
| 19 | .8277 | .6864 | .5703 | .4746 | .3957 | .3305 | .2765 |
| 20 | .8195 | .6730 | .5537 | .4564 | .3769 | .3118 | .2584 |
| 21 | .8114 | .6598 | .5375 | .4388 | .3589 | .2942 | .2415 |
| 22 | .8034 | .6468 | .5219 | .4220 | .3419 | .2775 | .2257 |
| 23 | .7954 | .6342 | .5067 | .4057 | .3256 | .2618 | .2109 |
| 24 | .7876 | .6217 | .4919 | .3901 | .3101 | .2470 | .1971 |
| 25 | .7798 | .6095 | .4776 | .3751 | .2953 | .2330 | .1842 |
| 26 | .7720 | .5976 | .4637 | .3607 | .2812 | .2198 | .1722 |
| 27 | .7644 | .5859 | .4502 | .3468 | .2678 | .2074 | .1609 |
| 28 | .7568 | .5744 | .4371 | .3335 | .2551 | .1956 | .1504 |
| 29 | .7493 | .5631 | .4243 | .3207 | .2429 | .1846 | .1406 |
| 30 | .7419 | .5521 | .4120 | .3083 | .2314 | .1741 | .1314 |
| 31 | .7346 | .5412 | .4000 | .2965 | .2204 | .1643 | .1228 |
| 32 | .7273 | .5306 | .3883 | .2851 | .2099 | .1550 | .1147 |
| 33 | .7201 | .5202 | .3770 | .2741 | .1999 | .1462 | .1072 |
| 34 | .7130 | .5100 | .3660 | .2636 | .1904 | .1379 | .1002 |
| 35 | .7059 | .5000 | .3554 | .2534 | .1813 | .1301 | .0937 |
| 36 | .6989 | .4902 | .3450 | .2437 | .1727 | .1227 | .0875 |
| 37 | .6920 | .4806 | .3350 | .2343 | .1644 | .1158 | .0818 |
| 38 | .6858 | .4712 | .3252 | .2253 | .1566 | .1092 | .0765 |
| 39 | .6784 | .4619 | .3158 | .2166 | .1491 | .1031 | .0715 |
| 40 | .6717 | .4529 | .3066 | .2083 | .1420 | .0972 | .0668 |
| 41 | .6650 | .4440 | .2976 | .2003 | .1353 | .0917 | .0624 |
| 42 | .6584 | .4353 | .2890 | .1926 | .1288 | .0865 | .0583 |
| 43 | .6520 | .4268 | .2805 | .1852 | .1227 | .0816 | .0545 |
| 44 | .6454 | .4184 | .2724 | .1780 | .1169 | .0770 | .0509 |
| 45 | .6391 | .4102 | .2644 | .1712 | .1113 | .0727 | .0476 |
| 46 | .6327 | .4022 | .2567 | .1646 | .1060 | .0685 | .0445 |
| 47 | .6265 | .3943 | .2493 | .1583 | .1009 | .0647 | .0416 |
| 48 | .6203 | .3865 | .2420 | .1522 | .0961 | .0610 | .0389 |
| 49 | .6141 | .3790 | .2350 | .1463 | .0916 | .0575 | .0363 |
| 50 | .6080 | .3715 | .2281 | .1407 | .0872 | .0543 | .0339 |

PRESENT VALUE FACTORS

| Periods | 8% | 9% | 10% | 11% | 12% | 13% | 14% |
|---|---|---|---|---|---|---|---|
| 1 | .9259 | .9174 | .9091 | .9009 | .8929 | .8850 | .8772 |
| 2 | .8573 | .8417 | .8264 | .8116 | .7972 | .7831 | .7695 |
| 3 | .7938 | .7722 | .7513 | .7312 | .7118 | .6931 | .6750 |
| 4 | .7350 | .7084 | .6830 | .6587 | .6355 | .6133 | .5921 |
| 5 | .6806 | .6499 | .6209 | .5935 | .5674 | .5428 | .5194 |
| 6 | .6302 | .5963 | .5645 | .5346 | .5066 | .4803 | .4556 |
| 7 | .5835 | .5470 | .5132 | .4817 | .4523 | .4251 | .3996 |
| 8 | .5403 | .5019 | .4665 | .4339 | .4039 | .3762 | .3506 |
| 9 | .5002 | .4604 | .4241 | .3909 | .3606 | .3329 | .3075 |
| 10 | .4632 | .4224 | .3855 | .3522 | .3220 | .2946 | .2697 |
| 11 | .4289 | .3875 | .3505 | .3173 | .2875 | .2607 | .2366 |
| 12 | .3971 | .3555 | .3186 | .2858 | .2567 | .2307 | .2076 |
| 13 | .3677 | .3262 | .2897 | .2575 | .2292 | .2042 | .1821 |
| 14 | .3405 | .2992 | .2633 | .2320 | .2046 | .1807 | .1597 |
| 15 | .3152 | .2745 | .2394 | .2090 | .1827 | .1599 | .1401 |
| 16 | .2919 | .2519 | .2176 | .1883 | .1631 | .1415 | .1229 |
| 17 | .2703 | .2311 | .1978 | .1696 | .1456 | .1252 | .1078 |
| 18 | .2502 | .2120 | .1799 | .1528 | .1300 | .1108 | .0946 |
| 19 | .2317 | .1945 | .1635 | .1377 | .1161 | .0981 | .0829 |
| 20 | .2145 | .1784 | .1486 | .1240 | .1037 | .0868 | .0728 |
| 21 | .1987 | .1637 | .1351 | .1117 | .0926 | .0768 | .0638 |
| 22 | .1839 | .1502 | .1228 | .1007 | .0826 | .0680 | .0560 |
| 23 | .1703 | .1378 | .1117 | .0907 | .0738 | .0601 | .0491 |
| 24 | .1577 | .1264 | .1015 | .0817 | .0659 | .0532 | .0431 |
| 25 | .1460 | .1160 | .0923 | .0736 | .0588 | .0471 | .0378 |
| 26 | .1352 | .1064 | .0839 | .0663 | .0525 | .0417 | .0331 |
| 27 | .1252 | .0976 | .0763 | .0597 | .0469 | .0369 | .0291 |
| 28 | .1159 | .0895 | .0693 | .0538 | .0419 | .0326 | .0255 |
| 29 | .1073 | .0822 | .0630 | .0485 | .0374 | .0289 | .0224 |
| 30 | .0994 | .0754 | .0573 | .0437 | .0334 | .0256 | .0196 |
| 31 | .0920 | .0691 | .0521 | .0394 | .0298 | .0226 | .0172 |
| 32 | .0852 | .0634 | .0474 | .0355 | .0266 | .0200 | .0151 |
| 33 | .0789 | .0582 | .0431 | .0319 | .0238 | .0177 | .0132 |
| 34 | .0730 | .0534 | .0391 | .0288 | .0212 | .0157 | .0116 |
| 35 | .0676 | .0490 | .0356 | .0259 | .0189 | .0139 | .0102 |
| 36 | .0626 | .0449 | .0323 | .0234 | .0169 | .0123 | .0089 |
| 37 | .0580 | .0412 | .0294 | .0210 | .0151 | .0109 | .0078 |
| 38 | .0537 | .0378 | .0267 | .0190 | .0135 | .0096 | .0069 |
| 39 | .0497 | .0347 | .0243 | .0171 | .0120 | .0085 | .0060 |
| 40 | .0460 | .0318 | .0221 | .0154 | .0107 | .0075 | .0053 |
| 41 | .0426 | .0292 | .0201 | .0139 | .0096 | .0067 | .0046 |
| 42 | .0395 | .0268 | .0183 | .0125 | .0086 | .0059 | .0041 |
| 43 | .0365 | .0246 | .0166 | .0112 | .0076 | .0052 | .0036 |
| 44 | .0338 | .0226 | .0151 | .0101 | .0068 | .0046 | .0031 |
| 45 | .0313 | .0207 | .0137 | .0091 | .0061 | .0041 | .0028 |
| 46 | .0290 | .0190 | .0125 | .0082 | .0054 | .0036 | .0024 |
| 47 | .0269 | .0174 | .0113 | .0074 | .0059 | .0032 | .0021 |
| 48 | .0249 | .0160 | .0103 | .0067 | .0043 | .0028 | .0019 |
| 49 | .0230 | .0147 | .0094 | .0060 | .0039 | .0025 | .0016 |
| 50 | .0213 | .0134 | .0085 | .0054 | .0035 | .0022 | .0014 |

## PRESENT VALUE FACTORS

| Periods | 15% | 16% | 17% | 18% | 19% | 20% |
|---|---|---|---|---|---|---|
| 1 | .8696 | .8621. | .8547 | .8475 | .8403. | .8333 |
| 2 | .7561 | .7432 | .7305 | .7182 | .7062 | .6944 |
| 3 | .6575 | .6407 | .6244 | .6086 | .5934 | .5787 |
| 4 | .5718 | .5523 | .5337 | .5158 | .4987 | .4823 |
| 5 | .4972 | .4761 | .4561 | .4371 | .4190 | .4019 |
| 6 | .4323 | .4104 | .3898 | .3704 | .3521 | .3349 |
| 7 | .3759 | .3538 | .3332 | .3139 | .2959 | .2791 |
| 8 | .3269 | .3050 | .2848 | .2660 | .2487 | .2326 |
| 9 | .2843 | .2630 | .2434 | .2255 | .2090 | .1938 |
| 10 | .2472 | .2267 | .2080 | .1911 | .1756 | .1615 |
| 11 | .2149 | .1954 | .1778 | .1619 | .1476 | .1346 |
| 12 | .1869 | .1685 | .1520 | .1372 | .1240 | .1122 |
| 13 | .1625 | .1452 | .1299 | .1163 | .1042 | .0935 |
| 14 | .1413 | .1252 | .1110 | .0985 | .0876 | .0779 |
| 15 | .1229 | .1079 | .0949 | .0835 | .0736 | .0649 |
| 16 | .1069 | .0930 | .0811 | .0708 | .0618 | |
| 17 | .0929 | .0802 | .0693 | .0600 | .0520 | |
| 18 | .0808 | .0691 | .0592 | .0508 | .0437 | |
| 19 | .0703 | .0596 | .0506 | .0431 | .0367 | |
| 20 | .0611 | .0514 | .0433 | .0365 | .0308 | |
| 21 | .0531 | .0443 | .0370 | .0309 | .0259 | |
| 22 | .0462 | .0382 | .0316 | .0262 | .0218 | |
| 23 | .0402 | .0329 | .0270 | .0222 | .0183 | |
| 24 | .0349 | .0284 | .0231 | .0188 | .0154 | |
| 25 | .0304 | .0245 | .0197 | .0160 | .0129 | |
| 26 | .0264 | .0211 | .0169 | .0135 | .0109 | |
| 27 | .0230 | .0182 | .0144 | .0115 | .0091 | |
| 28 | .0200 | .0157 | .0123 | .0097 | .0077 | |
| 29 | .0174 | .0135 | .0105 | .0082 | .0064 | |
| 30 | .0151 | .0116 | .0090 | .0070 | .0054 | |
| 31 | .0131 | .0100 | .0077 | .0059 | .0046 | |
| 32 | .0114 | .0087 | .0066 | .0050 | .0038 | |
| 33 | .0099 | .0075 | .0056 | .0042 | .0032 | |
| 34 | .0086 | .0064 | .0048 | .0036 | .0027 | |
| 35 | .0075 | .0055 | .0041 | .0030 | .0023 | |
| 36 | .0065 | .0048 | .0035 | .0026 | .0019 | |
| 37 | .0057 | .0041 | .0030 | .0022 | .0016 | |
| 38 | .0049 | .0036 | .0026 | .0019 | .0013 | |
| 39 | .0043 | .0031 | .0022 | .0016 | .0011 | |
| 40 | .0037 | .0026 | .0019 | .0013 | .0010 | |
| 41 | .0032 | .0023 | .0016 | .0011 | .0008 | |
| 42 | .0028 | .0020 | .0014 | .0010 | .0007 | |
| 43 | .0025 | .0017 | .0012 | .0008 | .0006 | |
| 44 | .0021 | .0015 | .0010 | .0007 | .0005 | |
| 45 | .0019 | .0013 | .0009 | .0006 | .0004 | |
| 46 | .0016 | .0011 | .0007 | .0005 | .0003 | |
| 47 | .0014 | .0009 | .0006 | .0004 | .0003 | |
| 48 | .0012 | .0008 | .0005 | .0004 | .0002 | |
| 49 | .0011 | .0007 | .0005 | .0003 | .0002 | |
| 50 | .0009 | .0006 | .0004 | .0003 | .0002 | |

## FUTURE VALUE FACTORS

| Period | 1% | 2% | 3% | 4% | 5% | 6% | 7% |
|---|---|---|---|---|---|---|---|
| 1 | 1.0100 | 1.0200 | 1.0300 | 1.0400 | 1.0500 | 1.0600 | 1.0700 |
| 2 | 1.0201 | 1.0404 | 1.0609 | 1.0816 | 1.1025 | 1.1236 | 1.1449 |
| 3 | 1.0303 | 1.0612 | 1.0927 | 1.1249 | 1.1576 | 1.1910 | 1.2250 |
| 4 | 1.0406 | 1.0824 | 1.1255 | 1.1699 | 1.2155 | 1.2625 | 1.3108 |
| 5 | 1.0510 | 1.1041 | 1.1593 | 1.2167 | 1.2763 | 1.3382 | 1.4026 |
| 6 | 1.0615 | 1.1262 | 1.1941 | 1.2653 | 1.3401 | 1.4185 | 1.5007 |
| 7 | 1.0721 | 1.1487 | 1.2299 | 1.3159 | 1.4071 | 1.5036 | 1.6058 |
| 8 | 1.0829 | 1.1717 | 1.2668 | 1.3686 | 1.4775 | 1.5938 | 1.7182 |
| 9 | 1.0937 | 1.1951 | 1.3048 | 1.4233 | 1.5513 | 1.6895 | 1.8385 |
| 10 | 1.1046 | 1.2190 | 1.3439 | 1.4802 | 1.6289 | 1.7908 | 1.9672 |
| 11 | 1.1157 | 1.2434 | 1.3842 | 1.5395 | 1.7103 | 1.8983 | 2.1049 |
| 12 | 1.1268 | 1.2682 | 1.4258 | 1.6010 | 1.7959 | 2.0122 | 2.2522 |
| 13 | 1.1381 | 1.2936 | 1.4685 | 1.6651 | 1.8856 | 2.1329 | 2.4098 |
| 14 | 1.1495 | 1.3195 | 1.5126 | 1.7317 | 1.9799 | 2.2609 | 2.5785 |
| 15 | 1.1610 | 1.3459 | 1.5580 | 1.8009 | 2.0789 | 2.3966 | 2.7590 |
| 16 | 1.1726 | 1.3728 | 1.6047 | 1.8730 | 2.1829 | 2.5404 | 2.9522 |
| 17 | 1.1843 | 1.4002 | 1.6528 | 1.9479 | 2.2920 | 2.6928 | 3.1588 |
| 18 | 1.1961 | 1.4282 | 1.7024 | 2.0258 | 2.4066 | 2.8543 | 3.3799 |
| 19 | 1.2081 | 1.4568 | 1.7535 | 2.1068 | 2.5270 | 3.0256 | 3.6165 |
| 20 | 1.2202 | 1.4859 | 1.8061 | 2.1911 | 2.6533 | 3.2071 | 3.8697 |
| 21 | 1.2324 | 1.5157 | 1.8603 | 2.2788 | 2.7860 | 3.3996 | 4.1406 |
| 22 | 1.2447 | 1.5460 | 1.9161 | 2.3699 | 2.9253 | 3.6035 | 4.4304 |
| 23 | 1.2572 | 1.5769 | 1.9736 | 2.4647 | 3.0715 | 3.8197 | 4.7405 |
| 24 | 1.2697 | 1.6084 | 2.0328 | 2.5633 | 3.2251 | 4.0489 | 5.0724 |
| 25 | 1.2824 | 1.6406 | 2.0938 | 2.6658 | 3.3864 | 4.2919 | 5.4274 |
| 26 | 1.2953 | 1.6734 | 2.1566 | 2.7725 | 3.5557 | 4.5494 | 5.8074 |
| 27 | 1.3082 | 1.7069 | 2.2213 | 2.8834 | 3.7335 | 4.8223 | 6.2139 |
| 28 | 1.3213 | 1.7410 | 2.2879 | 2.9987 | 3.9201 | 5.1117 | 6.6488 |
| 29 | 1.3345 | 1.7758 | 2.3566 | 3.1187 | 4.1161 | 5.4184 | 7.1143 |
| 30 | 1.3478 | 1.8114 | 2.4273 | 3.2434 | 4.3219 | 5.7435 | 7.6123 |
| 31 | 1.3613 | 1.8476 | 2.5001 | 3.3731 | 4.5380 | 6.0881 | 8.1451 |
| 32 | 1.3749 | 1.8845 | 2.5751 | 3.5081 | 4.7649 | 6.4534 | 8.7153 |
| 33 | 1.3887 | 1.9222 | 2.6523 | 3.6484 | 5.0032 | 6.8406 | 9.3253 |
| 34 | 1.4026 | 1.9607 | 2.7319 | 3.7943 | 5.2533 | 7.2510 | 9.9781 |
| 35 | 1.4166 | 1.9999 | 2.8139 | 3.9461 | 5.5160 | 7.6861 | 10.6766 |
| 36 | 1.4308 | 2.0399 | 2.8983 | 4.1039 | 5.7918 | 8.1473 | 11.4239 |
| 37 | 1.4451 | 2.0807 | 2.9852 | 4.2681 | 6.0814 | 8.6361 | 12.2236 |
| 38 | 1.4595 | 2.1223 | 3.0748 | 4.4388 | 6.3855 | 9.1543 | 13.0793 |
| 39 | 1.4741 | 2.1647 | 3.1670 | 4.6164 | 6.7048 | 9.7035 | 13.9948 |
| 40 | 1.4889 | 2.2080 | 3.2620 | 4.8010 | 7.0400 | 10.2857 | 14.9745 |
| 41 | 1.5038 | 2.2522 | 3.3599 | 4.9931 | 7.3920 | 10.9029 | 16.0227 |
| 42 | 1.5188 | 2.2972 | 3.4607 | 5.1928 | 7.7616 | 11.5570 | 17.1443 |
| 43 | 1.5340 | 2.3432 | 3.5645 | 5.4005 | 8.1497 | 12.2505 | 18.3444 |
| 44 | 1.5493 | 2.3901 | 3.6715 | 5.6165 | 8.5572 | 12.9855 | 19.6285 |
| 45 | 1.5648 | 2.4379 | 3.7816 | 5.8412 | 8.9850 | 13.7646 | 21.0025 |
| 46 | 1.5805 | 2.4866 | 3.8950 | 6.0748 | 9.4343 | 14.5905 | 22.4726 |
| 47 | 1.5963 | 2.5363 | 4.0119 | 6.3178 | 9.9060 | 15.4659 | 24.0457 |
| 48 | 1.6122 | 2.5871 | 4.1323 | 6.5705 | 10.4013 | 16.3939 | 25.7289 |
| 49 | 1.6283 | 2.6388 | 4.2562 | 6.8333 | 10.9213 | 17.3775 | 27.5299 |
| 50 | 1.6446 | 2.6916 | 4.3839 | 7.1067 | 11.4674 | 18.4302 | 29.4570 |

## FUTURE VALUE FACTORS

| Period | 8% | 9% | 10% | 11% | 12% | 13% | 14% |
|---|---|---|---|---|---|---|---|
| 1 | 1.0800 | 1.0900 | 1.1000 | 1.1100 | 1.1200 | 1.1300 | 1.1400 |
| 2 | 1.1664 | 1.1881 | 1.2100 | 1.2321 | 1.2544 | 1.2769 | 1.2996 |
| 3 | 1.2597 | 1.2950 | 1.3310 | 1.3676 | 1.4049 | 1.4429 | 1.4815 |
| 4 | 1.3605 | 1.4116 | 1.4641 | 1.5181 | 1.5735 | 1.6305 | 1.6890 |
| 5 | 1.4693 | 1.5386 | 1.6105 | 1.6851 | 1.7623 | 1.8424 | 1.9254 |
| 6 | 1.5869 | 1.6771 | 1.7716 | 1.8704 | 1.9738 | 2.0820 | 2.1950 |
| 7 | 1.7138 | 1.8280 | 1.9487 | 2.0762 | 2.2107 | 2.3526 | 2.5023 |
| 8 | 1.8509 | 1.9926 | 2.1436 | 2.3045 | 2.4760 | 2.6584 | 2.8526 |
| 9 | 1.9990 | 2.1719 | 2.3579 | 2.5580 | 2.7731 | 3.0040 | 3.2519 |
| 10 | 2.1589 | 2.3674 | 2.5937 | 2.8394 | 3.1058 | 3.3946 | 3.7072 |
| 11 | 2.3316 | 2.5804 | 2.8531 | 3.1518 | 3.4786 | 3.8359 | 4.2263 |
| 12 | 2.5182 | 2.8127 | 3.1384 | 3.4985 | 3.8960 | 4.3345 | 4.8179 |
| 13 | 2.7196 | 3.0658 | 3.4523 | 3.8833 | 4.3635 | 4.8981 | 5.4924 |
| 14 | 2.9372 | 3.3417 | 3.7975 | 4.3104 | 4.8871 | 5.5348 | 6.2613 |
| 15 | 3.1722 | 3.6425 | 4.1772 | 4.7846 | 5.4736 | 6.2543 | 7.1379 |
| 16 | 3.4259 | 3.9703 | 4.5950 | 5.3109 | 6.1304 | 7.0673 | 8.1372 |
| 17 | 3.7000 | 4.3276 | 5.0545 | 5.8951 | 6.8660 | 7.9861 | 9.2765 |
| 18 | 3.0000 | 4.7171 | 5.5599 | 6.5436 | 7.6900 | 9.0243 | 10.5752 |
| 19 | 4.3157 | 5.1417 | 6.1159 | 7.2633 | 8.6128 | 10.1974 | 12.0557 |
| 20 | 4.6610 | 5.6044 | 6.7275 | 8.0623 | 9.6463 | 11.5231 | 13.7435 |
| 21 | 5.0338 | 6.1088 | 7.4003 | 8.9492 | 10.8038 | 13.0211 | 15.6676 |
| 22 | 5.4365 | 6.6586 | 8.1403 | 9.9336 | 12.1003 | 14.7138 | 17.8610 |
| 23 | 5.8715 | 7.2579 | 8.9543 | 11.0263 | 13.5523 | 16.6266 | 20.3616 |
| 24 | 6.3412 | 7.9111 | 9.8497 | 12.2392 | 15.1786 | 18.7881 | 23.2122 |
| 25 | 6.8485 | 8.6231 | 10.8347 | 13.5855 | 17.0001 | 21.2305 | 26.4619 |
| 26 | 7.3964 | 9.3992 | 11.9182 | 15.0799 | 19.0401 | 23.9905 | 30.1666 |
| 27 | 7.9881 | 10.2451 | 13.1100 | 16.7387 | 21.3249 | 27.1093 | 34.3899 |
| 28 | 8.6271 | 11.1671 | 14.4210 | 18.5799 | 23.8839 | 30.6335 | 39.2045 |
| 29 | 9.3173 | 12.1722 | 15.8631 | 20.6237 | 26.7499 | 34.6158 | 44.6931 |
| 30 | 10.0627 | 13.2677 | 17.4494 | 22.8923 | 29.9599 | 39.1159 | 50.9502 |
| 31 | 10.8677 | 14.4618 | 19.1943 | 25.4104 | 33.5551 | 44.2010 | 58.0832 |
| 32 | 11.7371 | 15.7633 | 21.1138 | 28.2056 | 37.5817 | 49.9471 | 66.2148 |
| 33 | 12.6761 | 17.1820 | 23.2252 | 31.3082 | 42.0915 | 56.4402 | 75.4849 |
| 34 | 13.6901 | 18.7284 | 25.5477 | 34.7521 | 47.1425 | 63.7774 | 86.0528 |
| 35 | 14.7853 | 20.4140 | 28.1024 | 38.5749 | 52.7996 | 72.0685 | 98.1002 |
| 36 | 15.9682 | 22.2512 | 30.9128 | 42.8181 | 59.1356 | 81.4374 | 111.8342 |
| 37 | 17.2456 | 24.2538 | 34.0039 | 47.5281 | 66.2318 | 92.0243 | 127.4910 |
| 38 | 18.6253 | 26.4367 | 37.4043 | 52.7562 | 74.1797 | 103.9874 | 145.3397 |
| 39 | 20.1153 | 28.8160 | 41.1448 | 58.5593 | 83.0812 | 117.5058 | 165.6873 |
| 40 | 21.7245 | 31.4094 | 45.2593 | 65.0009 | 93.0510 | 132.7816 | 188.8835 |
| 41 | 23.4625 | 34.2363 | 49.7852 | 72.1510 | 104.2171 | 150.0432 | 215.3272 |
| 42 | 25.3395 | 37.3175 | 54.7637 | 80.0876 | 116.7231 | 169.5488 | 245.4730 |
| 43 | 27.3666 | 40.6761 | 60.2401 | 88.8972 | 130.7299 | 191.5901 | 279.8392 |
| 44 | 29.5560 | 44.3370 | 66.2641 | 98.6759 | 146.4175 | 216.4968 | 319.0167 |
| 45 | 31.9204 | 48.3273 | 72.8905 | 109.5302 | 163.9876 | 244.6414 | 363.6791 |
| 46 | 34.4741 | 52.6767 | 80.1795 | 121.5786 | 183.6661 | 276.4448 | 414.5941 |
| 47 | 37.2320 | 57.4176 | 88.1975 | 134.9522 | 205.7061 | 312.3826 | 472.6373 |
| 48 | 40.2106 | 62.5852 | 97.0172 | 149.7970 | 230.3908 | 352.9923 | 538.8065 |
| 49 | 43.4274 | 68.2179 | 106.7190 | 166.2746 | 258.0377 | 398.8814 | 614.2395 |
| 50 | 46.9016 | 74.3575 | 117.3909 | 184.5648 | 289.0022 | 450.7359 | 700.2330 |

FUTURE VALUE FACTORS

| Period | 15% | 16% | 17% | 18% | 19% | 20% |
|---|---|---|---|---|---|---|
| 1 | 1.1500 | 1.1600 | 1.1700 | 1.1800 | 1.1900 | 1.2000 |
| 2 | 1.3225 | 1.3456 | 1.3689 | 1.3924 | 1.4161 | 1.4400 |
| 3 | 1.5209 | 1.5609 | 1.6016 | 1.6430 | 1.6852 | 1.7280 |
| 4 | 1.7490 | 1.8106 | 1.8739 | 1.9388 | 2.0053 | 2.0736 |
| 5 | 2.0114 | 2.1003 | 2.1924 | 2.2878 | 2.3864 | 2.4883 |
| 6 | 2.3131 | 2.4364 | 2.5652 | 2.6996 | 2.8398 | 2.9860 |
| 7 | 2.6600 | 2.8262 | 3.0012 | 3.1855 | 3.3793 | 3.5832 |
| 8 | 3.0590 | 3.2784 | 3.5115 | 3.7589 | 4.0214 | 4.2998 |
| 9 | 3.5179 | 3.8030 | 4.1084 | 4.4355 | 4.7854 | 5.1598 |
| 10 | 4.0456 | 4.4114 | 4.8068 | 5.2338 | 5.6947 | 6.1917 |
| 11 | 4.6524 | 5.1173 | 5.6240 | 6.1759 | 6.7767 | 7.4301 |
| 12 | 5.3503 | 5.9360 | 6.5801 | 7.2876 | 8.0642 | 8.9161 |
| 13 | 6.1528 | 6.8858 | 7.6987 | 8.5994 | 9.5964 | 10.6993 |
| 14 | 7.0757 | 7.9875 | 9.0075 | 10.1472 | 11.4198 | 12.8392 |
| 15 | 8.1371 | 9.2655 | 10.5387 | 11.9737 | 13.5895 | 15.4070 |
| 16 | 9.3576 | 10.7480 | 12.3303 | 14.1290 | 16.1715 | |
| 17 | 10.7613 | 12.4677 | 14.4264 | 16.6722 | 19.2441 | |
| 18 | 12.3755 | 14.4625 | 16.8790 | 19.6733 | 22.9005 | |
| 19 | 14.2318 | 16.7765 | 19.7484 | 23.2144 | 27.2516 | |
| 20 | 16.3665 | 19.4608 | 23.1056 | 27.3930 | 32.4294 | |
| 21 | 18.8215 | 22.5745 | 27.0336 | 32.3238 | 38.5910 | |
| 22 | 21.6447 | 26.1864 | 31.6293 | 38.1421 | 45.9233 | |
| 23 | 24.8915 | 30.3762 | 37.0062 | 45.0076 | 54.6487 | |
| 24 | 28.6252 | 35.2364 | 43.2973 | 53.1090 | 65.0320 | |
| 25 | 32.9190 | 40.8742 | 50.6578 | 62.6686 | 77.3881 | |
| 26 | 37.8568 | 47.4141 | 59.2697 | 73.9490 | 92.0918 | |
| 27 | 43.5353 | 55.0004 | 69.3455 | 87.2598 | 109.5893 | |
| 28 | 50.0656 | 63.8004 | 81.1342 | 102.9666 | 130.4112 | |
| 29 | 57.5755 | 74.0085 | 94.9271 | 121.5005 | 155.1893 | |
| 30 | 66.2118 | 85.8499 | 111.0647 | 143.3706 | 184.6753 | |
| 31 | 76.1435 | 99.5859 | 129.9456 | 169.1774 | 219.7636 | |
| 32 | 87.5651 | 115.5196 | 152.0364 | 199.6293 | 261.5187 | |
| 33 | 100.6998 | 134.0027 | 177.8826 | 235.5625 | 311.2073 | |
| 34 | 115.8048 | 155.4432 | 208.1226 | 277.9638 | 370.3366 | |
| 35 | 133.1755 | 180.3141 | 243.5035 | 327.9973 | 440.7006 | |
| 36 | 153.1519 | 209.1643 | 284.8990 | 387.0368 | 524.4337 | |
| 37 | 176.1246 | 242.6306 | 333.3319 | 456.7034 | 624.0761 | |
| 38 | 202.5433 | 281.4515 | 389.9983 | 538.9100 | 742.6506 | |
| 39 | 232.9248 | 326.4838 | 456.2980 | 635.9139 | 883.7542 | |
| 40 | 267.8635 | 378.7212 | 533.8687 | 750.3783 | 1051.6675 | |
| 41 | 308.0431 | 439.3165 | 624.6264 | 885.4464 | 1251.4843 | |
| 42 | 354.2495 | 509.6072 | 730.8129 | 1044.8268 | 1489.2664 | |
| 43 | 407.3870 | 591.1443 | 855.0511 | 1232.8956 | 1772.2270 | |
| 44 | 468.4950 | 685.7274 | 1000.4098 | 1454.8168 | 2108.9501 | |
| 45 | 538.7693 | 795.4438 | 1170.4794 | 1716.6839 | 2509.6506 | |
| 46 | 619.5847 | 922.7148 | 1369.4609 | 2025.6870 | 2986.4842 | |
| 47 | 712.5224 | 1070.3492 | 1602.2693 | 2390.3106 | 3553.9162 | |
| 48 | 819.4007 | 1241.6051 | 1874.6550 | 2820.5665 | 4229.1603 | |
| 49 | 942.3108 | 1440.2619 | 2193.3464 | 3328.2685 | 5032.7008 | |
| 50 | 1083.6574 | 1670.7038 | 2566.2153 | 3927.3569 | 5988.9139 | |

# Index

## ESTATE PLANNING & PROBATE

### Plan Your Estate With a Living Trust

*Attorney Denis Clifford*
*National 1st Edition*

This book covers every significant aspect of estate planning and gives detailed specific, instructions for preparing a living trust, a document that lets your family avoid expensive and lengthy probate court proceedings after your death. *Plan Your Estate* includes all the tear-out forms and step-by-step instructions to let you prepare an estate plan designed for your special needs.

**$19.95/NEST**

### Nolo's Simple Will Book

*Attorney Denis Clifford*
*National 2nd Edition*

It's easy to write a legally valid will using this book. The instructions and forms enable people to draft a will for all needs, including naming a personal guardian for minor children, leaving property to minor children or young adults and updating a will when necessary. Good in all states except Louisiana.

**$17.95/SWIL**

### The Power of Attorney Book

*Attorney Denis Clifford*
*National 4th Edition*

Who will take care of your affairs, and make your financial and medical decisions if you can't? With this book you can appoint someone you trust to carry out your wishes and stipulate exactly what kind of care you want or don't want. Includes Durable Power of Attorney and Living Will Forms.

**$19.95/POA**

### How to Probate an Estate

*Julia Nissley*
*California 6th Edition*

If you find yourself responsible for winding up the legal and financial affairs of a deceased family member or friend, you can often save costly attorneys' fees by handling the probate process yourself. This book shows you the simple procedures you can use to transfer assets that don't require probate, including property held in joint tenancy or living trusts or as community property.

**$29.95/PAE**

### The Conservatorship Book

*Lisa Goldoftas & Attorney Carolyn Farren*
*California 1st Edition*

When a family member or close relative becomes incapacitated due to illness or age, it may be necessary to name a conservator for taking charge of their medical and financial affairs. *The Conservatorship Book* will help you determine when and what kind of conservatorship is necessary. The book comes with complete instructions and all the forms necessary to file conservatorship documents, appear in court, be appointed conservator and end a conservatorship when it is no longer necessary.

**$24.95/CON**

## LEGAL REFORM

### Legal Breakdown: 40 Ways to Fix Our Legal System

*Nolo Press Editors and Staff*
*National 1st Edition*

*Legal Breakdown* presents 40 common sense proposals to make our legal system fairer, faster, cheaper and more accessible. It explains such things as why we should abolish probate, take divorce out of court, treat jurors better and give them more power, and make a host of other fundamental changes.

**$8.95/LEG**

## GOING TO COURT

### Everybody's Guide to Small Claims Court

*Attorney Ralph Warner*
*National 5th Edition*
*California 9th Edition*

These books will help you decide if you should sue in small claims court, show you how to file and serve papers, tell you what to bring to court and how to collect a judgment.

**National $15.95/NSCC**
**California $14.95/ CSCC**

### Fight Your Ticket

*Attorney David Brown*
*California 4th Edition*

This book shows you how to fight an unfair traffic ticket—when you're stopped, at arraignment, at trial and on appeal.

**$17.95/FYT**

### Collect Your Court Judgment

*Gini Graham Scott, Attorney Stephen Elias & Lisa Goldoftas*
*California 2nd Edition*

This book contains step-by-step instructions and all the forms you need to collect a court judgment from the debtor's bank accounts, wages, business receipts, real estate or other assets.

**$19.95/JUDG**

### How to Change Your Name

*Attorneys David Loeb & David Brown*
*California 5th Edition*

This book explains how to change your name legally and provides all the necessary court forms with detailed instructions on how to fill them out.

**$19.95/NAME**

### The Criminal Records Book

*Attorney Warren Siegel*
*California 3rd Edition*

This book shows you step-by-step how to seal criminal records, dismiss convictions, destroy marijuana records and reduce felony convictions.

**$19.95/CRIM**

## MONEY MATTERS

### Barbara Kaufman's Consumer Action Guide
*Barbara Kaufman*
*California 1st Edition*
This practical handbook is filled with information on hundreds of consumer topics. Barbara Kaufman, the Bay Area's award-winning host and producer of KCBS Radio's *Call for Action*, gives consumers access to their legal rights, providing addresses and phone numbers of where to complain where things to wrong, and providing resources if more help is necessary.
**$14.95/CAG**

### Money Troubles: Legal Strategies to Cope With Your Debts
*Attorney Robin Leonard*
*National 1st Edition*
Are you behind on your credit card bills or loan payments? If you are, then *Money Troubles* is exactly what you need. Covering everything from knowing what your rights are—and asserting them to helping you evaluate your individual situation, this practical, straightforward book is for anyone who needs help understanding and dealing with the complex and often scary topic of debts.
**$16.95/MT**

### How to File for Bankruptcy
*Attorneys Stephen Elias, Albin Renauer & Robin Leonard*
*National 3rd Edition*
Trying to decide whether or not filing for bankruptcy makes sense? *How to File for Bankruptcy* contains an overview of the process and all the forms plus step-by-step instructions on the procedures to follow.
**$24.95/HFB**

### Simple Contracts for Personal Use
*Attorney Stephen Elias & Marcia Stewart*
*National 2nd Edition*
This book contains clearly written legal form contracts to buy and sell property, borrow and lend money, store and lend personal property, release others from personal liability, or pay a contractor to do home repairs. Includes agreements to arrange child care and contract with caterers, photographers and other service providers for special events.
**$16.95/CONT**

## FAMILY MATTERS

### The Living Together Kit
*Attorneys Toni Ihara & Ralph Warner*
*National 6th Edition*
*The Living Together Kit* is a detailed guide designed to help the increasing number of unmarried couples living together understand the laws that affect them. Sample agreements and instructions are included.
**$17.95/LTK**

### A Legal Guide for Lesbian and Gay Couples
*Attorneys Hayden Curry & Denis Clifford*
*National 6th Edition*
Laws designed to regulate and protect unmarried couples don't apply to lesbian and gay couples. This book shows you step-by-step how to write a living-together contract, plan for medical emergencies, and plan your estates. Includes forms, sample agreements and lists of both national lesbian and gay legal organizations, and AIDS organizations.
**$17.95/LG**

### The Guardianship Book
*Lisa Goldoftas & Attorney David Brown*
*California 1st Edition*
*The Guardianship Book* provides step-by-step instructions and the forms needed to obtain a legal guardianship without a lawyer.
**$19.95/GB**

### How to Do Your Own Divorce
*Attorney Charles Sherman*
*(Texas Ed. by Sherman & Simons)*
*California 17th Edition & Texas 4th Edition*
These books contain all the forms and instructions you need to do your divorce without a lawyer.
**California $18.95/CDIV**
**Texas $17.95/TDIV**

### Practical Divorce Solutions
*Attorney Charles Sherman*
*California 2nd Edition*
This book is a valuable guide to the emotional aspects of divorce as well as an overview of the legal and financial decisions that must be made.
**$12.95/PDS**

### California Marriage & Divorce Law
*Attorneys Ralph Warner, Toni Ihara & Stephen Elias*
*California 11th Edition*
This book explains community property, pre-nuptial contracts, foreign marriages, buying a house, getting a divorce, dividing property, and more.
**$19.95/MARR**

### How to Adopt Your Stepchild in California
*Frank Zagone & Attorney Mary Randolph*
*California 4th Edition*
There are many emotional, financial and legal reasons to adopt a stepchild, but among the most pressing legal reasons is the need to avoid confusion over inheritance or guardianship. This book provides sample forms and step-by-step instructions for completing a simple uncontested adoption by a stepparent
**$19.95/ADOP**

# BUSINESS

### How to Write a Business Plan
*Mike McKeever*
*National 3rd Edition*
If you're thinking of starting a business or raising money to expand an existing one, this book will show you how to write the business plan and loan package necessary to finance your business and make it work.
**$17.95/SBS**

### Marketing Without Advertising
*Michael Phillips & Salli Rasberry*
*National 1st Edition*
This book outlines practical steps for building and expanding a small business without spending a lot of money on advertising.
**$14.00/MWAD**

### The Partnership Book
*Attorneys Denis Clifford & Ralph Warner*
*National 4th Edition*
This book shows you step-by-step how to write a solid partnership agreement that meets your needs. It covers initial contributions to the business, wages, profit-sharing, buy-outs, death or retirement of a partner and disputes.
**$24.95/PART**

### How to Form Your Own Nonprofit Corporation
*Attorney Anthony Mancuso*
*National 1st Edition*
This book explains the legal formalities involved and provides detailed information on the differences in the law among 50 states. It also contains forms for the Articles, Bylaws and Minutes you need, along with complete instructions for obtaining federal 501 (c) (3) tax exemptions and qualifying for public charity status.
**$24.95/NNP**

### The California Nonprofit Corporation Handbook
*Attorney Anthony Mancuso*
*California 6th Edition*
This book shows you step-by-step how to form and operate a nonprofit corporation in California. It includes the latest corporate and tax law changes, and the forms for the Articles, Bylaws and Minutes.
**$29.95/NON**

### How to Form Your Own Corporation
*Attorney Anthony Mancuso*
*California 7th Edition*
*New York 2nd Edition*
*Texas 4th Edition*
*Florida 3rd Edition*
These books contain the forms, instructions and tax information you need to incorporate a small business yourself and save hundreds of dollars in lawyers' fees.
**California $29.95/CCOR**
**New York $24.95/NYCO**
**Texas $24.95/TCOR**
**Florida $24.95/FLCO**

### The California Professional Corporation Handbook
*Attorney Anthony Mancuso*
*California 4th Edition*
Health care professionals, lawyers, accountants and members of certain other professions must fulfill special requirements when forming a corporation in California. This book contains up-to-date tax information plus all the forms and instructions necessary to form a California professional corporation.
**$34.95/PROF**

### The Independent Paralegal's Handbook
*Attorney Ralph Warner*
*National 2nd Edition*
*The Independent Paralegal's Handbook* provides legal and business guidelines for those who want to take routine legal work out of the law office and offer it for a reasonable fee in an independent business.
**$19.95/ PARA**

### Getting Started as an Independent Paralegal
*(Two Audio Tapes)*
*Attorney Ralph Warner*
*National 2nd Edition*
Approximately three hours in all, these tapes are a carefully edited version of a seminar given by Nolo Press founder Ralph Warner. They are designed to be used with *The Independent Paralegal's Handbook.*
**$44.95/GSIP**

# PATENT, COPYRIGHT & TRADEMARK

### Patent It Yourself
*Attorney David Pressman*
*National 2nd Edition*
From the patent search to the actual application, this book covers everything from use and licensing, successful marketing and how to deal with infringement.
**$29.95/PAT**

### The Inventor's Notebook
*Fred Grissom & Attorney David Pressman*
*National 1st Edition*
This book helps you document the process of successful independent inventing by providing forms, instructions, references to relevant areas of patent law, a bibliography of legal and non-legal aids and more.
**$19.95/INOT**

### How to Copyright Software
*Attorney M.J. Salone*
*National 3rd Edition*
This book tells you how to register your copyright for maximum protection and discusses who owns a copyright on software developed by more than one person.
**$39.95/COPY**

## THE NEIGHBORHOOD

### Neighbor Law:
### Fences, Trees, Boundaries & Noise
*Attorney Cora Jordan*
*National 1st Edition*
*Neighbor Law* answers common questions about the subjects that most often trigger disputes between neighbors: trees, fences, boundaries and noise. It explains how to find the law and resolve disputes without a nasty lawsuit.
**$14.95/NEI**

### Dog Law
*Attorney Mary Randolph*
*National 1st Edition*
*Dog Law* is a practical guide to the laws that affect dog owners and their neighbors. You'll find answers to common questions on such topics as biting, barking, veterinarians and more.
**$12.95/DOG**

## HOMEOWNERS

### How to Buy a House in California
*Attorney Ralph Warner, Ira Serkes &*
*George Devine*
*California 1st Edition*
This book shows you how to find a house, work with a real estate agent, make an offer and negotiate intelligently. Includes information on all types of mortgages as well as private financing options.
**$18.95/BHCA**

### For Sale By Owner
*George Devine*
*California 1st Edition*
*For Sale By Owner* provides essential information about pricing your house, marketing it, writing a contract and going through escrow.
**$24.95/FSBO**

### The Deeds Book
*Attorney Mary Randolph*
*California 1st Edition*
If you own real estate, you'll need to sign a new deed when you transfer the property or put it in trust as part of your estate planning. This book shows you how to find the right kind of deed, complete the tear-out forms and record them in the county recorder's public records.
**$15.95/DEED**

### Homestead Your House
*Attorneys Ralph Warner, Charles Sherman & Toni Ihara*
*California 8th Edition*
This book shows you how to file a Declaration of Homestead and includes complete instructions and tear-out forms.
**$9.95/HOME**

## LANDLORDS & TENANTS

### The Landlord's Law Book: Vol. 1, Rights & Responsibilities
*Attorneys David Brown & Ralph Warner*
*California 3rd Edition*
This book contains information on deposits, leases and rental agreements, inspections (tenant's privacy rights), habitability (rent withholding), ending a tenancy, liability and rent control.
**$29.95/LBRT**

### The Landlord's Law Book: Vol. 2, Evictions
*Attorney David Brown*
*California 3rd Edition*
Updated for 1991, this book will show you step-by-step how to go to court and get an eviction for a tenant who won't pay rent—and won't leave. Contains all the tear-out forms and necessary instructions.
**$29.95/LBEV**

### Tenant's Rights
*Attorneys Myron Moskovitz & Ralph Warner*
*California 11th Edition*
This book explains the best way to handle your relationship both your landlord and your legal rights when you find yourself in disagreement. A special section on rent control cities is included.
**$15.95/CTEN**

## OLDER AMERICANS

### Elder Care: Choosing & Financing Long-Term Care
*Attorney Joseph Matthews*
*National 1st Edition*
This book will guide you in choosing and paying for long-term care, alerting you to practical concerns and explaining laws that may affect your decisions.
**$16.95/ELD**

### Social Security, Medicare & Pensions
*Attorney Joseph Matthews with Dorothy Matthews Berman*
*National 5th Edition*
This book contains invaluable guidance through the current maze of rights and benefits for those 55 and over, including Medicare, Medicaid and Social Security retirement and disability benefits and age discrimination protections.
**$15.95/SOA**

## JUST FOR FUN

### 29 Reasons Not to Go to Law School
*Attorneys Ralph Warner & Toni Ihara*
*National 3rd Edition*
Filled with humor and piercing observations, this book can save you three years, $70,000 and your sanity.
**$9.95/29R**

### Devil's Advocates: The Unnatural History of Lawyers
*by Andrew & Jonathan Roth*
*National 1st Edition*
This book is a painless and hilarious education, tracing the legal profession. Careful attention is given to the world's worst lawyers, most preposterous cases and most ludicrous courtroom strategies.
**$12.95/DA**

### Poetic Justice: The Funniest, Meanest Things Ever Said About Lawyers
*Edited by Jonathan & Andrew Roth*
*National 1st Edition*
A great gift for anyone in the legal profession who has managed to maintain a sense of humor.
**$8.95/PJ**

# RESEARCH & REFERENCE

### Legal Research: How to Find and Understand the Law
*Attorney Stephen Elias*
*National 3rd Edition*
A valuable tool on its own or as a companion to just about every other Nolo book. This book gives easy-to-use, step-by-step instructions on how to find legal information.
**$14.95/LRES**

### Family Law Dictionary
*Attorneys Robin Leonard & Stephen Elias*
*National 2nd Edition*
Finally, a legal dictionary that's written in plain English, not "legalese"! *The Family Law Dictionary* is designed to help the nonlawyer who has a question or problem involving family law—marriage, divorce, adoption or living together.
**$13.95/FLD**

### Legal Research Made Easy: A Roadmap Through the Law Library Maze
*2-1/2 hr. videotape and 40-page manual*
*Nolo Press/Legal Star Communications*
If you're a law student, paralegal or librarian—or just want to look up the law for yourself—this video is for you. University of California law professor Bob Berring explains how to use all the basic legal research tools in your local law library with an easy-to-follow six-step research plan and a sense of humor.
**$89.95/LRME**

# SOFTWARE

### WillMaker
*Nolo Press/Legisoft*
*National 4th Edition*
This easy-to-use software program lets you prepare and update a legal will—safely, privately and without the expense of a lawyer. Leading you step-by-step in a question-and-answer format, *WillMaker* builds a will around your answers, taking into account your state of residence. *WillMaker* comes with a 200-page legal manual which provides the legal background necessary to make sound choices. Good in all states except Louisiana.
**IBM PC**
**(3-1/2 & 5-1/4 disks included) $69.95/WI4**
**MACINTOSH $69.95/WM4**

### For the Record
*Carol Pladsen & Attorney Ralph Warner*
*National 2nd Edition*
*For the Record* program provides a single place to keep a complete inventory of all your important legal, financial, personal and family records. It can compute your net worth and also create inventories of all insured property to protect your assets in the event of fire or theft. Includes a 200-page manual filled with practical and legal advice.
**IBM PC**
**(3-1/2 & 5-1/4 disks included) $59.95/FRI2**
**MACINTOSH $59.95/FRM2**

### California Incorporator
*Attorney Anthony Mancuso/Legisoft*
*California 1st Edition*
Answer the questions on the screen and this software program will print out the 35-40 pages of documents you need to make your California corporation legal. Comes with a 200-page manual which explains the incorporation process.
**IBM PC**
**(3-1/2 & 5-1/4 disks included) $129.00/INCI**

### The California Nonprofit Corporation Handbook
*(computer edition)*
*Attorney Anthony Mancuso*
*California 1st Edition*
This book/software package shows you step-by-step how to form and operate a nonprofit corporation in California. Included on disk are the forms for the Articles, Bylaws and Minutes.
**IBM PC 5-1/4 $69.95/NPI**
**IBM PC 3-1/2 $69.95/NP3I**
**MACINTOSH $69.95/NPM**

### How to Form Your Own New York Corporation &
### How to Form Your Own Texas Corporation
*Computer Editions*
*Attorney Anthony Mancuso*
These book/software packages contain the instructions and tax information and forms you need to incorporate a small business and save hundreds of dollars in lawyers' fees. All organizational forms are on disk. Both come with a 250-page manual.

**New York 1st Edition**
**IBM PC 5-1/4 $69.95/NYCI**
**IBM PC 3-1/2 $69.95/NYC3I**
**MACINTOSH $69.95/NYCM**

**Texas 1st Edition**
**IBM PC 5-1/4 $69.95/TCI**
**IBM PC 3-1/2 $69.95/TC3I**
**MACINTOSH $69.95/TCM**

## VISIT OUR STORE

If you live in the Bay Area, be sure to visit the Nolo Press Bookstore on the corner of 9th & Parker Streets in West Berkeley. You'll find our complete line of books and software—new and "damaged"—all at a discount. We also have t-shirts, posters and a selection of business and legal self-help books from other publishers.

### HOURS

| | |
|---|---|
| Monday to Friday | 10 a.m. to 5 p.m. |
| Thursdays | Until 6 p.m |
| Saturdays | 10 a.m. to 4:30 p.m. |
| Sundays | 10 a.m. to 3 p.m. |

950 Parker St., Berkeley, California 94710

# ORDER FORM

Name

Address (UPS to street address, Priority Mail to P.O. boxes)

| Catalog Code | Quantity | Item | Unit price | Total |
|---|---|---|---|---|
| | | | | |
| | | | | |
| | | | | |
| | | | | |
| | | | | |

| | | |
|---|---|---|
| Subtotal | | |
| Sales tax (California residents only) | | |
| Shipping & handling | | |
| 2nd day UPS | | |
| TOTAL | | |

**PRICES SUBJECT TO CHANGE**

### SALES TAX
California residents add your local tax:
7 1/4%, 7 3/4%, or 8-1/4%

### SHIPPING & HANDLING
$4.00    1 item
$5.00    2-3 items
+$.50    each additional item
Allow 2-3 weeks for delivery

### IN A HURRY?
UPS 2nd day delivery is available:
Add $5.00 (contiguous states) or
$8.00 (Alaska & Hawaii) to your regular shipping and handling charges

### FOR FASTER SERVICE, USE YOUR CREDIT CARD AND OUR TOLL-FREE NUMBERS:
Monday-Friday, 7 a.m. to 5 p.m. Pacific Time

| | |
|---|---|
| US | 1 (800) 992-6656 |
| CA   (outside 510 area code) | 1 (800) 640-6656 |
| (inside 510 area code) | 549-1976 |
| General Information | 1 (510) 549-1976 |
| Fax us your order | 1 (510) 548-5902 |

### METHOD OF PAYMENT
☐ Check enclosed
☐ VISA  ☐ Mastercard  ☐ Discover Card  ☐ American Express

Account #          Expiration Date

Signature Authorizing

Phone

DIMO

**N O L O   P R E S S   /   9 5 0   P A R K E R   S T R E E T   /   B E R K E L E Y   C A   9 4 7 1 0**

# Update Service

### Recycle your out-of-date books and get 25% off your next purchase

It's important to have the most current legal information. Because laws and legal procedures change often, we update our books regularly. To help keep you up-to-date, we are extending this special offer: Send or bring us the title portion of the cover of any old Nolo book and we'll give you a 25% discount off the retail price of any new Nolo book! You'll find current prices and an order form at the back of this book. Generally speaking, any book more than two years old is of questionable value. Books more than four or five years old are usually a menace. This offer is to individuals only.

## OUT-OF-DATE = DANGEROUS